CONGRESSMAN FROM MISSISSIPPI

CONGRESSMAN

from

MISSISSIPPI

Frank E. Smith

CAPRICORN BOOKS

NEW YORK

PRINTED IN THE UNITED STATES OF AMERICA

FOR

Helen, Kathy, and Fred

Preface

This book is largely about race, because race has been the overriding element in Mississippi politics for more than a century. In a larger sense, it is an apology for hypocrisy. I was a member of Congress representing the Third Congressional District of Mississippi. This book is the result of my twelve years in that office.

You will find here no wide and pillared verandas, no blossom-laden magnolias, no julep-sparked soirees. If that concept of the South ever dominated Mississippi, the time had passed before I was born. Neither will you find the tobacco roads; in the main they, too, have passed. There is still great poverty in Mississippi, perhaps more than anywhere else in the nation, but there, as elsewhere in the South, the grinding and hopeless poverty that once blanketed the people is no longer universal.

This book states the burden of conscience that I carried without public comment during my entire political career. When I sought election to the House of Representatives, it was because I knew full well that there were enough spokesmen for the segregated way of life in Mississippi, but there appeared to be few spokesmen whose concern was for the total welfare of Mississippi or who refused to pander to the state's obsession with race. I believed that by working for economic progress, without adding my voice to the racial clamor, I could make some genuine contribution to the gradual elimination of discrimination. This was the view with which I approached the electorate and this was my course of conduct in office.

As a condition to holding my office, I made obeisance to "the Southern way of life." Like the rest of my colleagues from Mississippi and the South, I went on record with speeches against every civil rights measure that came up during my tenure. Annually, I wrote a newsletter on civil rights, and on the occasions when expediency demanded it, I "voted right."

Incongruous as it may seem, I believed then and I believe today that my conduct of office served a useful purpose. If, in the interest of survival, I evaded my responsibility to bring home to my constituents the absolute urgency of finding solutions to the racial problems that beset us, I also saved my state the added inflammation and dishonor of yet another racist representative.

As a product of an entirely Mississippi background, both personal and political, I know well and work closely with many of the thoughtful and, like me, troubled people who are not misled by the demagogues. But because too many minds in Mississippi are too bitterly closed on all matters relating to race, I have not taken the liberty of identifying them. If it seems that names are missing where names should be, it is because I do not wish to subject those good people to embarrassments or recriminations.

I am deeply indebted to many friends who helped refresh my memory of some of the events described, or otherwise added valuable contributions in the preparation of this book. First mention should go to Bill Peters, who first aroused my interest in writing it. My wife, Helen, was an accomplished proofreader for the old Greenwood *Morning Star*, and she has undertaken that chore for this manuscript. My secretary, Mrs. Mary F. Knurr, typed the manuscript and was very helpful with many other tasks that were part of the preparation.

During most of my service in the House of Representatives, Mrs. Audrey G. Warren was my executive secretary or administrative assistant and trusted adviser. She is entitled to much of the credit for most of the achievements I immodestly claim for that period. She will also have to assume a good share of the credit, or the blame, for this book, for she has provided invaluable assistance in preparing the manuscript.

The article originally published in *The New Republic*, in Chapter 7, is reprinted with the permission of the magazine. A brief excerpt from "Congress Makes a Law," by Stephen K. Bailey (Columbia University Press), in Chapter 6, is reprinted with permission of the copyright owner.

The telling of this story will have been well worth the effort if it in any way hastens the day when Mississippi, and all the South, can throw aside its self-imposed shackles of race and enter unreservedly into the national life, and when Mississippi's representatives in the Congress can fully represent all the people of Mississippi and be, in truth, United States Congressmen.

FRANK E. SMITH

Knoxville, Tennessee
February 1964

Contents

CONGRESSMAN FROM MISSISSIPPI

Chapter I

AN AFTERNOON

IN JULY

July afternoons in the Mississippi Delta are always hot. In the days before air conditioning, however, summer heat was the norm and left little impression. My recollections as an eight-year-old on a July day in 1926 are not of heat, but of the abrupt destruction of the pattern of life. I was playing with a neighbor boy when my mother called me home to say that she had to go to the hospital. My father had been shot.

"He was shot in the arm," Mama told me. The hospital must have told her that to soften the shock of the news. Daddy had been shot in the arm but also twice in the body, a bullet entering from each side. A neighbor lady came to take my younger brother and baby sister to her house, and my playmate and I speculated as to which arm of my father had been shot, as we went to tell his mother the news. Half an hour later I was the only one at home when a carload of men turned into Crockett Street and pulled up before our house.

"Where are Frank's guns?" two of the men shouted as they came to the porch. "We're going out to help get the nigger that shot your daddy, and we haven't got a gun for everybody in the car."

I led the two men, father and son, whom I vaguely knew as distant cousins, into the house to claim my father's shotguns. A deputy sheriff might have little money, but there was always available to him a wide choice of confiscated weapons.

All through the rest of the afternoon I knew little more. My little brother Fred and I stayed with one neighbor, and another cared for our six-month-old sister, while Mama was at my father's bedside. In the early morning of the second day, Daddy's best friend, a fellow deputy, came to tell me that he had died during the night. I learned the full story as the days and the years went by.

Frank Smith was the chief deputy in the Leflore County sheriff's office. On that July day he came home to dinner (then, as it often still is, the word for the midday meal in Mississippi) and afterwards played with his baby Sadie for a few minutes in the shade of the screen porch. Then he drove off in his Ford touring car to serve a jury summons in the northern part of the county.

As he drove along the gravel road toward the town of Money, just north of the Tallahatchie river, Daddy came on a Negro carrying a suitcase, walking in the same direction as he was driving. Daddy stopped to pick the man up, as he automatically did for all he passed on the road in a day before hitchhiking had become customary.

The Negro came to the right side of the car, and then stooped to pick up his suitcase and swing it into the car. His face seemed vaguely familiar to Daddy, who said, "Wait a minute!" and reached to his shirt pocket for the packet of postcard pictures of escapees from the state prison which he always carried while out on the job. (There was an automatic fifty dollar reward for any prisoner returned to Parchman.)

When Daddy looked up again, the Negro (whose name turned out to be Sylvester Mackey) had a revolver in his hand. Mackey fired, and the bullet entered Daddy's right side. Daddy desperately grabbed for his own gun, which he never wore in the car but always placed down beside the driver's seat on his left side. Weakened and stunned, he could not pull the gun from its holster with his left hand, so he opened the car door and sprawled to the ground at the car's side. He tried to crawl away across the road. This moment of respite had come only because Mackey's gun had jammed after one shot. The assailant now ran behind the car and came around to the driver's side, where he picked up Daddy's gun and shot him a second time through his left side.

At this moment another car rounded the curve, carrying a Negro farmer and his wife. Panic struck Mackey, and he ran away across the nearby cotton field. The farmer and his wife picked up Daddy and drove him to Greenwood and the hospital.

Daddy was still conscious, being prepared for surgery that the doctors hoped would save him, when Mama arrived at the hospital. He told her what had happened, and then asked her to tell Sheriff Ed Crippen to do everything he could to make sure there was no lynching.

"I've been a deputy trying to enforce the law too long for us not to try to enforce it now," he said.

Ed Crippen had sent another deputy to the hospital to check about Frank before he joined the groups searching for the assailant. Mama gave him Daddy's message and added her own appeal to his.

The Leflore County peace officers honored the request, in a day and era when lynchings were still commonplace. The sheriff arrived at the scene of the shooting with Paul White, the assistant police chief in Greenwood. The leaderless group, gathered largely from Greenwood, had had no great trouble in cornering Sylvester Mackey. Plantation Negroes had spotted the fugitive running across the fields and then taking refuge in a sharecropper's cabin that stood alone in the midst of a field of knee-high cotton. The posse, in that moment of indecision between remaining a crowd or becoming a mob, milled around the cabin. Sylvester Mackey was inside with a gun, and no one wanted to move in after him immediately. There was talk of burning him out, but decisions for action were slow.

The one quick, sure way to avert a lynching was to arrest the cornered assailant and to get him safely to the county jail in Greenwood. After a few minutes of discussion, Paul White volunteered to go in and take the man. When the policeman entered the one main room of the cabin, it was obvious that the gunman must be hiding under the bed. White plunged under after him, and Mackey fired at the officer. He missed, but the pistol was so close that powder burns singed White's face. In another moment he grabbed Mackey and pulled him out. The posse made no attempt to take the prisoner or change its course when Sheriff Crippen told them that it was Frank Smith who wanted the law enforced. The Greenwood *Commonwealth* made the same plea editorially, again in the name of the wounded deputy. Even after Daddy died, no more talk of mob vengeance came out into the open.

Sylvester Mackey was tried within a few weeks and hanged for the murder. His only statement about the crime was "I didn't know he was an officer," and no real motive was ever discovered for the senseless killing. He was from the southern part of the state and had never lived in the Delta. As far as the Leflore County authorities ever learned, he was not being sought by police anywhere else in the country. Sylvester Mackey, like Frank Smith, was a victim of the nameless terror, the fear and suspicion between white and black that always has walked in the shadows with the people of Mississippi.

My father had died, and I had had my first serious encounter with the race problem. But learning to live with the relationship between white man and black man was and is part of the experience of growing up in Mississippi. It leaves its imprint on us all, white and black, rich and poor.

Chapter II

S I D O N

Sidon, where I was born in 1918, came into being in the 1830's as a boat landing on the Yazoo river, built by a man named Marion to serve the farmers in the hill country that began ten miles to the east. Marion's Landing was one of the first towns in the Delta. It was located on part of a large plantation named Sidon, and after Marion himself departed, the village became known as Sidon.

In those early years, most of the Delta was believed to be uninhabitable. A flat land of swamps and cypress brakes, even its higher ridges periodically awash in the floodwaters of its rivers, bogues and bayous, it stretched a brooding seventy to eighty miles from the hills on the east to the Mississippi on the west. Geologists now refer to it as the alluvial plain of the Mississippi valley. In the 250 years following De Soto's agonies at the hands of this all but impassable terrain, the white men who came skirted it to north and south, content to leave the tangled forest of cypress and cottonwood, cane and creepers, to the Indians, while they traveled on to wrest new homes and fortunes from less treacherous territory.

One generation's scorn becomes another's challenge, however, and profit is a strong stimulant. That this soil was wildly fertile was evident even to people who had never farmed, and as the lands to the east grew weary and crowded, men decided it would be no harder to clear this verdant earth for the riches of cotton than it was to claw a crop from the sterile slopes they would leave behind them. There were some ridges that never seemed to be under water and others that drained in time for spring planting, and gradually the Delta was opened up to provide new cotton land.

The large Delta plantations owed their beginnings to the sons of planters from Virginia, Kentucky, South Carolina, and Tennessee, and while they—and their slaves—were clearing their lands, the small nonslaveholding family farmers who were to become the Delta's major source of new population after the Civil War were still in the hills. In the almost half-century between statehood and fraternal conflict, more and more of them moved down, seduced by the rich earth, the warm rains, and the long hours of sunlight that were, and are, the paramount elements in this cotton economy.

There are fifty or sixty plantation towns much like Sidon scattered all over the Delta, but Sidon has special distinctions in my mind, and in memory it was the best of all small towns. The story of Sidon in the years of my youth is the story of Mississippi (and the Mississippi Delta) in the years of its youth; a hundred years lay between Mississippi's entry into the Union in full statehood and my entry into the human family, but social conditions were not too different in both periods. And if an understanding of those formative years is essential to evaluate the road I traveled, it is equally essential to an evaluation of the fate that has befallen Mississippi.

Until a generation ago, all but a handful of Mississippi's people lived on farms, and the towns that served the farms were, for the most part, plantation villages like Sidon, remote even from the county seat. The little towns were the center of life for at least half the Delta's white people, and for most of the Negroes they were the only relief from cabin and field. The pattern has changed in the last twenty years, but the change is so recent that it is not relevant to an understanding of why Mississippi continues to stand in isolation from the outside world.

As complete as my identification with Sidon was as a boy, my recollection of those years is empty of anything that would suggest a knowledge of the whole community. Like most of the white people of the town, I was aware of the Negro community without knowing anything about it. In Sidon there were things apart from race for both children and adults to talk about. Perhaps this was because the people lacked the pretensions of those who imagined themselves successors to the planter aristocracy, who talked about it in defense and apology; and they lacked, certainly, the savagery of those who talked about it as proof of their superiority. Sidon was a plantation town, but it saw little of the fabled plantations of many thousands of acres. Most of the nearby farmers were not the type who thought of themselves as "planters." They farmed a "place." They fitted well into the everyday middle-class life of the community.

Today's sociologist might argue that a white community that saw but did not see its Negro neighbors was as guilty, in its way, as the two groups at the extremes of the white spectrum. But had I not been raised on that fortunate middle ground between profitable paternalism and baiting hatred, my life would almost certainly have been very different, and the chain of events that made this book could not have been.

My father was born on a farm in the Carroll County hills, a place too small to bring wealth but big enough—with hard work—to pay for a basic education for a large family. Daddy was sent to a boarding school to get high-school training. His grandfather, Doug Smith, had been the first of the family in Mississippi, a dozen or so years before the Civil War. Doug Smith was born in North Carolina, but his family took him to Tennessee as a boy, and when he struck out on his own, it was to work as an overseer on the new Mississippi plantations. A lot of thrift and a few years later, he had acquired a small farm and a school teacher from New York state for a wife.

He owned two slave families and, like other small slaveholders, loaned them out for a fee to work on other farms when they were not needed at home. The slaves reported that one of the neighbors for whom they worked badly abused them, and the issue came to a head not long after the Civil War began. The neighbor was warned, but the abuse persisted. The showdown came, and Grandfather Smith shot the man down. More in fear of revenge from the dead man's family than of the law, he fled to Arkansas and stayed away from home for more than a year. He came back to become something of a neighborhood patriarch in his community of small hill farmers.

In 1948, when I went to Jackson as a member of the Mississippi State Senate, I was invited to dinner with one of the state's distinguished retired lawyers, General J. N. Flowers, who was a native of Carroll County. After I explained my own tie to Carroll County, General Flowers exclaimed: "Why, I know you. Your grandfather killed Will McCarty's grandfather!" (Will McCarty was a Jackson grocery tycoon, founder of the Jitney Jungle chain.) He was wrong a generation; it was my great-grandfather.

By the time my father came to manhood, the chance for a young man was down the creeks and into the Delta. Sidon, a village of ten stores and a sawmill, was the nearest Delta town, and during my boyhood it became the center for the whole Smith family. The Frank Smith branch came into being when a young school teacher from West, a hill town in Holmes County twenty miles to the east, came to Sidon. Sadie Ellis' people were from a background very much like the Smith's, with perhaps a few years more in Mississippi. Mama's father, T. Q. Ellis, spent his life as a store clerk and bank clerk in West, but I remember him best as the one who helped me to learn to read newspapers in the period when he came to live with us after his health broke.

When Frank Smith married Sadie Ellis in 1917, he had worked with his brothers in operating a general store at Cruger, a few miles south of Sidon; he had clerked in Sidon stores, and he had operated small cotton farms on a cash rental basis. In 1919, Will Vardaman, younger brother of the fading "Great White Chief" James K., was elected sheriff of Leflore County, and he selected Frank Smith to be one of his deputies. Daddy maintained his residence in Sidon, and on the strength of his new job made the down payment on a 200-acre farm southeast of town. 1920 seemed a good year to raise cotton; the price was hovering around a dollar a pound. Naturally, cotton farmland was selling at relatively high prices.

Daddy's ambition was to become the county sheriff when the chance came for him to run. In 1923 his friend Ed Crippen was elected sheriff, and Daddy was named his chief deputy. This necessitated moving to Greenwood, for the county seat would be a better base for campaigning. I was five when we moved to Greenwood, so most of my boyhood memories of Sidon are of the years after the move, but they all help to make up the picture of Mississippi before World War II, mechanized agriculture, and industrialization.

Though we lived in Greenwood, we spent a lot of time in Sidon, too, and it was like growing up in the country and the small town combined. In Sidon, I remember first living in a house by the railroad and on warm nights sitting on the porch with Mama. A deputy sheriff naturally had a spotlight on his Ford, and Daddy always turned his on for us as he turned up the incline over the railroad. There had to be a fire in the stove to heat water, and after one late homecoming, sparks from the flue set the house on fire in the night after we were all asleep. Daddy saved Mama's piano with the help of the first neighbor who gave the alarm, but that was all. The bucket brigade was the only way to fight a fire, and any fire usually meant the end of the building.

At the house we moved to after the fire, I went to the door one night and opened it on a Negro man whose whole torso seemed to be red and bleeding. "Tell Mr. Frank, Lizzie done cut me up," he said. He was Mack Ransom, who through the years had been an employee of some member of the family. Mack survived, and so did his and Lizzie's marriage.

The days spent on the farm were usually timed so that I could ride the five miles into town on a wagonload of cotton headed for the gin. Once I was enthusiastically helping to push the cotton toward the funnel that sucked it up into the gin, and lost a relatively new cap. The cap was wool, but we figured it didn't hurt the cotton too much.

Sidon's population fell from 370 in 1920 to 320 in 1930. There were 214 whites and 106 Negroes in that census, but by 1940 farming and relief program changes had raised the population to 418, of whom 201 were Negroes. The Negroes who had regular jobs worked at the sawmill, at menial jobs at the stores, and in the homes of the whites. Others "chopped" cotton in the summer when the crop needed hoeing, and picked it in the fall and winter. In the twenties most of the farm work was still being done by sharecroppers and tenants, with little hired labor, but there was enough demand for occasional workers to keep a surplus the year round in Sidon.

There were ten or twelve stores in Sidon then; they were to dwindle to five or six by 1940. Before the good roads and the chain stores, the white residents and most of the nearby white farmers bought their groceries and most of their clothing in the local stores. The Negroes, in town and on the farm, dependent on wagons for transportation, could rarely go anywhere else to spend money even when they had it. For most of them, their shopping was limited to the store which had a credit arrangement with the farm owner for whom they worked. It was a slight modification of the old plantation commissary system, and it was used by most of the farms in the Sidon area, partly because it was simpler than maintaining a commissary and partly because it was more popular with the sharecroppers themselves.

The old commissary system still existed on scattered farms, however. I remember one Sidon man who had been a plantation bookkeeper telling me of the times his employer had come in after disastrous poker games with orders to charge all the families on the place with another barrel of flour. "I can't let Mrs. ———— and the children have to pay for last night," he would explain.

Before the paved roads opened an easy route to Greenwood and beyond, organized recreation in Sidon centered around the churches and the school, in the manner of rural areas everywhere. There were two white churches, a Baptist and a Methodist, and two Negro churches of the same denominations. In the first thirty years of the century, both the white churches maintained full-time ministers; the Sidon charge usually had a higher rating among the ministers than those of the other small towns. Religious fervor rose and fell more or less spontaneously. The sudden determination of one influential person to be more active in church work could have as much influence as the annual revival. The revivals were universally attended by the townspeople of both denominations.

Depression, and the drift to Greenwood of both townspeople and farmers, changed the pattern, and there has been no full-time pastor for these last thirty years. The time came when each church held services on alternate Sundays, so that there was a service in town every Sunday. Eventually the two women's missionary organizations combined (though they naturally retained their separate identities for purposes of district conventions and the like), and union prayer meetings also started, but there never was any talk of resolving the economic problems by uniting the two churches.

Sidon's Negro churches survived in more regular fashion, although they must have had some of the same depression-born financial problems. The highlight of their year, for both the white and colored communities, was the baptizing in the river with white robes and melodious spirituals. Some of the white people may have come to look for the ludicrous, but I don't believe they often found it in the atmosphere of "Swing Low, Sweet Chariot."

Negroes and whites played together as small children, if they happened to be in the same neighborhood, and they sometimes continued these friendships into their teens. Houston's mother was the cook for a family that included some very good young baseball players, and Houston became a star in both white and colored circles. When the town boys were playing each other, Houston usually played. When his gang became old enough and skilled enough to be part of a team that played for Sidon against neighboring towns, the members wanted to include him too, but the older heads said no. Baseball was nearly a year-round sport, white and black, on the school grounds or in pastures at the edge of town. The resident who had seen a Southern League game in Memphis never ceased to tell about it, and boys learned early to follow the major leagues, the Southern League, and the Cotton States League in the sports pages of the Memphis *Commercial Appeal*. Baseball careers were the dream of all the white boys, and my Uncle Grady Roberts had a brother who pitched in the International League until he was thrown out for using a spitter.

The only Negroes who were ever allowed to break traditional barriers were the very old with strong characters and strong attachments to families for whom they had worked many years. For instance, the door that I opened to answer the call of the bleeding Mack Ransom was the front door. A strange Negro would not have come to the front door even in a far greater emergency. Another privileged character was Aunt "Zoury" (a contraction of Missouri, where her mother was supposed to have come from). She could scare the daylights out of any child, white or black, with stories of a small boy lost in the woods who sat down on a log to rest, only to discover that the log was an alligator. At least that was what the boy said who got back home with one foot, and never disobeyed his mother again, or talked back to Aunt Zoury. Alligators were often seen in the Yazoo, and every now and then someone snagged one on a trotline. Aunt Zoury was the first one to tell me about the Yankees, those soldiers who came to Sidon during the Confederate War. Her Yankees were good Yankees, for they let the slaves go free and gave them and their children lumps of sugar.

There always seemed to be some sort of "not speaking to each other" feud going on among some part of the white community of Sidon, but the relative isolation, before the advent of good transportation, served to make most of these feuds short-lived. In the pre-World War I days most of the long-standing families of the community had made one or more marriages into another similar family, and the connections sometimes seemed to double back. I remember making a rough tabulation when I was about twelve and deciding that I was kin to half the people in the town. My family lived in Greenwood from 1924 on, but the warmest memories of my childhood are the every-Sunday-after-church visits to Sidon for Sunday dinner and Sunday afternoon playing and visiting. We were always both Sidon and Greenwood folks.

Men and boys played baseball, and the ladies attended all the social activities of both churches and even progressed eventually to a bridge club, but the favorite recreation in Sidon was always gossip. Very few details of the lives of its citizens, from the most casual to the most intimate, failed to become public property in fairly rapid fashion, if any other Sidon citizen happened to learn about them, and they always did. Perhaps the most interesting aspect of the whole busy grapevine was that even its worst victims never seemed to question its right to existence.

After prohibition put the town's two saloons out of business, the drugstores became the male loafing centers. The drugstores eventually became general stores. In time, the town could boast of two cafés, the "Red Onion" and the "Green Front," both with a white counter and a colored counter. Their menus did not go far beyond hamburgers and fried eggs, but the pocketbooks of their customers could go no further, either. For ten years after beer was legalized the

Green Front was the only one which maintained a license to sell it, and the names of the men who dropped in there were items worthy of mention in the daily gossip. Through the years, local pressures have prevented a bootlegger from operating within the actual limits of Sidon—the active church-goers have strongly disapproved, and the customers prefer a place on the highway far enough from town so that their visits will at least not be tabulated daily.

The Sidon school system never included a high school. After the eighth grade the children were sent to Greenwood High School. The temptation to drop out of high school was usually too great for the poor white farm children of the area, but the town children themselves had a good record of going on to complete high school. In the 1930's, nearly all Sidon students who managed to finish high school continued through at least one year in college. This was primarily because of the existence of Sunflower Junior College at Moorhead, an institution which Leflore County partly supported in return for free tuition for Leflore students. The percentage of college graduation was relatively low.

During my childhood, I doubt if more than a handful of Sidon's Negro students ever received anything even approaching a high-school education. As the changing farm pattern brought more Negroes into town, the Negro school became badly crowded. In the late thirties, enrollment averaged over 300, but there were only three teachers. The principal worked out a system of shifts, with half the pupils coming in the morning and the other half in the afternoon. It was a fair-sized teaching load by any standard.

Despite these obvious deficiencies, the Sidon Negro school was regarded as one of the best in the county because of the qualities of the principal. He was an intelligent man who developed more respect and support for his work among the white community than any previous principal. There was even some respect for a certain dignity for himself which he obviously sought to preserve and for the way he tried to avoid degrading his position as the town's most prominent Negro. In the flush of new-sought values after World War II, he took the further step of going to Greenwood and registering and qualifying as a voter. He was fired on short notice.

On the surface that a young boy could see, Sidon was calm and contented through the 1920's—prosperous enough, if measured by sumptuous Sunday dinners. But underneath, in the adult world the young boy couldn't see, it was feeling the pangs of cotton's distress. The story of one of my uncles by marriage is descriptive of what happened to a great many.

As a young man, Uncle John worked on railroads in Mississippi and Texas. In 1920 he came back home, and with his carefully hoarded savings, made the down payment on a 300-acre farm near Sidon. He was foreclosed there in 1926, and farmed for the next four years as a cash renter. There had been a family residence on the farm he had bought and lost, but as a renter he could not live there; he had to take his family back to a house in Sidon. He was a good farmer and a hard worker, so in 1930 he found someone willing to extend enough credit for him to buy a 500-acre farm thirty miles to the south. He averaged a good yield of cotton on that place, but the rock-bottom price for the commodity during the next three years made it impossible for him to meet a single note, and he was foreclosed again.

Once more he settled his family in Sidon and went back to cash renting. Now the New Deal farm program was beginning to stabilize and improve the outlook for cotton farmers, but it also had adverse effects for Uncle John. Thanks to the better conditions, cotton land was harder to come by, and for the rest of his life 300 acres was the largest farm he could rent. Only twice in eight years was he able to rent the same land two years in succession. The renter who could keep competent sharecroppers to make a crop with him had a major asset, but two or three times Uncle John "lost his labor" because he was unable to rent land by Christmas and, on the basis of this rental contract, borrow the money with which to make an advance to the sharecroppers for their Christmas spending. A man twice burned grows extremely cautious, so he passed up several chances to buy good farms because he thought they were overpriced, only to see gradually inflating values prove them to have been underpriced.

The New Deal cotton program changed the population structure of Sidon. Cotton acreage reductions lessened the need for farm tenants—some went to Greenwood, some came to Sidon. The proportion of Negroes within the town itself increased. Phillipston Plantation, four or five miles southwest of town, was purchased by the Farm Security Administration and broken up into small tracts for the resettlement of white farmers. As always with Sidon, most of these came from the nearby hills. Some of them became solidly accepted citizens of the community; others were a new element of "white trash" who faded from Phillipston after failing to meet the standards of FSA and its successor agency, the Farmers Home Administration.

The several farm programs of the first eight Roosevelt years brought a stable and relatively prosperous farm economy to Leflore County, and in the process they almost entirely wiped out the plantation village. Consequently, they exerted a great long-range influence on my little town.

The most immediate benefits of the New Deal on Sidon, however, came from the WPA and its allied relief projects.

Throughout the surplus commodity program, more than two-thirds of the townspeople qualified to receive them. Relief from summer dust came for the first time in the hundred years of the town's existence when the WPA blacktopped the two main streets.

At various times there were from 15 to 25 white people with WPA jobs. Most of these were heads of families, but some were girls and women in clerical work. The number of Negro WPA workers varied with specific projects, because they all had to be employed as laborers. Widow and maiden ladies, previously without hope of earning a living, proudly found some niche with the government programs among the "white folks" jobs. For most of them it meant commuting to Greenwood, which was area headquarters for a number of the relief programs. For a few, there was work in Sidon itself. One of the best jobs was the running of the WPA library, set up in a vacant store building. A small permanent collection of books and magazines was donated locally, but the bulk of the circulating books was borrowed from the Greenwood Public Library. During most of its existence, the Sidon WPA library had the largest per capita circulation of any WPA library in the county.

For five or six years, the WPA budget allowed for a recreation supervisor for the Sidon area, and those years will be long remembered. A weekly square dance was held in the summer months the first two years of the program. The first year the event brought an enthusiastic response from the middle-aged and up throughout the southern part of the county, but in the second year the vigor of that first revival began to dull, and response was not considered good enough to carry on the program. "Round" dances, which had been only an occasional part of the square dance program, took their place. The entire youth crop of Sidon regularly turned out for these dances, in addition to both planters and sharecroppers from the country. Half of Sidon's mothers were usually on hand to enjoy the proceedings and lend a chaperoning eye. None of the town girls ever danced with the sharecropper, or "poor white" or "resettlement farm" folks, but many a Sidon boy took advantage of the opportunity to strike up an acquaintanceship with some of the poor white daughters.

The days of WPA, NYA, and distribution of surplus food commodities were the first that Sidon ever knew without sharp pockets of poverty and even just plain hunger in some corners of the community. Even in the prosperous times of recent years, the surplus commodity program has been the only way that many of the Negro families stayed ahead of hunger during the hard winter months of no farm work and little casual labor. The permanent government welfare programs, including old-age assistance, social security, and aid to dependent children, plus veterans' benefits, have virtually eliminated all but the emergency cases of real suffering. There are still those who are hard-pressed to find employment in a rural economy, of course, and they longingly look back to WPA days when there was a job for them.

From 1940 on, my ties to Sidon began to unravel. The paved highway had gone a long way toward making it primarily a bedroom suburb of Greenwood; postwar economic forces completed the process. By 1960 the population was 410, with slightly more whites than Negroes. Cotton is still the center of the economy, which is stable and relatively prosperous. Most of the present clients of the Farmers Home Administration on Phillipston Plantation are successful small farmers—some have acquired additional land, others have turned to work in town as a main source of income for their families. Negro farm labor today has to be at the level of skilled tractor drivers, at least. There is far less dependence on casual labor, even for the peaks of seasonal demand—hoeing and picking. The wages paid are still well below the minimum in any other type work, but they reflect a steadier, more certain income than the old haphazard potentials of sharecropping. Some farmers still use the tenant system, but it has been modified to fit the mechanized operations. Turnover in farm ownership is relatively limited, with opportunities for purchase arising primarily from death or retirement. Government credit programs are ready to move in with assistance when adverse weather conditions cause crop failures and upset normal financing arrangements.

Federal money is fundamental to Sidon's economic existence today, as much as it was in the 1930's. Cotton programs may change, but they still control cotton farming, and the Delta is still cotton-obsessed. Government pension and welfare checks are the main source of day-to-day business for the handful of stores still operating in Sidon.

The postwar years have brought an annual attraction for the older families, common to hill communities built around a church but rare in the Delta. The Sidon Cemetery Association, which maintains the town's white cemetery, has an annual meeting each spring to conduct its business and collect dues from families whose relatives are buried there. The meeting is also a homecoming for former Sidon residents throughout the state and from even more distant points. It is held on the school grounds, with each family contributing to an old-fashioned dinner-on-the-grounds style picnic, improved by the serving facilities of the school cafeteria.

In race relations there has been virtually no change. A Citizens Council was formed at Sidon when the movement started, but as in most small towns, there hasn't been much for such an organization to do. The Negroes have no organization. If they contribute to the effort for better conditions, it is through their friends in Greenwood. Both sides assume that changes in racial patterns will come last to plantation villages such as Sidon, and, like all of the Delta, Sidon today uneasily awaits them.

Chapter III

G R E E N W O O D

In the winter of 1923 we moved to Greenwood, from the village to the town. Greenwood had started—a little before Sidon, but in much the same manner—as a steamboat landing on the Yazoo to serve the hill country to the east. The town was named for Greenwood Leflore, the former Choctaw chief who was the largest landholder in neighboring Carroll County as well as one of the most romantic and colorful figures in early Mississippi history.

As a county seat, Greenwood eclipsed all rivals as a river trading center. In 1924 the town had a population of about 10,000, and its growth had been steady for fifty years. It was a city of shaded streets. Houses came lot by lot, with room to leave the old trees and rich soil for new ones to grow. The exception was in the Negro sections. Gritney and Baptist Town were made up of shotgun houses so close together that there was rarely room to leave the old trees, let alone room for new ones.

We moved into a quiet part of North Greenwood, across the Yazoo from the business district. In the post-World War II build-up, North Greenwood was to be the part of town where most of the residential expansion took place, but in the time of my childhood it was small enough to be served by a four-room schoolhouse with six grades. Everybody walked to school, except for a lucky few who had bicycles.

While I was in the second grade, the North Greenwood teachers decided it would be best for me to skip half a grade, and that meant that the rest of my grammar school days were spent with the uneven graders across the river in Jefferson Davis School, which served the main part of town. A few of my classmates were skip-graders like me, but most of them were boys and girls who had been set back one or more times. Consequently, most of them were two, three, or four years older than I. None of my classmates lived in my part of North Greenwood, and I lost out on most of the classic schoolmates-growing-up-together sagas of childhood, but I also came firsthand to a side of Greenwood life from which the children of North Greenwood were sheltered. Perhaps all of this contributed to an introverted shyness that has been with me all my life.

When Daddy died, he left $1,000 in insurance and a very small equity in the farm below Sidon. Mama rented the farm on shares during the next few years but was never able to meet all the payments. She lost the whole investment in 1932, the year before a federal farm program came into being and ended the torrent of farm bankruptcies. Mama's school teaching of ten years before had been done without the preparation of a college degree, so returning to that as a means of providing for her family was not possible. She invested her capital in a business college course.

Daddy had been the universal favorite to win the sheriff's election of 1927. After his death, most of the candidates who now came into the race made giving Mama a job as office deputy part of their platform. She went to work for $100 a month, and after long years, the pay finally became $150. There was no margin for luxuries raising a family on this income, but neither was there the suffering that the depression brought to many others. Because the job was subject to change with a new sheriff every four years, however, Mama never felt any real sense of security in it. My father's brother Harry was twice sheriff during the period, but even his political opponents kept Mama on their staff. She worked too hard and was too popular with the voters for them to consider any other course.

After Daddy was killed, the people of Leflore County had raised money by public subscription, carried on through the columns of the local paper, for us to buy a house. It was a generous spontaneous reaction to the way of his passing. Mama chose a house in North Greenwood two blocks from where we had been living, this time on Claiborne Street, on the river front. Along Claiborne, west toward the bridge and downtown, there were houses. To the east a cotton farm began that surrounded us, even to the extent of a vacant lot on the west. The actual river channel was a quarter of a mile in front of our house, and we could see the river only in times of high water. A strip of that stretch was high enough to be farmed most of the time, but much of the area was wooded wasteland, an ideal place for boys to play.

The road past our house led on to a large plantation, the property of Congressman Will M. Whittington. As boys, my brother and I came to know all of the regular tenants. We either picked cotton for them in the fall at a penny a pound, caught rides with them on their cotton wagons headed for the Whittington gin across town, or played with their children in the pastures along the river bank. Our house, inhabited by three children, my mother and her mother, stood a few feet from a road over which hundreds of Negroes passed regularly, and through all hours on Saturday night, but I don't think our peace was ever disturbed. We never thought of locking the door at night.

The 1927 flood which broke the main Mississippi levee damaged a good part of the west Delta, but very little of its overflow bothered people in the Greenwood area. This flood awakened the country to the necessity of having the federal government take responsibility for flood protection of the Mississippi, a policy written into law in 1928. The Flood Control Act of 1936 extended the responsibility throughout the country. The Delta's ever-recurrent battle with the water first came home to me in 1932, when the Yazoo flooded and water covered nearly all of North Greenwood. We stayed in our Claiborne Street house until the water was just a foot below the floors, and then moved out with the help of an ice wagon that rode high above most of the water. Our place of refuge was the judge's chambers in the top story of the courthouse. One year later the first major public works project in our area was an earth levee around North Greenwood. From that time forward our view was the levee, not the stretch of land to the river.

When I was eleven years old, I got the only job I ever had as a schoolboy—the only one that was available in town and the one I kept until the summer after I was graduated from high school. The *Greenwood Commonwealth* paid its carriers a flat sum, not a commission on each subscriber, and it never gave a pay raise. My pay was $1.50 a week for five years. It was a magnificent sum for a boy my age in Greenwood at that time, but it grew much smaller as I advanced into high school. But it was all there was, and its actuality made a boyhood in Greenwood far more meaningful. Through the years most of it went into books and magazines and a growing concept of the world outside.

Reading was something that began with the legend on oatmeal boxes, before even starting to school at Sidon. When we first moved to Greenwood, Grandfather Ellis had come to live with us for the year or so before he died. He helped me read the newspaper headlines, and talked to me about them. I remember asking him, "Who was William Jennings Bryan?" when the headlines in the *Commercial Appeal* told of the death of the Great Commoner at Dayton. "He was a man too good to be President," Daddy Ellis replied.

One of the advantages of going to Davis School uptown was that the Greenwood Public Library was along the way to school. Thanks to the generosity of the Carnegie Fund, Greenwood had a library that looked big and inspiring to a small boy. Before I had finished high school, it had begun to seem small, for I had read practically all the volumes of history and biography, and a large part of the fiction. In the depression days the library budget for new books was limited to the income from "overdue" fines, although there may have been some grants from the WPA in return for assistance to the WPA community libraries. Regardless of its limitations, the Greenwood library was good for Frank Smith. There was a basement reading room, wonderfully cool in the summer, where the magazines were kept, together with most of the personal library of the late Senator J. Z. George, whose daughter lived next door. The library introduced me to many of the current magazines, but the discovery of *The New Re-*

public and *The Nation* probably made the strongest impression. Here were two magazines which devoted most of their space to politics and public affairs. They were something to revel in and eventually to subscribe to in order to be sure I had them every Monday.

The library, of course, did not satisfy all my reading needs. In my high-school days, with my income of $1.50 per week, for a couple of years I belonged to both the Book-of-the-Month Club and the Literary Guild, in addition to subscribing to *The New Republic* and *The Nation*, patronizing a lending library that two young women had opened in a drugstore downtown, and buying magazines such as *Story* and other odd items that reached the newsstands in the local drugstores.

The first magic of the newsstand for me as an eleven-year-old was the *Open Road for Boys*. The stories seemed more vivid than those in *Youth's Companion* and *American Boy*. The pulp magazines were all exciting, but for a few years during this period the only one that got my fifteen cents every week was Street and Smith's *Wild West Weekly*. The comic books have destroyed both the boy's magazines and the pulps, and I think they have taken something out of the lives of our sons thereby. It was from the advertisements in the *Open Road* that I was introduced to the world of boys' amateur journalism. Papers put out by teen-age editors were being published in every corner of the country, printed by companies who would produce 100 copies of your paper on a 2 x 4 folder for a couple of dollars and half the space for their own ads. The productions of these schoolboy editors varied from the near professional to the rankest amateur, but they also published each other's pieces and were the source of most of the mail circulation of each other's papers. My own efforts found print in some of these brother publications, but the big production was my own paper, printed through the services of the G. Blake Printing Company of Burlington, Iowa. I'm sure that none of the editors who worked over the G. Blake imprint ever paid their expenses—I've often wondered since then whether the G. Blake Company itself, which sounded so professional to me, paid its way either.

The only copy of the *Boy's Friend* that has survived the years is Volume I, Number 4, for February 1930. We had graduated from G. Blake to twelve pages (still 2 x 4) prepared by another printer who must have been Hubert Motsinger of Route 3, Marion, Illinois, because he had a full-page ad for printing. The subscription price of the *Boy's Friend* was a bargain—six months for 20 cents or 35 cents for a full year. By the time that I had developed enough talent to produce a semiprofessional-looking edition, I had outgrown their appeal, but that must have been the normal cycle for the boy publishers.

The Greenwood school system for white children was probably well above the average in Mississippi. What it was for Negro children I had no way of knowing, and there was not much chance of the average white adult's finding out anything about it either. On the plantation to our east the children attended a one-room country school, probably as good or better than schools on the other plantations of the county, but not likely to encourage even an ambitious student to struggle with the difficulties of traveling every day to the other side of Greenwood to go to high school. There were no school buses for Negroes—Mississippi had not yet been driven to embracing the "equal" part of the "separate but equal" doctrine. Richard Wright has written an eloquent account of a talented Negro boy's growing up in Mississippi in the years just ahead of me in his book *Black Boy*.

Any member of Sadie Smith's family was an active member and participant in the affairs of the First Methodist

Church. Both the church and the Sunday school were a major part of my life. The people in the church were the people I knew first in town, except for our few immediate neighbors in North Greenwood, until the years of delivering papers made all the *Commonwealth*'s subscribers part of my daily circle. For several years the boys in my age group had a rich old retired farmer and businessman as Sunday school teacher. He liked us because we afforded him a captive audience, and we liked him because every Sunday he would award two or three nickels to the boys who had memorized the Scripture best or who could give the best answers to the series of questions in the Sunday school lesson book. One Saturday morning there was a fairly large crowd on the courthouse lawn, and the big topic of conversation was the capture of two Negroes, accused of a recent murder, who were in the county jail in the courthouse annex. Old Mr. Jones was in the crowd, and I listened on the edge of his circle to what he had to say:

"They have no business locking those black sonsfabitches up and keeping 'em out of our hands. Stringing them up right now would be cheapest and easiest way to handle this."

I don't know whether I was shocked more by the profanity of the Sunday school teacher or by his advocacy of lynching. Lynching, I had learned from my father and from the other members of my family who had become peace officers, was wrong. We had had no lessons or sermons in the church on Christian race relations, but the whole concept of Christianity to which I was constantly exposed was a contradiction of the racial pattern in which I was growing up. In the process of my intellectual development there is nothing I can put my finger on as having made my views on race different from those of my friends and neighbors. It was a gradual accumulation of influences, and having been raised in the sheriff's office and regularly attending Sunday school were two of the significant ones. There were many other people who felt the same influences and wound up with different attitudes. I think in most cases they recognized the influences but did not have enough inherent independence to respond to them in the face of the ingrained community pressures.

Growing up in the Delta involved a constant awareness of race. The Delta had been opened up to cotton, and the original plantation system survived here longer than anywhere else. Two-thirds of the people were Negroes, and from the days of Reconstruction the white population had unquestioningly accepted the doctrine that their economic and social order could not survive unless the Negroes were rigidly controlled by being excluded from any voice in the political system and rigidly segregated in their participation in all other forms of community life.

Outsiders who looked at the Delta were universally impressed by the white and colored caste system, and what they saw was a white society so stratified by class consciousness that its rigid bounds scarred those at every level, leaving no man or woman free to function in a manner of their own choosing. The class system was actually far more flexible than it appeared—most of the Delta was only two or three generations old, and large land-ownership before the New Deal was never stable enough to develop the traditional landed aristocracy of a rural society. Plantation ownership was the mark of the Delta's upper class, but there were few cases of inherited opulence for more than one generation in the 1920's and 1930's. At every hand there were examples of "planters" who had started as sharecroppers, and quite often there were paupers who had been planters. This flexibility did not breach support of the caste system, however, which all whites accepted as an inviolate part of the social order. To express the simplest accurate explanation, the Negro was regarded as an inferior being, beyond the pale of religious and political doctrines of brotherhood and equality.

In the Greenwood of my youth, cotton completely dominated the economy. Poor prices for cotton could sometimes be offset by seasons of good yield, but when both yield and price were poor, everyone felt the result. The size rather than the price of the crop influenced the demand for cotton choppers and pickers among the town's Negro population. In good crop years, anywhere from 1,500 to 2,000 Greenwood Negroes would be hauled to fields each day to pick cotton. This total included probably 90 percent of the town's maids, cooks, and children's nurses. The cotton economy of the times demanded a surplus of Negro population available for seasonal farm work.

Greenwood was the narrow world in which I first learned politics. Through the years my family was always in local politics and consequently never took an active role in state elections (Mississippi elects all its county and state officials, from constable to governor, every four years, and local candidates just don't have the time to get involved in state campaigns, not to mention their disinclination to risk alienating their own voters by supporting a possibly unpopular state candidate). But political activity at any level begets an interest in the whole spectrum. I lived part of the excitement of all of it—in the state candidates' rallies, in the columns of the Memphis *Commercial Appeal*, the Jackson *Daily News* and the *Commonwealth*, and in the overheard conversations of my elders.

Greenwood was a traditional Delta town as far as most politics went, which meant that it seldom offered a candidate the big audiences for speeches typical of the hill country where politics was the sport of all the people. The town and county vote was big enough, however, for all the candidates to have to speak in Greenwood, and sometimes twice. I still remember a remark I heard from one listener as we filed out after hearing my first Bilbo speech in 1927— "That man can make you believe him even when you know he's lying." There wasn't a political rally in town, from 1927 until I went to college in 1934, without me as part of the audience. I listened to all the state politicians and their local supporters who showed up for their appearances, but I don't think I ever was forward enough to go up and shake the hand of one of the candidates until I was a local candidate speaking on the program myself.

In many of the hill counties there are organized speaking tours for county candidates that cover each major voting precinct in the county. Leflore County candidates didn't follow this, but there were occasional barbecues and Brunswick stews built around the campaign—sometimes strictly community affairs and sometimes special efforts to promote state or district candidates. Perhaps there is no relationship, but Brunswick stew has always been my favorite among distinctively Southern dishes.

Leflore County didn't have a political machine in the traditional sense. There were sometimes factions built around one man or one family, but they were transitory. Candidates won elections by having a reputation that was respected by the people who knew them and building from this by energetically getting to know the individual voters. The man with special influence was the one paying large blocs of poll taxes for voters who otherwise would not have gotten around to it. As the years went by, "getting to know the people" came to be virtually a house-to-house canvass of the white residents of the county, but knowing the people was actually much more than this for the really successful politician. It required knowing something about a man's family, the background of his people before they came to the Delta, the history of his farm, the bank and the merchants with whom he traded. More activity was expected in election years, of course, but the successful politician had to know his people and be sure they knew he knew them, all the time; he lived his campaign, more or less without letup, year in and year out.

The sheriff's office changed every four years (by law, the sheriff cannot succeed himself in Mississippi), but other county offices rarely changed hands. This could have led to a machine-type "courthouse ring," but it didn't, at least not in Leflore County. There were natural friendships that developed through long association, but the officeholders were too concerned about their own welfare to risk alienating voters for someone else's sake.

My mother took a plunge into politics on her own in 1935 and ran against the circuit court clerk, who had held his office for more than twenty years. She ran into hundreds of voters whose marriage licenses had been supplied with a waiver of the fee by the clerk, and another large group who thought a lady that had a steady job in the sheriff's office didn't need the job as badly as her opponent did—a combination which resulted in her losing by a heartbreaking couple of hundred votes. The immediate bitterness of the defeat didn't last, though, and eight years later Mama went to work for the man she had tried to oust from office.

That defeat was much harder for me to take than my own 27 years later. If she had won, I would have been able to go on to senior college—I had already made plans to study journalism at Emory University. But more than that, I simply could not understand how the voters could turn her down. What in the world did they want for that office?

There was a Senate campaign in 1928 that failed to register any lasting imprint. I remember that Congressman T.

Webber Wilson made a speech everyone called impressive, but it failed to dislodge Senator Hubert Stephens, and I probably wouldn't remember that much of it were it not for the fact that Wilson spent the night with the Johnstons next door. A man from up in the north Delta ran against Congressman Whittington on a platform calling for legal beer, but he couldn't get over the levees that Mr. Whittington was making his trade-mark.

The state campaign I remember best was in 1934, when Senator Stephens was turned out of office for not being a wholehearted New Dealer. Ex-Governor Theodore G. Bilbo was the one who turned him out, but I was heart and soul for the man who ran third, Congressman Ross Collins of Meridian. For several years Collins had been engaged in a seesaw battle with the War Department over what he considered its wasteful weapons system and its failure to build up air strength. Collins' stand, based on the normally politically sound assertion that he opposed military waste, attracted the attention of the national press and brought applause from people such as Oswald Garrison Villard in *The Nation*. It was the first favorable comment I had ever seen in *The Nation* or *The New Republic* about a Mississippian, and it immediately put me in the Collins camp. Unadulterated vanity is the hallmark of the young, and I was no exception. I promptly wrote a letter to Mr. Villard, praising his support of Collins' position and vowing that I would be a candidate for the legislature when I reached 21. What a relief it must have been to Villard thus to be assured that his opinions were sound and that the state of Mississippi stood but five short years removed from political salvation! At sixteen, my conceit must have been exceeded only by my optimism—it seems unlikely, however, that Mr. Villard suffered unduly through the eight extra years it took me to get to the legislature.

Ross Collins came to Greenwood, and his speech was intelligent, more than could be said for his opponents; intelligence, unfortunately, was no weapon to carry into the rough and tumble of a contest against the pseudo-evangelistic vulgarities and federal spending promises by which Bilbo won the support of the mass of voters who so blindly supported him in that bleak depression year.

Theodore Bilbo was Mississippi's personality politics at its worst—vulgar, vain, corrupt, contemptuous of both knowledge and outside refinements—but he was a past master at reading the winds of voter sentiment. That year, Mississippi voters wanted someone who would help Franklin Roosevelt end the depression. Bilbo promised to be a "100 percent New Dealer," and that was enough.

Mr. Collins is still alive at this writing. His is one of many cases of influential House careers lost to Senate ambitions. Defeated in that 1934 senatorial campaign, he regained his House seat in 1936, but he couldn't get it back after he gave it up in 1942 to run against—and lose to—James O. Eastland. If he had remained in the House, he would have had a long stay as chairman of the Committee on Appropriations; that is, assuming he could have survived the Dixiecrats of 1948 and the Know-Nothings of 1962, movements with which he could have found no common ground save race.

The fourth candidate for the Senate in 1934 was a joke to most of the political writers, but when he spoke in Greenwood it seemed to me that he knew the heartfelt needs of the people of Mississippi better than anybody. State Senator Frank Harper was also something of a joke down in the legislature, but no one doubted his sincerity. During the campaign, he hitchhiked from one speech to the next, listing in detail and by individual example the vast poverty of the state of Mississippi and enumerating all the good that more government money would do. He had no plan to solve everything. His only wish was to get money into the hands of people who had none. In the hard year of 1934, money from the government was what most people in Mississippi wanted. They simply made the obvious choice that Washington-wise Bilbo could get it for them better than good old Frank Harper.

In those days national politics in Greenwood usually meant agreeing with the national Democratic leadership. Roosevelt's election in 1932 and his New Deal programs won almost unanimous support among Mississippians. Today Mississippians in Congress vote almost automatically against any welfare or subsidy programs except for farmers. In the 1930's, however, the people demanded the New Deal measures which brought money to the state. All of Mississippi was in desperate straits—from the top of the caste structure to the bottom, the people were bowed low, victims of an already unhealthy local economic system made worse by a national economic disaster. The New Deal promised to ease the burden, and it did. Not until the prosperity of World War II and the postwar reaction of 1946 did the name of Franklin D. Roosevelt fail to provoke ringing applause in a Mississippi audience. As the years went by and Mississippi became more and more antigovernment (while the state's economy benefited more and more from government funds), it became popular to picture Roosevelt as the sinister conspirator who had laid the foundations for all of the South's woes.

Keeping up with politics involved reading every line about it that was available in the newspapers that came to Greenwood. The editor of the local *Commonwealth*, Littleton Upshur, was a lean and wiry man with unkempt black hair, an introvert who loved politics as much as I did. Being editor of the *Commonwealth* also required doing odd jobs in the press room and circulation department, so as a boy I got to know Mr. Upshur as well as I knew any of the prominent men of the town. He was, on the surface, strongly conservative in national politics, but he knew the deficiencies of the local economy and worked for action to meet some of the problems. Mr. Upshur had already had one spell of tuberculosis when I first knew him, and he had severe attacks from time to time which eventually forced him to give up his work at the *Commonwealth*. After his departure, the *Commonwealth* lost all personality, used nothing but "canned" editorials and AP features, and never made a positive comment on politics, local or national.

The paper with a larger circulation in Greenwood than the *Commonwealth* was the Memphis *Commercial Appeal*, which carried a fair coverage of national news and thoroughly covered Mississippi—in both respects much better than the two Jackson papers. During the early 1920's its most famous editor, C. P. J. Mooney, won a Pulitzer Prize for his outspoken opposition to the Ku Klux Klan, but since Mooney died the *Commercial* has undertaken no crusades that might arouse any major opposition within its circulation territory of west Tennessee, north Mississippi, east Arkansas, southeast Missouri, and southwestern Kentucky. In 1933, from my fifteen-year-old ivory tower, I sent the *Commercial* a long letter protesting its conservatism and lack of originality. There was enough sensitivity to such protests for the publisher to send one of his staff men to see me. Beyond his holding out illusory promises of campus correspondent jobs to pay my way through Ole Miss or Millsaps, nothing came of it. Shortly thereafter, the *Commercial Appeal* was sold to Scripps-Howard, giving that chain a monopoly in Memphis (it already owned the *Press-Scimitar*). The *Commercial Ap-*

peal retained its outward identity as an independent paper—and became even more conservative. It remains so today.

The Jackson morning paper was the *Clarion-Ledger*, a colorless publication always politically identified with future governor Paul Johnson, Sr., because of his long-time personal ties with the newspaper's owners, the Hederman brothers; otherwise, the paper's only claim to fame was its position as the state's chief advocate of prohibition, both state and national. The Jackson *Daily News*, the capital city afternoon paper, personal organ of editor Fred Sullens, was filled with Sullens' personal politics—on the editorial page, in his front-page column "The Lowdown on the Higher-Ups," and in his news columns themselves during campaigns. Sullens was a hard-core conservative on practically every economic issue, but personality always dictated his choice in state elections. His editorial flamboyance was rivaled only by Bilbo on the stump—the mutual trade-mark being a long assortment of big and unpleasant adjectives to further describe an unpleasant descriptive noun such as scoundrel, liar, jackass, or nincompoop. Sullens was always anti-Bilbo, but he was even more anti-Johnson and anti-Hederman. He and Governor Johnson came to blows in a hotel lobby one day, and Sullens claimed to have broken a cane over the governor's back. I have often wondered with what crowning irony this vitriolic old man who had been the scourge of so many must have addressed himself when, in the 1950's, harassed by advancing years and family stockholder squabbles, he was forced to acquiesce in the sale of his newspaper to his lifelong professional enemies, the Hedermans, thereby giving that family a newspaper monopoly in the state capital.

During my first years in school, I had made fair grades in all my work. Before long, however, the only work that held my attention was what could be absorbed by reading, when I could spare the time from the endless extracurricular reading in which I was always absorbed. In junior high and high school the Greenwood school system had some wonderful teachers, like Rosa Spann, Mary McCain and Willie Mae Williford, with the will and ability to encourage rebellious and disdainful students, and I benefited from them. In retrospect, my efforts to show off superior knowledge must have been tiresome. In those days, the school system over the Delta had annual "literary field meets," in which students competed in written examinations with representatives of other schools. I was proud to represent Greenwood in history, and very unhappy one year to be shunted to "current events" in favor of a girl who never argued with that year's history teacher. One of my field-meet opponents from the town of Goodman was a future Pulitzer Prize historian, David Donald.

My brother Fred never found a way to adapt to school. He was made for the woods and the fields. No boy ever loved hunting more. I know his soul today rambles over fields and streams, calling to his dog, waiting for a squirrel to reveal himself by fluttering a leaf, or patiently tracking a covey of quail. One of Fred's few scholastic triumphs was a junior-high essay contest on how America could keep the peace. At my suggestion, he concluded the paper by appropriating a slogan I had found in a publication of the American League Against War and Fascism—"The way to keep America out of war is to keep war out of the world." I thought of that when the news first came to us that Fred had gone down in the South Pacific with the cruiser *Juneau*.

Perhaps the high point of my school career in Greenwood was in the columns of "The Bulldog Broadcast" rather than in the classroom. I don't remember where the idea originated, but I do remember that I gloried in the prestige of a weekly column, "Frankly Speaking." It was a series of one-paragraph barbs, largely about school or current events. "The Bulldog Broadcast" was printed as a weekly page in the *Commonwealth*, so my readers included a good many adults. One of those adult readers was the town's most distinguished lawyer, A. F. Gardner. Several times he spoke to my mother in the courthouse about one of my columns, and then one day he asked me to come to his house and inspect his library, which contained a great many volumes of history and biography that weren't in the public library.

Mr. Gardner was one of the supporting cast, as chief counsel for the defense, at one of the few times a Greenwood dateline appeared in the national news before the tragedy of Emmett Till. A lady doctor was being tried for (and convicted of) the poison murder of another doctor, and the trial brought big-time reporters to Greenwood. One of them was Herbert Asbury, who had written two or three books, at least one of which I had read. The courtroom was packed every day with people absorbed in the dramatic stories from the witnesses, but the real drama for me was watching the two full press tables in operation.

During our 1932 flood, most of the newspapermen had covered the story by telephone, but the newsreel cameramen did show up. I was disillusioned to discover that when they went out in their boats to make pictures, they took along two Negro men who were used as props in the scenes they set up depicting dramatic rescues from the roofs of marooned houses. Had they come a little sooner, and looked a little closer, of course, they wouldn't have had any staging problems.

Working your way through college is a fine American tradition, but the chance to do it in Mississippi at the peak of the depression took more than the mere will to work. For a few months, I pursued the vain hope of a newspaper correspondent's job that would provide enough for me to get by at one of the four-year schools, and I applied for every conceivable scholarship or job. The scholarships were just nibbles, and the jobs for a freshman, age 16, were strictly part-time. There was no job at any of the four-year schools that didn't require enrollment fees, book buying, and other supplements of job income that were entirely out of reach of my mother's pocketbook or borrowing potential.

The one institution that kept the situation from being hopeless was Sunflower Junior College, 25 miles west of Greenwood at Moorhead, and partly supported by Leflore County. Except for the sports pages, most of my reading about colleges had been of Harvard and Yale, Chicago and Columbia. I was too much of a realist to have entertained any thought of a school outside Mississippi, but one long dream was badly shattered when I had to resign myself to the fact that my only chance of going to college was to go to Moorhead. In so many ways, going there was not going to be much of a break with Greenwood, but it would bring me at least one step closer to that outside world which had been the chief inspiration of my life to that time.

Chapter IV

MISSISSIPPI AND

THE WORLD

The Mississippi junior college system was superimposed upon an earlier system of agricultural high schools which were first established to give farm children a chance to attend a good high school through the use of boarding facilities at a time when good roads and school buses didn't exist. Junior college has thus offered additional formal education to many students who otherwise could have gone no further than high school. In my own generation, they led to college graduation, complete with degree, for many who could not go direct from high school into a four-year college.

I went to Moorhead, as we commonly referred to Sunflower Junior College (in 1961 it was renamed Mississippi Delta Junior College), because any other college was financially out of the question. Most of the other students were there for the same reason. With the spur that added maturity lends to personal effort, and the enhanced opportunity to borrow money for the junior and senior years, the majority of my classmates continued on to graduate from a four-year college after leaving Moorhead.

Even before the days of the National Youth Administration college program, Moorhead was a working school. Except for teaching and administration, all the work required to maintain the school was done by the students, who got credit for it against their board bill, the largest item of school expense. Those without regularly assigned jobs worked on the school farm at an hourly rate. Board was sixteen dollars a month, and books and other fees probably didn't come to more than fifty dollars a semester. In addition to the school work program, after 1933 there were fifty or sixty NYA jobs, each with a maximum allowance of ten dollars a month. I was the school publicity man, acting as correspondent for all the Jackson and Memphis newspapers in the name of the school president. For the first several months, the president wanted to see everything that I sent out, but eventually we found ways to work around this requirement which made for more working and less waiting on my part. My first year at Moorhead probably cost my mother close to a hundred dollars. The next year, I knew my way around much better, and the cost was held down to ten dollars.

The rudimentary required courses for degrees, such as mathematics and languages, are usually taken in the freshman and sophomore years, and they were probably as well presented at Moorhead as at any of the senior colleges in the state. More creative work, or study that required the use of research materials, was another question. The students who learned or developed most had to strike out on their own for this. The boarding-school disciplinary system was rigid—

study hours every night until the lights-out bell, compulsory church attendance on Sunday, no dating except at school functions on week ends. Other than sports events, the social life was restricted to a movie in the auditorium each Friday night and an occasional concert. Dancing was barred. Visits home were limited to three or four a year, and then only with specific permission from the president. The rules were enforced by stern penalties requiring so many hours' work clearing "new ground" (drained swampland, never before farmed). Sometimes the chores might be the same jobs that other students were doing for pay. Since most of those students who weren't at Moorhead because of financial necessity were there because their parents thought they needed some of this heavy discipline, and the rest of us were having to hang on for whatever chance at school we could—the system seemed to work. Transgressors lined up every Monday morning to receive their sentences to so many hours of new-ground work.

One spring afternoon when President Vandiver was out of town, another boy and I took advantage of his absence to hitchhike to Greenwood to see Carl Hubbell of the Giants pitch against the Cleveland Indians in a major league baseball exhibition. It was a good game, but dusk found us stranded at Itta Bena, a town only halfway back to school. We were flagging every car that approached in the twilight, when finally one stopped. The door opened and it was President Vandiver. "Twenty-five hours," were his only words.

I became a columnist for the *Sunflower Petals*, the school paper, and turned around the title of Fred Sullens' Jackson *Daily News* column to make mine "The Higher-Down on the Lower-Ups." I had some forthright and sometimes very pat answers for most state and national problems. There were several which I would hate to have to reprint, such as the one in which I said a war with Japan would be impossible because there was no way they could get to us. Some of the other paragraphs still look fairly good:

> The death of Huey Long at the hands of an assassin is an event that forebodes evil for the rest of the country as well as Louisiana, if it means that Americans have begun to use assassination as a political weapon. There is no doubt that Long invited death through his wholesale use of bodyguards and the ruthlessness with which he destroyed men, but political murder cannot be condoned under any such conditions.

> Long advocated many worthy measures, but his methods were leading straight toward an American brand of fascism. The reason men of his type have been in public office is because they have been able to play, sincerely or not, on the discontent of the disinherited masses of the South. The only way we can avoid making the South completely fascist is to change the system which allows for such inequalities without chance for advancement.

> It is hard to believe much about the progress of education when one has to hear daily the most ignorant prejudices and hatreds being voiced by college students. It does seem that some education should instill a little tolerance into the young people who will be the deciding influence in the country's affairs a few years hence. This is supposed to be a Christian nation, yet the most un-Christian ideas and practices are being openly condoned by so-called Christians. The trouble is this—the churches and schools were created to improve mankind; yet they are afraid to ask for improvement for fear that mankind will do away with them. You can't quench your hunger with crumbs that fall off the table; you've got to eat off the table.

In my sophomore year at Sunflower, I was editor of the *Petals*, in addition to being columnist. David Holloman was the business manager of the paper, Willie Ruth Townsend was assistant editor, and we also took on the same jobs in re-establishing a school yearbook. We talked of newspaper ventures together in the future, after we dug up the capital in some obscure and indefinite way. My journalistic effort at Moorhead was good experience, but it added up to no more than that when I tried to translate it into a newspaper job. There was no way to go on to another college, and I wanted to go into newspaper work if this was the time to strike out to earn my living.

I applied to nearly every newspaper in the mid-South area, but in 1936 openings were practically nonexistent. One prospect developed with the *Clarion-Ledger* at Jackson, which was looking for a reporter to be hired at ten dollars per week. I got down to the finals in the competition for this job, but in the end lost out to a young fellow who had been working on his home-town paper. Fourteen years later he was the high-powered publicity man furnished to my opponent in the runoff of my nomination to Congress.

After working during the summer measuring cotton under the AAA crop-reduction program, I got a job in the fall of 1936 as general assistant in the engineering department of Supreme Instruments Corporation, Greenwood's sole manufacturing plant. Supreme Instruments made several types of electronic testing equipment, and my principal job was to make blueprints, which I did with the sun on clear days, and an old arc machine that gave a nasty shock on rainy days. Then the firm acquired a modern blueprinter, and I became one of automation's earliest casualties. For a few days they tried to find a place for me on the assembly line, wiring instrument testers, but I showed little prospect of ever acquiring that skill.

No other job immediately turned up, but I didn't look very hard. I set up my portable typewriter on the dining room table, determined to earn my living as a free-lance writer. I had been reading *Writer's Digest* for several months and struck out with that publication as my principal guide to markets. For three or four months my only income was from two- and three-dollar items for business trade journals, or the two to five dollars a month I received as the Mississippi correspondent for the Religious News Service. Then an article about the Civil War which I had submitted to *Esquire* was bought by *Coronet* for $100. *Reader's Digest* reprinted a half-page of it for $25, and the die was cast. For the next two-and-a-half years I eked out an existence as a free-lance writer, concentrating primarily on articles about Mississippi, but willing to tackle any subject that might bring in a few dollars. The hours were longer, but in those two years my writing earned me more than the pay checks from Supreme Instruments would have been.

I did a fantastic amount of writing during the period, ranging from more than half the historical material in the mammoth centennial edition of the *Clarion-Ledger*, for which I was paid at the space rate of a dollar per column, to an article in *Liberty* about the emerging "chemurgic" industry (chemically processed farm products), for which I was paid $200 and for which I secured the byline of Mississippi's Governor Hugh White. The state advertising commission paid me a bonus of $50 because the article gave Mississippi some favorable publicity. But, as with most unarrived magazine writers, the big story of my career was not the articles published or sold, but the ones that almost sold. It was strictly a buyer's market, and editors had no qualms about setting forth minutely detailed requirements for material being prepared purely on speculation. The articles that demanded the greatest preparation and generated the highest hopes might eventually bring a personal letter of refusal instead of a form rejection slip, but they rarely brought any money. I'm sure that my writing often lacked a professional quality, but the biggest problem was that national magazine editors simply didn't have much interest in the South in general or Mississippi in particular.

The most carefully prepared of all my unpublished efforts even included the plans of my collaborators to leave their home town upon its publication. *Esquire* announced plans for a new magazine to be called *Ken*, with sensational factual articles as its main attraction. For these, its announcement said, payment would be at least $1,000. I queried the editor about the possibility of an article giving a detailed factual account of a lynching, in which the mob had taken a Negro prisoner from the jail when it appeared that he might not be convicted of first-degree murder. The lynching had never been officially solved, and nobody had ever been arrested in connection with it. Our article would name all the principal members of the mob and tell how they had planned and executed the murder. The lynching had taken place in a town nearly 100 miles from Greenwood, but two friends of mine there knew most of the story and were in a position to help me dig up the rest of it without the knowledge of the mob leaders, who were fairly prominent people in the community. We prepared the article with meticulous accuracy and the firm faith that $333 would be enough for each of us to make a new start somewhere else. Then some other factor entered the picture—probably *Ken's* libel lawyers—and the article was turned down with no explanation.

In that first period of writing for a living, articles about the South were not as popular as they were to become after World War II, and any emphasis on race problems or attitudes was discouraged. The "true detective" magazines as a trade practice turned down any story in which a Negro was a major character, either as criminal or victim. I prepared an article describing in considerable detail (and with substantial evidence) a lynching technique which then was being widely used in the South—"killed while resisting arrest"—by law-enforcement officers who in other days would have co-operated with lynch mobs. The strongly developing reaction against lynching, at home as well as across the nation, led to the subterfuge of prisoners' being killed when first arrested, allegedly attempting to escape when they were being taken to jail. None of the magazines would buy this story either, but I believe Religious News Service used a very brief item about it.

I will always remember the account of the murder of one Negro youth that I uncovered while digging up the material for the lynching article. Just before the mob members shot him, the youth shouted into their faces: "Joe Louis!"

One of the publications for which I wrote book reviews back in 1938 and 1939 was the *North Georgia Review*, edited by Lillian Smith and Paula Snelling. One day editors Smith and Snelling showed up in Greenwood as part of a tour of the South. I went with them on my first visit to a cooperative farm southeast of Cruger, bought with money raised by a Northern group aroused by the plight of sharecroppers turned off plantations in the cotton acreage cutbacks. I had tried unsuccessfully to get a national magazine interested in an article about the farm. Four or five years later, Miss Smith jumped into national prominence when her novel *Strange Fruit* became a best-seller. Her visit, with Miss Snelling, was the only personal contact I had with the editorial world during my two-and-a-half years of free-lancing. Everything else was done by mail.

My writing resulted in considerable travel over Mississippi, the one area in which I could claim broader background and knowledge than most other practicing free-lance writers, but it brought very little real contact beyond the normal orbit of Greenwood. A successful series of sales, big by Mississippi standards, seemed always on the verge, but they never quite materialized. I decided to change my goal to teaching history and writing on the side; and the first step in this plan was to return to college and get a degree. The NYA still offered student employment, and I now found that there were student loan agencies willing to advance money to students closing in on a degree. I went back to college, entering the University of Mississippi at midyear in February 1940.

I went to Ole Miss because it was the state university, with the only liberal arts degree within my reach that would be a satisfactory basis for graduate work. The forced choice turned out to be a fortunate one, however, for I accidentally joined up with the best three-man history faculty in the country. The trio were Bell I. Wiley, J. J. Mathews, and James W. Silver, all young and all capable of transmitting the excitement of history to others. In their classes, and in the general atmosphere that centered around their work, my vague ideas about making a career in history became specific and scholastic. In sociology, where there were two good teachers named Paul Foreman and Morton King, I gained solid background for much of the subject matter about which I had been writing over the preceding three years.

Ole Miss was a relatively small school, as state universities go, but its horizons were much wider than those of Moorhead and Greenwood, even for a student like me, slightly above the average age and with considerably more experience in self-employment. For the first time there were people interested enough and informed enough to welcome, and encourage, free-ranging talk about the problems of the economy and the society of Mississippi. As on many university campuses, Ole Miss students gave priority to campus activities, and few of them were concerned about the derisive "country club" label their fellow students at other Mississippi schools gave the university. Scattered throughout the student body, however, were serious minds interested in all problems. Here was no ferment of reform or revolution, but neither were there taboos on subjects for learning or discussion. Most of those serious students understood the objectives, if not the intricate working details, of the New Deal program, and they were able to relate the purposes and the results to Mississippi, and to the advantages that would accrue to Mississippi and to themselves.

While most of the college students of the late thirties were pursuing their happy-go-lucky ways, oblivious or indifferent to the fact that the torch had been laid to the life we knew, some of the crusading breed of students were busy whipping up a shortsighted enthusiasm for pacifism. The youth protests of the thirties were completely unrealistic, but they were a reflection of the isolationist posture that had characterized our national sentiment and governmental policies for many a year. A good part of the attack was against military service, of course, and most of the adherents were more enamored of the seeming nobility of their cause than they were interested in trying to understand the appalling forces that had to be halted. There was a vague general belief throughout the United States that the decision to fight or abstain was strictly up to us; the student peace groups owed no apology to their not-so-wise elders. Back at Moorhead, I had expressed editorial approval of the "Veterans of Future Wars" organization among college students. I attended a statewide church youth meeting, climaxed by a massed affirmation of the Oxford oath against participation in military service.

As with the original Oxford students, the oath and everything that lay behind it was promptly forgotten when war became a reality. At Ole Miss, by 1940, I had abandoned all my antiwar ideas in the rising anxiety about Hitler. A good part of the country felt we could sustain neutrality in perfect safety. My own position had become interventionist by 1940, but I must have retained an element of belief that we could help without actually becoming physically involved, because at the same time I was still thinking of my own future in terms of peacetime pursuits. I passed up the graduation exercises at which I was awarded my B.A. degree in the summer of 1941 so that I could take a state merit system examination scheduled for the same day; that exam might lead to some future job. In November 1941, after having already tried unsuccessfully to enlist in the Navy, and with several applications for commissions submitted, I went to Atlanta to a meeting of the Southern Historical Association, to meet people and to look for schools that wanted candidates for doctorates in history. I had qualified for some sort of fellowship for the fall of 1942 and was tentatively planning to enter graduate school at the University of North Carolina.

Most of the campus "wheels" at Ole Miss qualified for second lieutenant's commissions through the ROTC program, and more than two dozen of the best of them became figures in the high casualty rates of infantry line officers. It is interesting to observe the attitudes and standards, today, of those who survived their war service. All of them were raised in the traditional Mississippi atmosphere of "keeping the nigger in his place," but very few were subjected to the stifling climate of blatant racism and all-out pressure for conformity that exists today. A number are prominent in professional, business, and political life, and perhaps half of them are active in organizations such as the Citizens Councils and their political satellites. All of them should know better, merely from their exposure to enlightenment when they were in college.

Those former students who are active today in the re-
gressive forces which control Mississippi may seem an ex-
ceptionally high percentage, but that is because they are the
ones who stayed at home; a large number of the prominent
students of the day chose to follow careers elsewhere, with
considerable success. Despite the fact that the state university
is the normal college choice for young people who have ready-
made careers ahead of them at home through family connections, a large proportion of Ole Miss's outstanding students of that period did not return following World War II;
if they did, they left shortly thereafter. None of them that I
know of, in his present career outside Mississippi, is waving
any flags for the kind of society Mississippi stands for today.

I had planned to pay part of my expenses at Ole Miss by
continuing my free-lance writing, but I found that the pressures of keeping up on campus left little time for such efforts.
Perhaps the discovery that I could squeeze by through the
combined efforts of the NYA, my family, and a philanthropic
Mississippi loan fund called the Field Foundation contributed
to my abandonment of writing for pay, but there were also
literary demands on the campus which seemed more immediately compelling.

One of my good friends in the town of Oxford was Dale
Mullen, the son of the publisher of the *Oxford Eagle*, then the
best weekly newspaper in Mississippi. Dale and his brother
Phil had briefly published, largely through the courtesy of
their father, a "little" magazine which they called *River*.
Copies of *River* would be collector's items today, because it
first printed the works of several to-be-famous writers, including Eudora Welty and Tennessee Williams. The literary
magazine bug stayed with Dale, and I helped him develop the
Mississippi Literary Review, which was the joint product of
half a dozen of us on the campus with similar inclinations. We

had had the idea for a long time, but we sprang into action when the young man who had the cigarette advertising contract for the campus humor magazine left school hurriedly and we were able to grab this particular asset. The maiden issue was notable, to us, for one of the first serious studies of the works of William Faulkner, done by a faculty member, and a ghastly short story contributed by John Faulkner. To the Ole Miss English faculty it was notable primarily for its multiplicity of typographical errors. With so many editors, nobody had the responsibility of proofreading. The first issue came out about December 1, 1941. There was no second issue. There was Pearl Harbor instead.

During the week after Pearl Harbor, Dale and I tried to join the Navy together, but at that stage the Navy was still demanding better physical specimens. I had been classified as 4-F by Selective Service for about a year because of overweight and a badly perforated eardrum. In January there was another Selective Service examination, this time on a mass basis. The doctor didn't look at my right ear, and by then the Army was willing to take on the job of weight reduction. In early February 1942, I was in the Army.

The Army never had a softer, more out-of-shape specimen to work on. Almost my sole recollection of basic training at Fort Bragg was my daily failure to keep up with the rest of my battery in the morning calisthenics, and the awful necessity of staying in bed nearly every Saturday afternoon and Sunday to cool a fever or recuperate the energy necessary for the coming week. By a variety of near-misses and near-miracles, I survived. I had been a poor student of arithmetic and all subsequent mathematics from the fifth grade onward, but on the basis of the way the punch cards fell, the Army sent me from the induction center at Camp Shelby to a training battery in survey and instruments at the Field Artillery

Basic Training Center at Fort Bragg. We had day and night trigonometry classes. It was a period when the acute shortage of officers to meet the needs of the vastly expanding Army was recognized, so four months after I got to Fort Bragg, I was on my way to the Artillery Officer's Training School at Fort Sill, with corporal's stripes on my sleeve.

If I had been unprepared for basic training, I was overwhelmed with a feeling of inadequacy when I reported to OCS. Our class was huge, but the people we knew intimately were the 25 men in our platoon. More than half of the men in mine were high-ranking NCO's from the Regular Army or National Guard outfits, and most of the others were draftees of at least a year's service. The only other man in the platoon who had been in the Army no longer than I had had two years of ROTC in college. I was irreducibly overweight and had never learned properly to execute a smart about-face or some of the other elements of military drill. The rumors of the fierce attrition in OCS were thick, and in the first few weeks I lived in daily dread of being the first to go. Oklahoma summers are just as warm as Mississippi summers, but I had never spent one in Mississippi double-timing through a twelve-hour-a-day schedule and then spending two or three hours studying at night in a tent with five other men. One of the tactical officers told me during the first week of our ninety days that I would have to secure a waiver of my excess weight before I could receive a commission. One day I missed a command during close-order drill, and the officer in charge accused me of being weak from cutting down on meals in order to lose weight. I told him that I wasn't, but this interest encouraged me to open up about my bigger fear—that in the individual rating that we in the platoon were required to give each other from time to time, my lack of military bearing and aptitudes would put me so far down on the list that I would be the obvious choice for elimination.

"Don't let that bother you," I was told. "You've been high up on the list from the start." New-found confidence made the second half of OCS much easier than the first, though the day of completion was a major goal, like the end of a war or the end of a political campaign. I had uncovered a natural talent for shooting an artillery piece—not the actual firing of the howitzer, but conducting fire through observation of the target and calculating adjustments in firing data from round to round to put shells on target. Our last course was in tactics, and that was no great problem to a long-time student of history.

OCS at Fort Sill was a revolutionary experience to those of us from the South, and probably to a good many others from outside the South. Negro officer candidates were scattered among us wherever they happened to fall in the alphabetical list. There were two in my platoon, and that was probably the general distribution over the class. As far as I know, the only element involved in determining their number was the need to staff the Negro divisions and units being formed. There was some talk about the novelty of being in a platoon or in a tent with Negroes, but there were no complaints that I heard. The Southerners who expressed themselves to me said they had no objections, and some even voiced approval. Everybody knew that integration was the official Fort Sill policy, and nobody was bucking the tide. I knew then that changes in racial patterns would be generally accepted when authority backed acceptance and when resistance would mean resistance to compelling authority. Unfortunately for some of its future programs, the Army did not integrate its other major OCS systems. All the results at Fort Sill were good.

With my new gold bars I was sent to help establish a new unit, the 243rd Field Artillery Battalion, at Camp Shelby, Mississippi. I was to stay with the 243rd through months of stateside training and eventual shipment to Europe in time to add our eight-inch guns to the Third Army artillery for General Patton's campaign in France. Part of life in the Third Army was constant fear of Patton's wrath over some trivial incident that he would not allow explained. There were too many stories of these incidents for some of them not to have been based on fact. A common saying was "Our blood and his guts." After the race across France began, however, being in Patton's army was a paramount source of pride. On balance, I believe that Patton's theatrics benefited morale so much that this more than offset his other failings as an army commander. I'm proud of my Third Army patch.

Our gun was an improvised weapon, the tube of an eight-inch naval gun mounted on a 240 howitzer carriage. It had a range of twenty miles but was highly erratic at all distances. To offset this we had a well-trained, hard-working, high-morale outfit led by an aggressive and energetic commander, Lieutenant Colonel Jo Rucks. These factors made the 243rd stand out over other heavy artillery units and put us in support of many actions where we rendered effective help. Beginning at Brest, we got in the habit of handling 240- and 8-inch howitzer battalions through our fire direction center, because we already had the observers out and a fire direction unit that was fast and efficient. It was a small item in the mass of fire power, but the 243rd's extra contribution was part of what I believe is a special quality of the best-led troops.

Two of the highlights of combat I remember still. One was the outpouring of French civilians along the highway from Saint-Malo and Dinard to Brest on the Sunday when we moved from one clean-up to another. This was the actual celebration of liberation by people in their black Sunday best, and all of us knew it. The other was the thousands of freed slave laborers, walking west toward France in March of 1945, as we moved across the Palatinate toward the Rhine. They must have been hoarse and tired beyond belief, but they seemed to wave and cheer at every Army vehicle they met.

When the war was over in Europe, everyone wanted to get home and get out. I thought of the changes that the war had made in my smaller world. My brother Fred was gone. In January 1943 I had been sent to Miami to make preparations for one of our batteries to take on an assignment with the Eastern Defense Command. In the Pullman berth that night, after the train was moving out to Jacksonville, I opened up the paper I had bought and read that the five Sullivan brothers had been lost together in the Pacific. I knew they were on the *Juneau* with Fred, and I had to wait the rest of that sleepless night before I could call Mama from the Jacksonville station and learn that he had gone with them. David Holloman, my best friend since Moorhead days, had gone down with a B-29 over Japan. Baby Sister Sadie had grown up while I was gone. She had married an airman from Indiana, and that would be her future home.

Military life had no appeal for me, but I decided the United States had invested too much in my training for me to get out of the Army before it was all over with Japan too. I volunteered to stay for the duration. During the last weeks of the war, with the Third Army stretched too far out behind armor to need heavy artillery, the 243rd was assigned MP duty. Immediately after the surrender we took on the job of guarding prisoners of war. For several weeks we had thousands at Regensburg, then the location of Third Army headquarters, including a special cage of field marshals. I knew that Regensburg was the site of the battle of Ratisbon, but I

didn't know until we were there that it was also the site o
Mad King Ludwig's Valhalla, a Greek-style temple high
above the Danube. Two other officers, Malcolm Harrison and
Jim Henderson, and I went up to look at Valhalla. As we
approached the front door, it opened and General Patton
walked out, preceded by his aide. We saluted and froze. Pat
ton returned the salute and passed by, then turned back and
spoke. "What kind of transportation are you up here in?" he
asked in his high-pitched voice. I had visions of being court
martialed for wasting government gasoline, but I had to an
swer: "A jeep, sir."

"Well, there are a lot of unsightly gas cans strewn along
the road coming up this hill," Patton said. "We'll attend to
that right away, sir," I replied, needing no further hint. Three
captains collected a jeep-full of empty gas cans on the way
back down the bluff; it was the only direct order I received
from General Patton during my service in the Third Army
The temple contained Ludwig's idea of the great of all ages
down to and including him. There were busts of these other
immortals and a life-size statue of Ludwig. There were also
several vacant pedestals. Looking in the basement, we found
the missing busts. They were of Jews who must have been
banished to suit Hitler.

The last stand of the 243rd was at an old German air base
near Bad Aibling, roughly halfway between Munich and
Salzburg. Here, with the help of CIC, we processed more
than 300,000 German prisoners. For a few weeks in the sum
mer, we moved down the Autobahn a few miles beside a
pretty little Bavarian lake, Seeham See, and trained to go to
Japan. When the war ended in the Pacific, we went back to
Bad Aibling to process prisoners from Italy and wait to go
home.

Our men with the longest service and the most depend

ents were high on the point release system, so a number of them had been sent home while we were still waiting for Japan. By now I was also acting as battalion adjutant, in charge of personnel assignments. As fast as a vacancy for noncommissioned rank appeared on our table of organization, we promoted one of the old 243rd veterans. Before I was transferred, every man but one who had been with us during combat had also received the orders starting him home. Almost all of them were going home at least one grade up in rank, with new stripes to show off and more terminal pay to draw. The one man who didn't go out with us had been a PFC at war's end, acting as orderly for the battalion headquarters battery. We left him as battalion sergeant major. It was the best send-off I could provide for the good men who had been the 243rd Field Artillery Battalion. The name may still be on paper somewhere, and it may come alive again someday, but it will never see the equal of its original band.

Chapter V

POSTWAR FERVOR

More young men came home from World War II with a sense of purpose than from any other American venture. I was one of them.

Military training and combat gave many of us a confidence in our own abilities that almost certainly would never have developed in the limited sphere that was the civilian world of 1940. We had been given the responsibility of acting to determine the war's outcome. We had not planned the strategy, but we had helped to make effective the life-or-death decisions that led to victory. If we could play that role, we felt we were equally capable of decisive action in the new world that the war had made. I wanted to be a part of it, and for me the main interest was Washington. I decided that I wanted to return to writing, and to write about Washington.

There was a personal arrangement of paramount importance involved in all this. A few months before going overseas I had met, at Columbia, South Carolina, the girl I was going to marry. She was Helen McPhaul, originally from Brewton, Alabama, but then working for the Tennessee Valley Authority on an Army mapping project. In preparation for our postwar plans, Helen transferred from TVA to a job in Washington with the Coast Guard. Letters from Helen, and the chance to write back, were what kept me going in the long months across Europe, and the strength and devotion she gave to my every undertaking were to buttress an often flagging determination in the years ahead. There are wives, and there are wives, in politics. Every man needs his own kind. I needed the kind who would actively work in the political arena without trying to dominate it, and I was lucky—Helen is that kind of wife. Feminine to the heart as she is, I'm sure my inability to express my profound feelings of love and gratitude has deprived her of many a compliment and reassurance she should have had but kept right on going without. Let them all be said now. I couldn't have made the climb, nor taken the falls, without her—and even if I could have, without her it wouldn't have been worth the effort. We were married a few weeks after I returned from Europe and moved to a cubby-hole apartment in Alexandria, Virginia. I opened up my typewriter and began to write, by courtesy of Helen's salary and my stipend as a part-time GI student at American University.

I started looking for things to write about in Washington, but half of Washington in that spring of 1946 seemed to be looking at Mississippi. Bilbo was up for re-election that year, and whether he would be returned to the Senate was the universal topic. There was grave concern about his increasingly wild agitation of every wind of racial fear and prejudice, but the well-meaning people who were concerned about him usually demonstrated their concern in a manner best suited to play into Bilbo's hands; he had built a picture of himself in Mississippi as the state's champion against outside attacks. I remember, one night, meeting an earnest young man who was making a career of picketing Bilbo's Washington apartment. I tried to tell him how his tactics were certainly helping to ensure Bilbo's re-election in Mississippi, but my arguments meant nothing. It was more important to be against Bilbo than to be rid of him.

I knew Mississippi, and I even knew Bilbo, better than I foresaw a chance to write with knowledge about Washington. Within a few months I began to look for something back home. It was obvious that my move in the postwar world should be made from a base in Mississippi. The chance came right in Greenwood. James Alsop was the son of a wealthy planter, reared on a farm near Cruger but in the orbit of Greenwood. He was about my age and had acquired the urge to write and report while at Ole Miss. In the Army he served for a while in the same Mississippi National Guard unit with Hodding Carter. Jimmy came back to work for a few months with Hodding at Greenville, and to plan a new daily paper at Greenwood which he recklessly labeled in advance as a "liberal" paper. They asked me to join the venture, and I landed full in the middle of the postwar Mississippi Delta. Bilbo was at the height of his campaign. He had to run against something or somebody stronger than his opponents and more personal than just "outsiders" or "niggers." Hodding Carter was ideal for this purpose, so Bilbo pitched a good part of his campaign against Hodding.

Thus, in addition to the standard problems of starting a new newspaper against the entrenched local opposition, the new Greenwood *Morning Star* came into being as the child of that villainous liberal, Hodding Carter. Actually, Hodding gave up his share of ownership in the *Star* shortly after we started, but we printed it for a year at his Greenville plant.

My title was managing editor, with Helen as my proof-reader, but my job was also desk man, reporter, copy boy, columnist, and make-up man. We took over the plant of the *Delta Democrat-Times* at 5 p.m., with the hope of getting our six- to eight-page paper out in time to truck it the sixty miles to Greenwood by daybreak. It was a time of frantic shortage of linotype operators, and many a day we were happy to settle for 8 a.m. delivery. Any morning was off to a good start if there were an editorial or two, and maybe a feature article, that I could lift in type from the *Democrat* to the next day's *Star*. There weren't many—Hodding was in the process of winning a Pulitzer Prize reputation for editorials on racial tolerance, which was no way for a new paper to win acceptance in Greenwood. The sixteen-hour days, six days a week, might have been more livable if printers had been more tractable. I had to learn that if I did not take abuse from tramp printers there wasn't going to be a paper the next morning, so I took it.

Not all days were sixteen-hour ones. There was an occasional twenty-hour stretch when I took on special reporting chores. President Truman (in the short-lived days before Truman hatred descended on Mississippi) was scheduled to address the annual meeting of the Delta Council at Cleveland in May 1947, but canceled out for some reason at the last minute. The substitute supplied was Under Secretary of State Dean Acheson. The speech Acheson made was the trial balloon for the Marshall Plan unveiled a few days later at the Harvard commencement, but only the Greenwood *Morning Star* (and, later in the afternoon, the *Delta Democrat-Times*) noticed anything unusual about the speech. The Associated

Press lead was something like this: "Under Secretary of State Dean Acheson hammered away at agricultural topics here in the cotton country today as he spoke to Mississippi Delta Council." My *Morning Star* lead said that the United States must aid its friends to restore economic stability to the world. Because the *Star* was a United Press paper (the service was cheaper), I supplied the UP local coverage for their national story, which they built from the State Department release on the speech.

The Associated Press national desk became concerned about the difference in emphasis between the two wire-service stories and eventually rewrote the AP story. There were not many analytical observers of the national press among the readers of the *Morning Star*, so nobody applauded our perception, but I have always been proud of our performance on an occasion that is worth a footnote in history. The AP reporter who flubbed the story eventually married a publisher's daughter and became a newspaper executive in the best American tradition.

Despite our problems as a "liberal" paper, the *Morning Star* began to succeed. Within a few months, our paid circulation passed that of our competitor, the *Commonwealth*, and slowly and painfully the advertising started coming in. Unfortunately, the rigors of nursing the *Star* for a year were beginning to tell on Jimmy Alsop. He was probably suffering even then from some of the ailments that struck him down with a brain hemorrhage a little more than a year later; gradually, it was becoming harder and harder to work with him. We were installed in a plant in Greenwood now, and conditions should have been a little better, but I had to call it all off one night when I suffered the final indignity of having the composing room foreman leave out my column rather than delay the make-up of a page. The *Star* eked out an existence for seven or eight years after Jimmy's death, but it finally expired without even the dignity of a merger. Two of its best known alumni are Charlie Pou, political writer for the *Atlanta Journal*, and John Herbers of *The New York Times*.

During the spring of 1947 I covered a service club speech at Greenwood by Circuit Judge John Stennis of DeKalb. Judge Stennis was a courtly, attractive man in the style of the Southern lawyer-scholar. A group of men who had been his classmates at Mississippi State College twenty-odd years before were interested in pushing him for statewide political office, and these service club luncheon speeches were one of the ways of making him known to the state.

The United Nations was the topic of the Stennis talk that day, and I thought it was the best expression of support for the UN that I had heard in Mississippi. Judge Stennis expressed the belief that UNESCO, with its potentialities for economic benefit for all of the undeveloped areas of the world, might make the greatest contribution to lasting peace of all the UN agencies. For the UN to achieve its great purpose, he declared, the American people must realize the possible necessity of having to yield some areas of national sovereignty to this international agency.

When Theodore G. Bilbo died in September of that year, John Stennis became the darkhorse candidate to succeed him. Two congressmen, W. M. Colmer and John Rankin, were in the race along with Paul B. Johnson, Jr., the son of a former governor fresh from a statewide campaign, and Forrest Jackson, a glib lawyer who was the heir to what there was of Bilbo's personal political machine because he had represented the Senator in his elections contest earlier in the year.

Rankin in his first years in Congress had been, even more than Bilbo, the heir apparent to the Vardaman strain of Populist doctrine in Mississippi. But change had come to him, too, and only "The Man" Bilbo was more skilled than he in hoisting the battle flags of racism. Jackson and Johnson tried to take on the Bilbo mantle, even though it was then a difficult fit for Johnson, whose father had been a Bilbo foe. Bill Colmer laid claim to being both the fitting heir to Bilbo and the chief exponent of conservatism in Mississippi at a time when the fight over the Taft-Hartley Act was giving rise to a new wave of antilabor sentiment in a state where the labor movement was almost nonexistent. John Stennis' base was the six counties of his judicial circuit and his friends among the Mississippi State alumni. This was a special election, and it would be on a high-man-wins basis.

I remembered the Stennis speech on the UN and told his friends in Greenwood that I wanted to help in the campaign. They suggested I might best be useful on the state campaign staff. About that time the man first hired to handle publicity turned out to be both too expensive and too infrequently available, so I was quickly taken on as a replacement. For the next six or seven weeks I slept in the hotel suite that was campaign headquarters and literally lived the campaign 24 hours a day. Before long I was general assistant to every division of the campaign.

Bilbo was lamented long and loud by most of the candidates throughout the canvass, but there were pockets of genuine revulsion to his demagoguery in every section of the state. It was to this vote that the Stennis appeal had to be directed. He secured what in any other state would have been called the liberal vote by campaigning without mentioning the race issue and by pledging to "plow a straight furrow down to the end of my row." The total Negro vote was no more than one or two thousand, and it was generally agreed that Stennis got the biggest share of it. As in any campaign there were side issues and distractions, but the home folks, the Mississippi

State alumni, and the moderates combined to elect John Stennis to the United States Senate by a margin of some 4,000 votes over Bill Colmer.

It was during this campaign that I had my first experience with the touch-and-go, hand-to-mouth character of most campaign financing. It was a short campaign, and relatively cheap, but I did not attempt to draw any of my agreed-upon compensation until a day or two before the election, when I had to have $100 to cover an election bet that I had made with Colmer's publicity manager. That extra $100 came in at just the right time—it covered the cost of preceding the Stennis party to Washington and setting up his Senate office.

My own first venture into politics had come a few months before, in the August primaries, when I ran for the State Senate while still an employee of the *Morning Star*. Under a so-called "gentleman's agreement" swap arrangement with neighboring Tallahatchie County, the two counties alternated in furnishing the senator. It was Leflore County's time in 1947. I jumped into the campaign early to try to head off as much opposition as possible. I had no illusions about my political attractions. My bread and butter job with the *Star* would give me practically no time for campaigning. I had engendered opposition by my association with the *Star*, and my relatively liberal attitudes were well known; these drawbacks might be offset by the recognition, through my newspaper writing, that I had some ability and some knowledge of Mississippi. My biggest assets were the good name of my father and the widespread friendships of my mother in every corner of the county. Mama had worked for sixteen years in the sheriff's office, collecting for automobile tags and taxes, *ad valorem* and poll, from at least one member of every voting family in the county. In 1944 she had left the sheriff's office to become deputy circuit clerk, working for the veteran officeholder she had been unable to dislodge back in 1935. There was no better-known or better-loved person in Leflore County, and the result was reflected in my nomination by a heavy margin over two opponents.

I came to the state capitol in Jackson for the opening of the legislative session in January 1948 with some of the glamour worn off by six weeks in Washington with the U.S. Senate, but it was still a moment that I remember as well as I do my first day in the U.S. House of Representatives. There were thirty or forty young veterans in the legislature, nearly a dozen of them still GI students at Ole Miss. I knew, either directly or indirectly, that most of them were idealists who hoped to have a part in making a better day. We had no illusions about completely remaking Mississippi, but we did believe we could contribute to its improvement. Before any of that new influence could get to its feet, a tidal movement against any change was mounted. Every man had to breast it as best he could.

Lieutenant Governor Fielding Wright had succeeded to the governorship upon the death of Tom Bailey, and he had then been elected to a full term in 1947. At a time when many state problems which had been postponed for five or six years because of the war, and many others which were being recognized for the first time, confronted Mississippi, Governor Wright felt no urgency about charting any new courses. The report of President Truman's Commission on Civil Rights a few months before gave the old guard the ammunition with which to open up a new attack on the national Democratic party, with Harry Truman as its particular target. Wright's inaugural address was devoted primarily to this attack, and to the unveiling of the scheme to defeat the Democrats in the electoral college. The Dixiecrat movement in 1948 was officially born at the beginning of our legislative session, and for the rest of our three months the Mississippi legislature was little more than a cheering section. There was virtually no program from the governor, and very little was generated by the legislature itself. We acted on the necessary appropriation bills, and spent the rest of the time passing resolutions attacking the national Democratic party and endorsing every fragment of opposition to it that showed up anywhere else in the South. I didn't join in the tumult, but nobody seemed to notice. Mississippi was too busy planning national salvation to take note of one dissident.

The one major exception to legislative inactivity was the passage of a workmen's compensation law, thereby making Mississippi the 48th state in the Union to adopt the program. Perhaps because we were last, the law we enacted was at that time something of a model. Several young members of the House were entitled to major credit for the law, but I was proud to have had an active part in getting it through the Senate. The day after the bill passed, one of my Greenwood constituents, a local manufacturer, called me on the phone to complain. I tried to mollify him: "Most people tell me that the compensation insurance they will have to carry will be cheaper than the liability insurance they've been paying."

"It won't be for me," he replied, "I've never carried any insurance. People who want to work for me know that I'm not going to stand for them suing me."

A new vocational college for Negroes had been authorized a few years earlier, and land had been donated for its site in Leflore County. I managed to get $250,000 appropriated for construction of the first buildings. Legislative achievement by a new man in the prevailing atmosphere was sharply limited, but I learned a lot from hard experience. One of my first bills to pass the Senate was a minor one relating to local tax assessments. The House Ways and Means Committee amended it, and the bill was referred to a conference committee, of which I was a member. The chairman of the House committee came to me one day with a conference report to sign, before we had ever had a meeting. "We changed the bill to do what you wanted," he said. "You sign the report right here." I automatically started to sign, but hesitated a moment and read the report. Instead of accomplishing my purpose, the new language had precisely the opposite effect. I refused to sign, and the conference report eventually withdrew the House amendment. After that I read all reports and every bill I voted on.

When the legislative session ended, I returned to Washington and my work as Senator Stennis' legislative assistant. As a Stennis staff man, and a Mississippi officeholder, I went to Philadelphia to observe my first Democratic national convention. The excitement and the glamour of big names were wonderful. My vantage point as the first session started was at the rail of the press box down beneath the main speaker's rostrum. As Dennis Cardinal Dougherty, Archbishop of Philadelphia, spoke the first invocation, my eyes were turned up in search of celebrities rather than bowed in supplication. There was a tug at my sleeve, and a voice said, "Everybody from Mississippi bow your heads." My admonisher was H. L. Mencken, to whom I had been introduced a few moments before. He laughed at the days twenty years before, when the *American Mercury* had been proclaiming Mississippi as the heart of the Bible Belt and the capital of illiteracy.

The Mississippi delegates, or rather the group in firm control of the delegation which was bound under the unit rule, came to Philadelphia prepared to proceed to Birmingham and organize the States' Rights party. The Mississippi movement, outlined earlier, was a direct offshoot of a scheme first promoted in Texas in 1944, which attempted to persuade electors already chosen, and on the ballot as Democrats, to announce that they would not cast their electoral votes for Franklin D. Roosevelt. The majority of the Mississippi electors back in 1944 had announced their opposition to Roosevelt a few days before the election, after the ballots had been printed and when they thought it was too late for the scheme to be thwarted. With popular indignation at a boiling point, Governor Bailey called a special session of the legislature, changed the election laws to allow a new and loyal slate of electors to be named, and new ballots were distributed barely in time by highway patrol cars. I had mailed my own absentee ballot from France, with votes for the defaulting electors. Fortunately, I had mailed it to my mother for delivery to the voting precinct, and she tore it up.

The 1948 Dixiecrat delegates had their reservations for Birmingham and devoted a good part of their time to arguing about who would be the strongest men for their ticket, but they spent the first three days at Philadelphia obsessed by the fear that they would have no excuse to walk out. The news that the platform committee had accepted a compromise, watered-down, civil rights plank, which the Mississippi delegate had to vote for, struck our group with dismay. They were saved by Hubert Humphrey's clarion call for a strong substitute civil rights plank, which carried on the floor at an early enough hour for the walkout to get the best coverage from the morning papers and the peak radio listening audience. (Complete TV coverage hadn't come yet.) While the Mississippi delegates walked out, I stayed for the rest of the excitement. Alben Barkley's great keynote speech and Harry Truman's fighting words on accepting the nomination, coupled with his dramatic call for a special session of Congress, fired me with far more optimism about Democratic chances in November than most people seemed to have.

But there were no Mississippians to whom I could say this. While the country marched one way, they had retreated another—to Birmingham. They are still there, in spirit if not in body.

Chapter VI

COMING TO CONGRESS

Any successful career in politics, at any level, owes a good deal to just plain good luck in timing. If Congressman Will M. Whittington had retired and thus left the Delta congressional seat open in 1948, my chances of succeeding him would have been almost zero. In 1948, youth and inexperience, which were to be handicaps in 1950, would have been major obstacles. More than anything else, however, the surge of the Dixiecrat movement in 1948 would almost certainly have made me a casualty, for it would have been impossible to conceal my lukewarm attitude toward that operation.

Mr. Whittington had announced early in 1948 that he was planning to retire after serving twelve terms. His announcement evoked loud protests instead of announcements of candidacies by would-be successors. I attended a meeting in Greenville one afternoon where a large delegation formally urged the Congressman to seek another term. He agreed to stay on the job. Before the year was out, the local leaders of the Dixiecrat movement were attacking him bitterly because of his failure to line up with the rest of the Mississippi delegation in campaigning for the Thurmond-Wright ticket.

A special session of the Mississippi legislature was called in late 1949, and I left my job with Senator Stennis in Washington to attend it. Since the regular 1950 session would follow immediately, I left Washington with no plans to return. A campaign by me for Congress was a possibility, but if that did not develop I had vague ideas about starting a newspaper supplement to cover the Delta, plus syndicating a weekly column about Mississippi government and politics. In December, after the special session, I went to New Orleans to sell the column idea to Clayton Fritchey, then the editor of the *New Orleans Item*. My friend Tom Sancton, who later became a novelist but was then a reporter for the *Item*, did a small feature story about my political forecasts for the coming year in Mississippi. I told him that my main effort would again be to repeal the state prohibition law. The wire services picked up the statement, and local papers in the Delta carried their story. I had worked for repeal in both 1948 and 1949, but by a quirk I got more publicity out of that casual report that I would try repeal again in 1950.

When Will Whittington announced on January 18, 1950, that he would not run again, the prospective candidates demonstrated no hesitancy whatever. State Senator Oscar Wolfe immediately announced as a candidate, and I said I was making a survey preliminary to announcing. The "survey" was essential to the campaign. I had to make the rounds of prominent people in my home town to ask their advice and then their support. It was mandatory to build up the strongest possible home-town backing. During the second week in February, I announced that I would be a candidate.

Oscar Wolfe had been a representative or senator from Bolivar County, like Leflore one of the largest in the Delta, for some twenty years. He was 59 years old. For at least ten years prior to 1950, Wolfe had been preparing for a campaign to succeed Will Whittington upon his retirement. He was a prominent leader in the Delta Council and in many other civic and business groups over the area. He was a farmer and cotton merchant, and for several years he had been a conference lay leader in the Methodist Church, visiting and conducting services in the churches of that denomination. In the legislature and in other affairs he had allied himself with the conservative group which dominated the state legislature and managed to come out on top in most gubernatorial campaigns. Because of his prominence, his wide contacts, and commitments of support from many influential individuals, Senator Wolfe was a heavy favorite to win the election, and he preempted the race from several would-be candidates who would have had to work the same fields for support.

I had first met Wolfe when I came to the Senate in 1948. I pledged to support him for Senate president *pro tem* because he was the only candidate from the Delta. Wolfe and his opponent for the post eventually compromised and divided their period of service. Of the 49 senators, so the story went, there were twenty senators pledged to each candidate, and nine pledged to both. The compromise ended embarrassment for all parties. Senator Wolfe was generally accepted as the leader of the Senate's old guard, and in 1948 we had voted on opposite sides on many questions. The big difference in 1950, however, was on a new highway program to be financed by an increase in the gas tax. Wolfe led the opposition to the program, and I voted for it. During the canvass that spring and summer, it seemed to me that every filling station operator in the district had been well informed about that vote.

The only other candidate to enter the race was a young lawyer from Marks, a year older than I, named Lomax Lamb. He was a personable son of prominent parents, a graduate of Yale and Yale Law School. Years before, at the request of his brother, I had tried to collaborate with him on a magazine article about his experiences in a Finnish sauna. His Ivy League manners attracted considerable attention, and so did his tireless campaigning from door to door over the district. My chief complaint about him was simply that he was in the race.

Stephen K. Bailey, one of the nation's most prominent political scientists, wrote this about the old Third Congressional District of Mississippi in a book called *Congress Makes a Law*, which he published in 1950 shortly before our campaign:

> The third Congressional district of Mississippi is roughly co-extensive with the so-called Mississippi Delta—a flat, bow-shaped area which stretches along the river from historic Vicksburg on the south to the Tennessee border on the north, and inland to a maximum depth of one hundred miles. Seventy-three percent Negro in population, one of the wealthiest cotton areas in the world, the Delta is dominated politically and economically by an aristocratic junta called the Delta Council, which is made up of the leading cotton growers, bankers, lawyers and businessmen in the area. . . .
> Whittington and the other leaders of the Delta Council have no use for the corrupt demagoguery of the Bilbo element in Mississippi. Almost without exception, the leaders of the Council are public-spirited, successful, gracious, and honest men, who are interested in what they consider to be the economic welfare and social stability of their little world. While believing in segregation and "keeping the Negro in

his place," they take an interest in the health and education of the colored population, and although that interest is in part motivated by economic factors, it is not without humanitarian overtones. . . .

In the last Congressional election, Whittington, unopposed, received 4,000 votes. There are over 435,000 people in the Third District, which means that less than one percent of the population took pains to, or were allowed to, vote. . . . This type of political behavior is "justified" by the fact that half the adult population has had less than five years of schooling, and only 10 percent have completed high school.

Bailey's analysis of the Delta district was largely correct, but he was overimpressed with the apparent political power of the Delta Council and its leaders. The Council itself was not directly involved in politics. If its leaders had controlled the Delta, I would never have been elected to Congress, because most of them opposed me in 1950. The situation in Mississippi had changed by 1962, when the majority of Council leaders supported me, but the Council itself still did not control politics.

From the time of Will Whittington's retirement announcement, the 1950 session of the State Senate was secondary to the congressional campaign. From Thursday night through Monday morning of each week end, I was busy with some type of campaign activity—visiting potentially influential supporters, writing letters, writing campaign material, and making tentative organization plans, mostly in my home county. The first primary was not until August 22, however, so there was a long way to go. I stayed with the legislative session until its adjournment in early April. Except for the highway program with its gas tax, there was no major legislative issue on which I had to cast a vote different from Wolfe's.

My campaign was operated largely from a home base.

Washington County (Greenville) had the largest number of voters, and Bolivar, the home of Senator Wolfe, had a few more than Leflore, but in a campaign battle that lacked the entertainment value of a spectacular personality, the strongest county would be the one where the best get-out-the-vote drive was organized. We worked up a very good one in Leflore County, and more than a third of my first primary vote came from there. At home my biggest assets were still my family name, and local pride in the fact that Greenwood had furnished the congressman for 26 years and ought to keep on doing it. In the ten other counties in the district, my biggest assets were relatives and former schoolmates at Sunflower Junior College. There were Smith and Ellis cousins of varying degree in all but the three smallest counties. Most of them were wonderfully helpful. There were dozens of classmates from Moorhead scattered in the same area, and I recall only one who did not support me. We had come through some of the roughest days of the depression years together, and we still were not in the Delta's top bracket. The sense of unity was still there and easy to arouse.

One important family asset had been added. In 1948 my mother had married L. C. Spencer, a farmer and merchant of McCarley, in Carroll County. Mama now actually lived outside the congressional district, but she and Mr. Spencer canvassed former Carroll County residents all over the Delta that summer. In addition, Mama made house-to-house calls in half the counties in the district. My stepbrother, Louie Spencer, was one of the prominent young businessmen of Greenwood, manager of the rural electric cooperative that served the surrounding territory. He became the bulwark of my campaign, and a chief pillar of support throughout the years in Congress—one of those mainstays whose value can never be properly expressed or rewarded.

My formal campaign opened on May 4, in the form of a press release. I promised to devote myself in Congress to working for adequate agricultural price supports and continuing progress in flood control measures for the Mississippi Delta. There were few formal speeches during the campaign, and my press releases were at first built around radio talks. When the *Commercial Appeal* (for which the releases were primarily written) made it clear that it made no difference to them whether a speech was actually made or not, I began to use press release datelines based on nothing more than visiting in the town named that day.

There had to be public "issues" for the press releases, but my chief argument against Wolfe was that he was too old to acquire the necessary seniority in Congress, and that his background in state politics would leave him too much beholden to the old guard political leaders and too little responsive to the ordinary citizen. Wolfe's case against me was that I was too young and inexperienced, and that there were many indications that I had a lot of liberal ideas and inclinations. On the surface there were no major differences in our approach to national and regional issues, but just beneath the surface there was a sharp awareness of some probable basic differences. We both pretty much ignored Lomax Lamb, worried at the indications of support he was receiving but assuming that he would finish third, and hoping that his vote would not be big enough to cause a runoff primary.

There were none of the traditional rallies in our first primary campaign, because there was no way to rouse up enough of an audience. All three of us got our biggest crowd of the campaign at a joint speaking held in Greenville and broadcast over a local radio station. The meeting was arranged by the Lamb supporters with the idea that it would benefit their candidate the most, but it turned out in my favor. Each of us spoke for ten minutes and then submitted to questions from the audience, which we answered in turn. All three of us planted some questions in the audience, and my plants turned out to be the best. Wolfe's friends asked questions designed to prove him the strongest segregationist, but Lamb and I both sidestepped those easily enough. My plants were designed to give me a chance to show a superior knowledge of some congressional issues. One of the questions planted for my side was how we stood on proposed changes in the Fair Labor Standards Act. Luckily the question came when it was my turn to answer last. Both Wolfe and Lamb tried to blur over an answer, but it was obvious that neither knew what the question was about. I then explained that the Fair Labor Standards Act was the Wage and Hour Law, and promised to protect Delta farmers and merchants from it.

Stirring up interest was the hardest job in the campaign. Except for a few counties where they were nominating local judges, our race was the only one on the ballot. The people who took the trouble to vote would be going to the polls for no other purpose than to select a congressman. From the start I had believed that personal contacts with individual voters would be the decisive factor in the contest, and I followed through with this idea to the end. In addition to the usual canvass of towns, I made a special effort to cover the isolated rural areas, with the idea that a call from the candidate would be more influential with an individual voter out here than in some of the towns. It was also good publicity to claim that I had walked down enough furrows and turnrows to have chopped forty acres of cotton.

We used volunteer workers in the campaign headquarters, but we had to hire typists and eventually organizers to work some of the other counties. My day began about 7 a.m. and ended when I got home anywhere from 8 to 10 p.m. My wife was the campaign office manager. Late at night we would review the problems that had developed in the office during the day, answer the mail, and prepare the next day's news release. There was no campaign manager.

The first primary ended with the usual predictions of victory on all sides. The weather was hot as usual on August 22, but some cloudiness broke the heat a little in the afternoon. Approximately 18,000 people voted. Wolfe and I each got just under 7,000 votes, and Lamb was third with 4,500. After three days, the final tabulation showed that I had led the ticket by seven votes. By that time we were well into the three-week runoff, with voting due September 12.

Most of the press releases and radio speeches during this time were charges and countercharges, with only an occasional reply. Late in the first primary, Wolfe had told a group that he was a better type citizen than his opponents, trying in some way to leave an implication of my alleged liberalism. I answered by asking on what grounds he challenged the patriotism of a combat veteran when he (Wolfe) had been of military age in World War I but had not seen service. The next charge against me was that I had been the author of a bill passed by the legislature and vetoed by Governor Wright because he feared it might open the door to integration of the Mississippi National Guard. This was true, but my answer was that the bill had been supported by the ranking officers of the Guard as part of a codification of state military law. The Guard's Judge Advocate General came to my defense, but there was not one word from one of the division's general officers who had asked me to introduce the legislation and was now serving as a campaign adviser for Wolfe. This charge died away after a few days, when they switched to "the dead cat candidate." I had introduced a bill in the legislature to encourage the killing of stray cats by game wardens and peace officers, as part of an effort to increase the population of quail and other game birds. When the bill came to the Senate floor, it became obvious that its opponents were going to ridicule it to death, so I shut off debate by getting it returned to committee. For two weeks, cartoons depicting Frank Smith attacking stray cats were distributed to prove that I was nothing more than the laughingstock of the state legislature.

I had a countercharge to throw into the fray. In the legislature I had introduced a bill which would have established a form of compulsory arbitration law in case of utility strikes. Remembering that, one of the state railroad brotherhoods now endorsed Wolfe for Congress. I publicized the endorsement, questioning Wolfe's claim to be the more conservative candidate yet seeking endorsement from the railroad unions.

Wolfe's tie to the old guard political leaders was my principal argument against him. Walter Sillers, Speaker of the State House of Representatives and chief symbol of the conservative forces which were dominant in Mississippi, actively entered Wolfe's campaign during the second primary, and we enlarged our attacks to include him. There was a large bloc of anti-Sillers voters in his home county of Bolivar, so we decided to bring them to our side by making the campaign as much against Sillers as Wolfe, as far as Bolivar County was concerned.

I had run third in Washington County in the first primary, and perhaps our biggest effort was put forth in that county. In his book *Where Main Street Meets the River*, Hodding Carter has a brief account of the campaign in Greenville, with this item about how it started:

> Frank was a natural politician. The first time we got together he accepted my offer of editorial support and printing credit, but suggested that the paper keep quiet until after

the first primary. He was sure that he would be in any run-off and he reasoned that when a newspaper gets behind any one candidate in a first primary field of three or more, the others double up on that candidate and the newspaper. Moreover, in our case, the danger was compounded because whoever my newspaper supported was tagged by his opponent as a nigger-lover by association. Frank thought we might as well put off that evil day for a while.

On the night before election, Walter Sillers gave the keynote speech at a Wolfe rally. He chose to hit back at our attacks on him by painting me as the tool of Hodding Carter, whom he termed "unfit to live in a decent white society." On that same night, Hodding was scheduled to address a meeting of the Negro Voter's League in Greenville. The invitation to talk to the Negro meeting had come several weeks before, with the request that it not include endorsement of any candidate. The *Democrat-Times* had come out in strong support of me editorially, but Hodding stuck to the nonpolitical tone. When he finished, he asked his audience for a show of hands by those who had heard the Sillers speech, which had been broadcast a half hour before the meeting started. Most of those present had heard it, and they roared when Hodding said if he ever left the Delta it wasn't going to be at the request of Walter Sillers. That was as much of an endorsement as I received from the Negro voters.

In the runoff I carried Washington County by several hundred votes, by contrast with the dismal third finish three weeks earlier. Of the three or four hundred Negro voters I am sure that 90 percent went for me—thanks to Walter Sillers. The results in Washington County were symbolic of the whole Delta. I carried seven of the eleven counties to win by a vote of 11,291 to 9,569. Instead of the usual slight decline shown by a second primary vote, we had stepped up the total by about 3,000. There was a Republican opponent in November. My vote was slightly over 4,000 and his a little more than 500. These vote totals were in a district which the census that year showed to have a population of 413,000.

For the rest of that year and through my first month in Washington, I had to live on charge accounts and borrowed money. The campaign had cost about $27,000. Part of this was raised in Greenwood as we went along, and a little more in Greenville and over the district in a "deficit campaign" after the election. Part of it came from the $3,000 savings and almost everything else that Helen and I owned, and another part came from the $5,000 in campaign debts which I repaid over the next four years out of my congressional salary.

Thanks to a great many factors rarely identified among those which make for political decisions in Washington, I had been elected to Congress. I was committed to support the traditional viewpoint of the white electorate of the Delta on racial issues, but my campaign had been conducted so that I was not completely bound to the extremists among them. I had made the customary homage to economy in government, and opposition to governmental regimentation, but I also knew that the largest portion of my supporters were people who felt that governmental economic activity in various forms was essential to their own economic security and the progress of the region.

The Delta district had voted about 95 percent for the Dixiecrat ticket in 1948, and in 1950 anything that could be labeled a Truman program was bad politically. I had to be against the Brannan plan, but I also had to be for a farm program that might involve as much or more in the way of government support, controls, and intervention. I had to be for rigid economy and against the mink coat and deep freeze scandals, but I also had to be for flood control programs that many big-city critics considered the ultimate in "pork barrel" waste. Perhaps no one but the man I was succeeding in Congress realized the inherent contradictions in the positions which had to be taken. I went to Congress well aware of the problems I would face in trying to reconcile the surface views of the voters of my district with legislation I would have to support if we were to achieve the economic progress that they wanted and that I sought as the primary objective of my service.

It was my belief that large-scale economic progress was the only avenue likely to lead to solution of the race problem in Mississippi. In 1950 I honestly believed that proposals like FEPC would only aggravate the situation in areas like the Delta, and states like Mississippi, and set back the small but significant progress which I had seen in my lifetime. Perhaps it was a rationalization forced by the political necessity of opposing all the civil rights legislation, but it was a common enough opinion among public officials and civic leaders of all shades of political complexion at the time. Along with work toward economic progress, I believed that the greatest contribution I could make to improved race relations in my congressional district, and in the country, was to refrain from inciting prejudice and to show as much respect as possible for the dignity of my Negro constituents as citizens of the United States, even if they were not voters and, hence, for the most part outside the normal constituent-congressman relationship.

My economic philosophy could be condensed to fairly simple terms—federal programs were necessary to get more money into the hands of the people. Few of my constituents would have expressed it like that, and neither did I, but both in practical terms and in speech-making generalities, it meant improving the standard of living by developing natural resources and enlarging economic opportunities for the South as a whole and the Delta in particular.

The Mississippi Delta was the richest part of non-industrial Mississippi, but it was still a section of the poorest state in the Union. Poor health and poorer education left the people of Mississippi unprepared for the productive and efficient labor essential to economic advancement. Thanks to already existing federal farm programs and the steady advance of mechanization, the Delta was moving away from some of the worst features of the old plantation-sharecropper system, but markets were still unstable and the agricultural credit system still needed help from government agencies. The economic development of the South required more capital, and there was little possibility of Mississippi's poor economy being able to engender the savings from which local capital comes. Mississippi's tax base simply wasn't big enough to produce the revenue required for development programs—it had to come from the federal government. Economic development would bring change, and in the Delta the power was in the hands of those most resistant to change because of their long ties to tradition, even though these same people would probably be the ones to profit most from the economic development.

My own study of the American economy and American history had been made as a student seeking an explanation of the impoverished South. I knew that the Constitution itself was a recognition of the need for a central government with the power to act in behalf of economic development, so there had never been anything wrong with government help to solve economic problems. Until the intervention of the New Deal, most government activity in economic affairs had worked against the economic interests of the South, either indirectly as in the case of not having a share in programs like Western land development, or directly as in the case of tariff policy through the years. The tariff policy and the freight rate structure served to prevent the South's becoming a full partner in American economic life.

Some of my own constituents who would reject with horror a United Nations program for undeveloped countries bearing the title "land reform" were among the chief beneficiaries of the federal government's land reforms, and I believed that policy should be carried even further. Land tenure was improving in the shift from the sharecropper to the day labor system, and there had been major improvements in farm credit and in marketing and research programs. Price supports were offering a form of assured income for the farmer, and soil conservation and flood control programs gave him confidence that his land not only would be protected from natural destruction but would be built back to fertility and productivity. All of the South, and especially the Mississippi Delta, had been a major beneficiary of a land reform program, and I believed it should be continued, with supplements like better roads and rural electrification.

From my experience in state government it was obvious that Mississippi, politically chained to a dual school system, would never be able to bring its expenditures for education up to the national average. The failure to do so created intolerable handicaps for Mississippi's future; it also saddled a large mass of almost illiterate citizenry on the states to which Mississippians migrated by the thousands each year. The only feasible solution I could see under existing circumstances was increased federal expenditures for education, achieved by whatever means it would take to satisfy the political elements involved. In the legislature I had been active in fights to increase state expenditures for education. Mississippi ranked first among the states in the proportion of personal income spent on education, but no matter what the proportion statistics showed, the educational system was not satisfactory either in expenditures per pupil or in the end results.

Coming to Congress, my problem was that of every congressman: how to work to achieve goals of national purpose, and at the same time keep my constituents satisfied that these efforts were in their best interest as well as the best interest of the country. I was well aware that the individual voter usually equates his own best interest and that of the country—"what is good for Joe Doakes is good for the country"—and that he would assess my legislative record strictly in that light. Most issues were almost certain to be evaluated in shades of gray, not in black and white. There would be accommodations of conscience on many issues, just as there always is in legislative bodies. With all these reservations, I firmly believed that I could serve the voters of the Third Congressional District of Mississippi as well as my own ideals to the best interest of both state and nation.

Chapter VII

TALKING NIGRA

One lovely Saturday afternoon in April of 1936, I flagged a ride with two men, strangers to me, from Moorhead to Greenwood. It was a new car with the still rare luxury of a radio. We listened to Bryan Fields describe Teufel winning the Wood Memorial Handicap, and then the driver opened a conversation with me:

"You're the editor of the *Sunflower Petals*, aren't you?"

I admitted the editorship of the college paper, and my host continued, "I hear you've been writing some pretty good editorials about the way we treat the nigras in Mississippi. I'm glad somebody is doing some talking about it."

His manner was cordial, and I accepted the implied invitation to talk—luckily with the caution natural to a reserved eighteen-year-old. I wound up expressing the hope that more and more of our people were going to help eliminate some of the inequities and injustices.

"They'll get no help from me," the driver replied. "We'll never help the black apes get one crumb." He turned his head slightly toward me. "If the niggers ever get a toehold in this country, it will be the people like you who have done it."

Fortunately, we were by then driving into Greenwood, and I was out of the car in a few minutes. I had been given another lesson on the penalty for expressing any view other than the traditional one on "the nigra question." I could talk freely about the Negro only within a very limited circle made up of a handful of people my own age, and I was 21 before I ever discussed the subject with any freedom with a grownup.

Half a century earlier, Joe Bailey had been a young lawyer in Mississippi before he moved to Texas, where he was elected first to the House of Representatives and then, in 1901, to the Senate. After Bailey's retirement from the Senate, while he was still relatively young, he practiced law in Texas but took time out to travel over the country occasionally. One day a friend asked him why he never returned for a visit to his native Mississippi.

"I'd like to go back," Bailey replied, "but I can't stand the conversation. Those people in Mississippi never want to talk about anything but niggers."

The tone and temper of Mississippi conversation has varied somewhat with details peculiar to the times, but if that was Senator Bailey's real reason for avoiding Mississippi, he would still not be able to go back. Mississippi's devotion to the topic has been unceasing. For instance, through the years of World War II, the housewives' favorite complaint was against "Eleanor clubs," and their husbands harangued the general belief that any economic advancement for the Negro was part of a plot to destroy the labor market and, hence, the South.

It was during the war years, too, that Senator Theodore Bilbo became nationally known for his white supremacy tirades. Bilbo had been re-elected to the Senate by a heavy majority in 1940, but the race issue was almost totally absent from that campaign. The live issue then was Bilbo's unswerving support of Roosevelt and the New Deal. The racial invective poured forth by Bilbo in the early forties became the state's best known trade-mark to Mississippians in service over the world. But even the Mississippi servicemen who felt constrained to defend Bilbo against some of the reaction to his extremism were having second thoughts about the patterns back home.

Mississippi had its fair share of the many training camps scattered over the South. Whether the views of Southerners were modified more than those of the non-Southerners who were being exposed for the first time to an aggressive segregationist position is a good question. *The New Republic* conducted a "Soldiers' Prose" essay contest for servicemen. In 1943 the magazine published a piece that I wrote, and a review of it is interesting today, especially for the tone of wartime optimism about everything but the race question:

YANKEE ARMY IN THE SOUTH

When the sociologists begin to decide how the war changed the people of the United States, one of the stories they will have to tell will be about how several million Yankees discovered the South and left it with a face somewhat altered. In Texas and the deep South, an area which provides the cheapest climate the army can find for its training establishment, there are scarcely more than a dozen towns with a population of 10,000 or more that do not have military installations of some nature. Thus far, the biggest effect of the war economy on the Southern town is still the juke-box variety of prosperity that has come from catering to the soldier's individual needs.

The soldier off duty looks principally for a meal, a girl, or something to drink. The commerce that has grown up as a result has brought more Southern and Northern people into contact with one another than anything that has gone before in our history. The resulting clash of standards and mores has brought about changes, on both sides, in long held ideas about the "outlander." The most obvious changes have taken place in the towns that have become suburbs of the major camps, Fayetteville, North Carolina; Columbus, Georgia; Hattiesburg, Mississippi, and as many more towns in Texas, have lost a major part of their Southern identity. There is a Yankee briskness about them that does not seem out of place now when matched with the babble of non-Southern accents on the streets, and in the stores and restaurants which are now so heavily staffed by army wives. The Southern mistrust of the Northerner, as such, has all but disappeared in the space of a few months. The Yankees have been seen and talked to; now they have become a familiar presence.

An interesting sidelight on Yankee-Rebel relations is the introduction of many Southern areas to first and second-generation Americans for the first time. The rural South, peopled by what the sociologists term Old American stock, had previously had very little contact with new Americans. In many cases, though not all, the Southern reaction has been a favorable one. Southerners have found some good friends among the first-generation group and vice versa. But sometimes inevitable clashes of personalities and folkways occur and serve only to reinforce the original prejudices about "foreigners," on one hand, and the Jeeter Lester stereotype of the Southerner, on the other.

One big discovery on the part of the South has been that many educated Easterners are as provincial in their own way as the backwoods sharecropper or the most confirmed Daughter of the Confederacy. That everything west of the

Hudson is not an uncharted province is something hard for many Easterners to realize; apparently, judging from many instances of tactlessness, it is even harder to conceal this lack of realization from the provincials. The provincials, who have been thoroughly educated by the Yankee radio, movies, magazines and books, are surprised to find that they know more about New York City than many a New Yorker knows about all of the rest of the country.

In the mutual exposure and exchange of prejudices, the South seems to be coming out ahead. A vast majority of the men from above the Mason and Dixon Line have followed the policy of behaving as the Romans in their relations with Negroes. Great numbers of Northerners who probably had no particular notions on the subject previously have acquired all of the more vicious Southern attitudes. One way in which Northerners absorb these attitudes—without the more humane paternalism which often is present in the Southerner's attitude toward the Negro—is by listening with dead-pan fascination to the "nigger stories" which Southerners tell—usually about their alleged experiences with public or private lynchings and beatings. Actually these stories are told chiefly because of the satisfaction of seeing and hearing the shock registering on the Northern listeners.

On the credit side, boys whose only knowledge of the South was a Hollywood, Gone-with-the-Wind conception, have learned some of the South's real virtues; for instance, that except for the tragic white-black abyss, it is a place of almost-classless warm and genuine friendliness. The marriage records in county clerks' offices throughout the South tell the story of the ease in establishing cordial mutual relations after the first shock of the army invasion had worn off. This, of course, has been the story of armies of occupation since the dawn of history. In many places in the South the records show as many marriages between Northern soldiers and Southern girls as army weddings involving home-town sweethearts, a most common phenomenon in these times, with hundreds of brides traveling down to the camp town for a wedding and honeymoon on a three-day pass. When the war is over, communities all over the land are going to feel the effect of the different outlook of Southern brides who have come North, and of ex-Yankee soldiers who elect to stay in the South with the in-laws.

Soldiers in the South get a good look at practically all of the seamy side of Dixie. Walking through the poverty of small towns or carrying on field maneuvers through dreary areas of eroded land and dilapidated cabins, Northerners see something of the bitter struggle for life that is the lot of such a large part of the people of this section. The reaction produced on many outsiders by these sights is merely distaste and a growing dislike for the region that the army has given them in which to train. But even the men who gain only this superficial reaction must be better prospects for the support of future national social legislation to relieve some of this distress in a large section of the country they are preparing to fight for. This is one of the most important possibilities of the training program in the South.

The look of the South is not so impressive to the average Southern boy who trains in it; but the reaction of the Northern troops has opened the eyes of many Southerners. The attitudes, "Leave us alone" and "Yankees don't understand," seem somehow meaningless when Northern and Southern soldiers, side by side, are watching the same undeniable evidence of poverty.

The Spanish-American and First World Wars have previously been looked on as landmarks in the long, slow process of dissolving the Civil War hatred between the North and South. Hatred was gone when this one started, but prejudice was still rampant. A great part of this prejudice will probably be gone when our soldiers return from the war. There will undoubtedly be a broader realization by millions of soldiers of the bigness and wholeness of the United States. Yankees and Southerners are acquiring each others' bad habits and ill founded prejudices, but by the same token they are absorbing something of the better characteristics of the different sectional cultures.

If our democratic process works at all after the war, it should result in Southern problems receiving more consideration in national affairs.

Lt. Frank Smith

The climate for a relatively liberal approach to the race issue in Mississippi was better just after World War II than at any time since the Civil War. Bilbo's election campaign of 1946 brought the moderates' hopes to a quick death. The only way the Senator could win re-election was to play the race issue for every possible vote, to run against the "outsiders" who denounced him and the "liberals" at home who opposed him. (The discovery of the depravity of the word moderate had not yet been made by the racists.)

Successive political events helped keep the Negro question at the top of the conversation list in Mississippi for the next few years—the Truman Civil Rights Commission report in 1947 and the Dixiecrat movement in 1948, forerunners of the school decisions six years later which made unacceptable any attitude not absolutely segregationist.

Despite this increasingly bitter climate, however, it was still possible in the years between 1948 and 1954 to maintain an at least halfway moderate position without risking personal and political ostracism. I campaigned for Congress in 1950. Opposition to President Truman's civil rights program was necessarily a part of my platform, but the publicity I received for my strong stand in support of education and economic advancement for the Negro was favorable. My known convictions on these points had been the basis for a good part of the opposition to my candidacy, but then it was opposition that could be overcome.

For that brief period, the entire political atmosphere in the state seemed to be improving. Paul B. Johnson, a young man with two unsuccessful campaigns for the governorship already behind him, tried to join the trend in 1953 and early 1954 with statements that Mississippi politicians had to quit capitalizing on the race issue, but the May 1954 school de-segregation decisions put "Little Paul" back on the right track for Mississippi, even though he had to wait until the violent climate of 1963 for the governorship.

Paul Johnson, Sr., the father of the present governor of Mississippi, was the closest approach to a "New Deal" governor that Mississippi had during the Roosevelt years. His free textbook program was a major advance for Negro education, and he proposed, albeit with no success, the repeal of the poll tax. In 1942, President Roosevelt talked with him about the necessity of improving conditions for Negroes as a morale builder to benefit the war effort. In response to this, Governor Johnson specifically asked a number of local leaders and officials to join him in improving relations between Negro soldiers and the civilian population and in preventing lynch-ings. One of those he consulted was my uncle, the sheriff of Leflore County.

Paul Johnson, Jr.'s respect for his father apparently did not transcend his desire to be Governor of Mississippi. To make palatable campaign fodder in 1963, Paul Jr. turned the whole episode inside out, gutting the memory of some of his father's fine qualities by declaring that the whole thing had been a massive FDR plot to capture the Negro vote which Paul Sr. had resisted.

If there had ever been any possibility that the Negro could be displaced as the prime topic of Mississippi conversa-tion, the 1954 Supreme Court decision killed it. It also created a major barrier to communication between me and many of my constituents. Segregation, symbol of "the Southern way of life," was the beginning and the end of their interest; it was not mine. Except for an annual newsletter report on the status of civil rights legislation, I refused to introduce the race issue into correspondence, conversation, or publicity. But almost every discussion with a constituent, whatever its initial purpose, eventually led to the Negro. To my insistent constituents, I tried to bring some light instead of more heat.

The favorite question was why didn't those of us in Congress expose the communist control of the NAACP. My answer was that while the Communists obviously were trying to exploit the race issue, the House Un-American Activities Committee had never found any communist control of the NAACP, and if there were any the House group had missed, Senator Jim Eastland would surely reveal it through his Subversive Activities Subcommittee. It was an answer, but it wasn't enough; it rarely satisfied any inquirer.

Shortly after I returned to Mississippi following the congressional session of 1954, I told a newspaperman that I had had more complaints from my constituents about current farm problems than I had received about the school integration decision. I was immediately flooded with telephone calls and letters, the first of many skirmishes with the newly organized Citizens Councils.

"Fight integration? Why, I've just begun to fight," a young farmer told me. "When I was on a beach in the South Pacific I was fighting and didn't know why. Now we know what we are fighting for, and nothing is going to hold us back." The saddest commentary on this call is that the man who said those words was a graduate of an out-of-state liberal arts college, and that his statements to me were endorsed by one of the local patriarchs, a school superintendent regarded as one of the area's leaders of opinion.

In June of 1954, as part of the first reaction to the Supreme Court decision, Robert B. Patterson, a former Mississippi State football star then farming near Indianola, wrote a letter to *Time* which was carried with other letters reacting to the Supreme Court decision. How much *Time* edited the letter I have no idea, but choice phrases like "red-blooded Southern Americans," "unconstitutional judge-made law," and "our Caucasian heritage of 60 centuries" made the points. This was the language being voiced by hate groups throughout the country, but rarely in literate enough form for the letter columns of national magazines. Before the Supreme Court decision, Negroes were just one of the hate objects—Jews, Catholics, labor unions, and Communists were indiscriminately intermingled in the literature of the haters.

Time probably published the letter as an example of Southern extremism, but the rash of mail Tut Patterson received in response from like-minded people over the country helped push the Citizens Council into being and established Patterson as one of its major-domos. The Council would see to it that Mississippians would have no chance to forget to talk about Negroes.

Mississippians are not alone, however. Talking about Negroes has probably been a conversational sport in Congress since the first discussions of slavery, but it became a major avocation during the middle years of my service in the House. This made it harder than ever to spend much time with my fellow Mississippians in Washington; talk turned more and more to the all-pervading question. Members of Congress from other areas assumed that the simplest way to establish concourse with a Mississippian was to open up with some gambit about his sympathies on the race issue. Even a great-grandson of Abraham Lincoln used this tact with me.

Among the other congressmen from the deep South there were half a dozen or so as obsessed with racism as any

Mississippian has ever been. Their presence in a cloakroom or lunch table group was a sure sign of how the conversation would go, for like all activists, they set the pattern and dominated the exchange. Even people like Judge Howard Smith, the acknowledged leader of Southern conservatism in the House, had, upon occasion, to make obeisance to the pattern. I particularly remember Judge Smith, halting and almost bashful, telling a story about the unofficial lynching of a Negro in rural Virginia. Rigid economic conservatism is the backbone of Judge Smith's philosophy of leadership in the House, but even the most powerful leaders occasionally have to prove that they, too, walk the "right" road, think the "right" way.

Extremism on the race issue didn't shock me very much—I had had to live with it for a long time—but even I was jolted by a cloakroom conversation one day during the Korean War. My colleague was complaining that integration had ruined the Army, and I replied that I didn't know of any other solution the armed services could use for Negro troops. His follow-up was a question: How were we, as Mississippi congressmen, going to explain the use of integrated troops?

"I tell the people that the Army in Korea is fighting for our country just as much as if they were fighting in California," I said.

"An integrated country's not worth defending," was his reply.

In many respects the most disheartening part of "talking Negro" in the Congress was the revelation of the attitude of many of those from outside the South. Too many members, both Democrat and Republican, whose voting records on civil rights satisfied every NAACP or ADA standard, went out of their way to tell me they agreed with the Southern position but couldn't vote for it. Some of them said it outright; some of them said it indirectly by producing a card from their wallet with a printed Negro joke or cartoon. It would be hard to assess the real feelings of a majority of the members of Congress on civil rights, but these evidences of covert sympathy have had a lot to do with the continued acceptability of extremist action and conversation by Southern members.

Part of the problem of being a congressman representing a quarter of a million nonvoting Negroes was how to fulfill my obligation to make every congressional service available to them and at the same time avoid censure from the voting white citizens for providing the service. Many of my colleagues got around this by simply not offering farm bulletins, baby books, and similar items to Negroes. I distributed the farm bulletin order blanks to all post office patrons, regardless of color, but on the blank I had to include a space for identification by race to avoid the problem of how to address the acknowledging letters. In Mississippi, addressing a Negro as "Mr." or "Mrs." is still a cardinal sin. (Business firms making special appeals to Negro customers have felt the wrath of the Citizens Councils when they put "Mr." on the outside of a letter to a customer. Postal employee members keep the Councils informed.)

I have seen the problem of how to write a salutation of a letter to a Negro or, what was worse, to someone whose race could not be determined, throw a congressional office into complete turmoil, with a solution that ended up like this:

> John Jones
> Hushpuckena, Miss.

John Jones:

"Dear John" was too familiar; indeed, any use of "Dear" was too familiar or respectful. I eliminated the quandary for my own staff by adopting a standard "Dear Friend" salutation, but even this gained me no credit points in the Council books. In fact, by the time the Councils achieved widespread influence, I had already gone beyond their code of acceptability by establishing the rule that "Mrs." was to be used in the salutation to all married women, white or black.

Talking nigger or nigra had changed from a custom to a necessity for acceptance in most circles by 1956, and among certain groups the loudest and the strongest talker could achieve a status otherwise unattainable.

One of those who followed this route to a certain type of community stature was a tobacco salesman in Greenwood, Byron De La Beckwith. Delay, as he was called, talked about the race issue loudly and endlessly. He always advocated whatever was the most extreme position then going the rounds. It helped sell tobacco; it also afforded him status in groups far more exclusive than the Citizens Council. Our district of the Sons of the American Revolution elected Delay treasurer, and he was a prominent member at most meetings.

Delay sent me a letter to transmit to President Eisenhower, violently protesting the integration of the armed forces. The letter was filled with abuse of both the President and the federal government, and it was uncommonly illiterate for an officer of the SAR and a former student of Mississippi State University. I knew that the White House staff was familiar with the views of my constituents, but I was ashamed to let them see this one, so I returned it to Delay. Later, a local lawyer helped him polish it up, and a newspaper printed it as one of the long line of incendiary letters which the Memphis *Commercial-Appeal* and the two (sometimes three) Jackson newspapers have published through the years. With this publicity among his home folks, Delay became an inveterate letter writer as well as talker on the race issue.

Once he came to see me at my Greenwood office, to

complain about the sins against Mississippi and the South. I'm sure he found my replies as unsatisfactory as I found his comments distasteful.

In the summer of 1963 Delay Beckwith was arrested by FBI agents and charged with the murder of Medgar Evers, the Mississippi NAACP leader. The case was actively prosecuted; the first trial ended in a mistrial, as did the second.

A century ago, the abolition of slavery was a plot by Abraham Lincoln; today, Lincoln is the chief figure cited by the Citizens Councils in their literature and talks, in quotations carefully culled from Lincoln-the-candidate in the Douglas debates (but almost never in quotations from Lincoln the President). Thirty years ago, Negro uppishness was all part of Franklin Roosevelt's ambition to control the country; today, Earl Warren has replaced FDR as the ideal candidate for impeachment. In 1948, Harry Truman wore Roosevelt's mantle and was the focus of even greater abuse than had been heaped upon his predecessor; in 1961 (in street corner conversation), Truman had become almost respectable again, thanks to his denunciation of the early sit-ins. In 1963, the Kennedy brothers were the new personification of evil, a team which not only masterminded the whole plot, but underwrote all its expenses, including those of all the political candidates who did not have the blessings of the Citizens Councils.

For all of the talking *about* Negroes done by the white people of Mississippi, there is virtually no real talking *to* them by these same people. As I have pointed out in other parts of this story, the paths of communication are now all closed, and very few were ever open. But this, disheartening as it is, is not the real tragedy for my people. Their anguish lies in the fact that, enslaved by their need to talk about the Negro, they cannot talk, or think, effectively, about anything else. It is an appalling dissipation of energy which could so much better be used to the economic and social advantage of the state.

The overriding obsession with the Negro question in my home state today is, of course, reflected in the almost total preoccupation with the issue as far as national political issues are concerned. But it is also a reflection of guilt, buried in most cases perhaps, but acutely close to the surface among the many who privately profess the national philosophy—the thousands of Southerners who, silently now but surely with voice in a rapidly approaching tomorrow, view their country, its traditions, and its future in a broader perspective.

Chapter VIII

THE POLITICS

OF RACE

Race has been a factor in political decisions since the time two men of different races first faced each other in the same territory. Race is obviously a vital influence in Asian and African political affairs today. Only in the Union of South Africa and in the American South, however, does race tower over all other political influences. In South Africa the national government does not pay lip service to the equality of men; it simply does not believe men are equal. In our American South, under a national government founded upon the premise that all men are equal, race is the controlling element in a political structure dedicated to the preservation of inequality among men.

The Reconstruction era following the Civil War was the inevitable aftermath of the Republican congressional leadership's determination to punish the active secessionists, to make the privileges of citizenship available to the newly freed slaves, and to ensure Republican majorities in presidential election years. Reconstruction lasted about ten years and ended for good in 1877, when President Hayes agreed to withdraw federal troops from the South in return for the Southern support which gave him his disputed election victory over Democrat Samuel Tilden. The post-Civil War period was one of vast readjustment in the South, economic and social as well as political. In view of the enormity of the changes, the Reconstruction governments were probably better than might have been expected. They were universally corrupt, but even more widespread corruption has existed from time to time in every one of the states involved. The Reconstruction governments all began programs designed to educate and improve the lot of the freed slaves—welfare activities that have been vastly expanded by white supremacy governments in later years.

Universal Negro voting and Republican control were made possible only by the presence of federal troops, and the presence of the troops was the irritant and spur which unified the white opposition. White control was won back in elections that employed a combination of fear, force, violence, and fraud. In Mississippi, victory was achieved in the "revolution of 1875" by these methods, aided by restrictions on use of the troops ordered by President Grant, who was feeling the pressure of Northern dissatisfaction with Radical tactics. The white supremacy victories might have been reversed if federal troops had been used again, but Northern acquiescence in the bargain with Hayes ended that possibility.

Intimidation on the one hand and lack of protection on the other reduced the number of Negro voters in Mississippi to insignificance after 1875, but the specter of their return, like the "bloody shirt" waved by Republicans in the North, was the paramount political weapon for the next fifteen years. Mississippi's Constitution of 1890 effectively established permanent white political supremacy, but the race issue boiled up from time to time afterward, primarily because it was an effective defense against the Populist threat. The Populists probably achieved less in Mississippi than in any other Southern state, even though the poverty in the red hills and pine barrens would normally have made the state fertile ground for that movement. The Populist forces were taken over by James K. Vardaman as a faction within the Democratic party, and to help defeat the Bourbon faction Vardaman not only poured forth all the Populist doctrine; he also promised to make the state the weapon of white supremacy. In the early 1900's, he spoke out not only against Negro voting, but against Negro education and any other improvement in the black man's lot.

Vardaman, "the great white chief," beat a loud drum, loud enough to put him in the governorship and the U.S. Senate, and the most resounding note he sounded was white supremacy, echoing across a state in which the Negro had stopped voting before 1890, where very little was spent on Negro education, and where segregation was already nailed down by force of state law. In 1911, most of the Vardaman faction passed to Theodore Bilbo, who was to be the hardiest personality in state politics for nearly forty years. The Negro issue was always close to the surface, and it erupted regularly in statewide elections (about every eight to ten years, from 1910 all the way down to today). In the 1927 gubernatorial campaign, for example, Dennis Murphree was governor, serving an unexpired term. He sought a full term in a runoff with Bilbo, who was running for his second term in the primaries that summer. In the midst of the campaign, Governor Murphree had to call out the National Guard to prevent a lynching in south Mississippi. Murphree always believed that that one act changed enough votes to defeat him; Bilbo won by a narrow margin.

By the mid-thirties, Congress had replaced the state governments as the major field on which battle could be waged by those who opposed governmental efforts to protect the Negroes' rights as citizens. The Dixiecrat movement was, in part, an attempt by state officials to move into this popular field, to keep it from being pre-empted by senators and representatives. The label has always been states' rights, but the actual purpose has always been plain. In the days following the school desegregation decision, state policy in racial matters became a clear issue in state politics, but for fifty years before this there was no major race policy issue within the states; on the Negro, everyone was agreed—the only open question was who could assert his agreement the loudest.

Race has thus been the major influence in Southern politics for the last hundred years. "Southern" in this case means more than the former states of the Confederacy—it includes border states like Maryland, West Virginia, Kentucky, and Oklahoma, and parts of states like Missouri and New Mexico. Of the old Confederate states, the rigid rules have not always applied in Tennessee, Florida, and Texas. In all race matters, the Mississippi position has been the most extreme, and one of the misfortunes of the politics of race is that all too often the Mississippi position has had perforce to be adopted by the rest of the South. For instance, all Southern senators had to defend Bilbo's right to a seat in 1947.

There were real economic issues in 1860 and 1861, and a lot of noble talk about the rights of the states, but in the final analysis the Southern states attempted to secede from the Union to defend the institution of slavery. The controlling planter aristocracy believed that the national government was about to destroy slavery and that the one way to preserve it was to take their states out of the Union. To those nonslaveholding whites who had little sympathy for the planters, and less for the Negro, the Confederacy based its appeal on race prejudice. Secession failed, and the rebellious states were forced to recognize the end of slavery and the right of Negroes to full citizenship in the constitutional amendments the Congress required them to ratify before they could be restored to full statehood. The outcome of the Civil War firmly established two fundamental principles: the impossibility of secession and the illegality of slavery. The corollary principle—the grant of the full rights of citizenship to Negroes—has been so successfully thwarted by the politics of race that it is not surprising some extremists in Mississippi in 1962 openly spoke up for another secession, and talked of being willing to shed blood to achieve it.

It is generally conceded that the Reconstruction tactics of postwar Republican leaders like Thaddeus Stevens were motivated by the desire to maintain a Radical Republican majority in Congress, in contrast to the idealistic goals of people like Charles Sumner, who sought to secure the specific rights of citizenship for the freed men. With no program to help prepare the ex-slaves for citizenship beyond the haphazard Freedmen's Bureau, it is small wonder that active support for the Negroes was short-lived in the North and fiercely resisted in the South.

The first civil rights bill to become a major issue was the so-called "force" bill of 1890. Senator Henry Cabot Lodge of Massachusetts was its best-known sponsor. The "force" bill provided for supervision of federal elections by the national government to protect Negro voters in the South against state measures to deprive them of the vote. There was still some political motivation, and some plainly political results that could be achieved through this legislation, and the result was that Southerners had many Northern Democratic allies fighting its enactment. The next active effort to secure federal intervention in behalf of civil rights came in the 1920's in the form of antilynching proposals. No charge of political motivation could be made against this proposal, but the mere suggestion that federal protection against mob violence should be given when none was given locally became the rallying point for racism for two decades. "States' rights," cried the opposition—as always—but the bills were opposed because they were designed to protect Negroes.

No antilynch bill ever became law; to that extent the racists were successful, but they also had the help of some conscientious senators who were genuinely concerned about the constitutional merits of the antilynch proposals. To the credit of the South, the effort to end lynching is the one area in which sincere and courageous Southern leadership won the fight at the local level. The history of the antilynch bills in Congress makes an interesting commentary on the tactics used in opposing them. When the legislation was first introduced, the opposition in Congress defended lynch law! Eventually, their argument became the assertion that the crime could best be eliminated by the states themselves, acting without the threat of federal action.

Historically, "states' rights" has been the rallying cry of the opponents of civil rights legislation, of executive action to implement civil rights, and of judicial action to secure the enforcement of civil rights through the courts. Before the Civil War, states' rights was more a doctrine for the defense of slavery than a fine constitutional question; the war itself proved that the states are subordinate to the national power. A doctrine that is entirely negative, and that has been used only to defend the denial of citizenship and elementary justice to citizens of the United States, has been clothed in too much respectability. Doctrinaire economic conservatives find it a catchy and convenient slogan to use against federal programs. Citizens have every duty to fight vigorously any federal program to which they are opposed, and even to fight new federal programs on the general theory that there is too much concentration of federal power. But when they use the shibboleth "states' rights," they show a weakness in their own position and give renewed respectability to a discredited political proposition that is identified foremost as an anti-civil rights stand.

When the Civil War took from the states the right to allow human slavery, no matter whether it was favored by a vast majority of the citizens of a state, it also took from the states the right to deny full citizenship to any American, no matter how popular that denial might be with the majority of the citizens of a state. In the century since the Civil War, the politics of race has been successfully dedicated to perpetuating the presumed state power to deny certain rights to certain citizens. This is the predominant characteristic of Southern politics. It would not have been as successful, however, if economic interests at the national level had not exploited the system to achieve their own particular purposes.

The Populist movement had its greatest success in the Midwest, but it would have been even more successful in the South if the race issue had not been used as a weapon against it. The conditions which begot the movement—abject poverty on farms and in the small towns of the countryside—were certainly even worse in the South than in the Western states. In some cases the Southern Populist leaders spoke up for better economic conditions for the Negro, and where they did not speak themselves, the opposition Bourbon Democrats tarred them with the position taken by national Populist leaders on the issue. Eventually, the Democrats ended the Populist threat by becoming more or less semi-Populist themselves, or including a Populist faction, but they had already succeeded in keeping race politics simmering for another generation.

Tom Watson, a Populist leader in Georgia who was later to become one of the worst racists, explained the system in very plain political language, talking to both whites and blacks:

> You are kept apart that you may be separately fleeced of your earnings. You are made to hate each other because upon that hatred is rested the keystone of the arch of financial despotism which enslaves you both. You are deceived and blinded that you may not see how this race antagonism perpetuates a monetary system which beggars both.

The Dixiecrat movement in 1948 had two bases of leadership and fundamental support—business interests who could not openly become avowed Republicans in their fight against the national Democratic party, and politicians who had to cling to the name Democrat for local and future use, but at the same time wanted to reap the immediate benefit of opposing Truman and being way out in front on the race issue. In public they talked of winning the election by throwing it into the House of Representatives, but the realists in the movement knew quite well that one of the two standard party candidates would win even if the fantastic long shot of preventing an electoral majority paid off. The fantasy of a Southern candidate's being elected President in this manner died after 1948, and the next step was to offer the pig-in-the-poke, "independent electors." Briefly, this means that a state chooses a slate of electors pledged to no candidate, free to vote for whomever they wish in the electoral college. The idea is founded on the well-known political cynicism that people would rather vote against someone than for someone. Putting it over is a tougher selling job though, because even the most irrational voter realizes that if he supports the pig-in-the-poke, he hands over his own suffrage to a chosen few.

For the local political leaders, however, the system is ideal. Since they have no candidate, they do not have to defend him against the attacks any candidate is inevitably exposed to. They run only against the Negro, who is in a very safe minority as a voter, and they also run against every other government policy about which the voter may be unhappy. The greatest advantage of the independent elector system comes after election. Whoever wins, the local politicians have been against him and thus cannot be forced to share any of the blame for the actions he takes. The racist politicians know that whoever wins will be unpopular with the voters, for he will have to take stands on race issues contrary to the stands of Mississippi and Alabama. To make sure that he is a proper bugaboo to the voters, the local politicians, the governor and the congressmen will join in the catcalls if necessary. They usually decide that it is necessary—to keep themselves in power—that their voices must be stronger than those of the other professional racists of the press, bar, pulpit, or lower political rank.

1952 was the only year since 1940 in which there was not some independent third party on the ballot in Mississippi. A few weeks before election, one of my congressional colleagues from Mississippi was admonished, "You'd better quit speaking against Eisenhower. He's going to be elected."

"That's why I'm going to come out harder against him," was the reply. "Next year I want everybody to know that I didn't help elect him." In 1956, this same man actively pushed the independent elector idea, on the theory that members of Congress could not afford to be associated with either national ticket. Through lack of support from the governor, the independent elector idea fell flat in Mississippi that year, and their candidates ranked third in the balloting.

It is not surprising that politicians use the race issue to get themselves into office and then to perpetuate themselves there. The significant and disheartening (and to non-Southerners, incomprehensible) factor in the politics of race is that they are allowed to get away with it time after time after time.

The racists in the South need constant reassurance that their position is popular and that it will succeed. Because there was no evidence that they were winning, the politicians gambled that they could win by a political trick (the Dixiecrat movement and the unpledged electors); it was the simplest way to be optimistic. Another way is to discredit the motives of all who favor civil rights legislation—to assert that it is nothing but an appeal for the political support of minority groups. In my own personal brush with the politics of race, I think the leaders of the Citizens Councils disliked more than anything else my refusal to reassure either them or my constituents that they were winning the fight for segregation, or that their tactics would ever win it.

With the rare exception of a few who represent urban or border districts, all members of Congress from the South for the past fifteen years have been identified as segregationists and opponents of civil rights legislation. There are no shades of moderation in the classification, because in the showdown the votes of all have been the same. The wide differences in viewpoint among the Southerners are well-known to all but surface observers, but the extremists set the standards of measurement and thereby prevent any concessions. Since the most moderate member has to vote like the most extreme member if he plans to seek re-election, there is no room for voices of moderation among the Southerners in

Congress, and their votes would belie their voices if they spoke. The extremist members are not only accepted as the spokesmen for the South, they are also in a position to keep forcing the Southern position to even further extremes. All other members are their prisoners, because no one can afford a vote which does not coincide with the racist opposition to all civil rights.

The disadvantage to the South of the inflexible position in which approximately 100 members of the House of Representatives are held should be obvious. The entire legislative process is one of arriving at a position acceptable to the majority. The Southerners have for many years had no voice in decisions as to the character of the legislation the majority will pass in the House. Because their votes are automatically written off as opposed to any civil rights bill, they quite naturally are not consulted concerning the specific legislation brought before the House. From the standpoint of the civil rights activist, always seeking the strongest possible civil rights bill, this has been helpful, because he does not have to consider the Southerners in working out the terms of the legislation. The controlling influence for him is that group of Northern moderates not deeply committed on the civil rights issue. In both 1957 and 1960, the inflexible position of Southern members of the House actually brought about slightly stronger provisions in the laws which passed, much to the disgust of some of the Southern leaders in the Senate who, given some degree of cooperation by Southern leaders in the House, could have had the provisions toned down. There was considerable sentiment in the House on the part of rank-and-file Southern members favoring that cooperation, but the virtual bondage in which they are held kept them from speaking out against their intransigent leadership.

The national tragedy of this polarization of position is

that for many years there has been lost a great opportunity to achieve steady, gradual progress toward full protection of all civil rights, which in all probability would have been acceptable to the Negro population (in contrast with getting nothing) and grudgingly accepted by the white South (in contrast to the present fierce resistance).

The negative effect of the "no middle ground" attitude on the civil rights question cannot all be blamed on the Southerners alone, however, for there are examples of polarization on the other side in the Congress. For some thirty years, the opponents of the poll tax refused to accept any legislation except a general law barring all poll taxes. They could have had, a good while ago, an amendment to the constitution barring poll taxes in federal elections, but they refused to settle for that. Only when President Kennedy and the congressional leadership broke the icejam in 1962 by scheduling action on the poll tax constitutional amendment did it pass the Congress. Regardless of the merits of the argument over law versus amendment, the poll tax in federal elections could have been abolished shortly after World War II if its principal opponents had been willing to accept less than a complete victory.

The to-the-death resistance which practically all Southerners in Congress are obliged to espouse may not be the cause of the bitter-end opposition to any form of integration in many communities, but it certainly has been a contributing factor. A generation from now, thoughtful Southerners will probably conclude that the worst result of race politics in Congress was the barriers it erected against gradualism in eliminating the legal bulwarks of segregation. If it had been possible to adopt moderate gradual approaches to the elimination of discrimination as a broad national goal in the period immediately after World War II, the adjustment would have been far easier and the scars of hatred could not have gone so deep. Today, of course, any degree of gradualism is impossible insofar as it concerns the commitment of federal law and the federal government. Injustice and discrimination will not be eliminated until they are erased from the minds and hearts of all Americans, but if we are to sustain the most noble of American ideals—the fundamental rights of our individual citizens—we can never again condone any form of injustice or discrimination.

The fact that the extreme Southern position on civil rights in the Congress sometimes serves to lose ground for the South, not only in the Congress but also among the general public, is well-known to most members of Congress, and it must also be well-known to the people who set policy for the anti-civil rights bloc. One reason such tactics are used is that they strengthen control over members on economic issues. The interjection of race saved the power of the Bourbon Democrats seventy years ago, and the politics of race is the strongest bulwark of economic conservatism in the Congress today. Most liberal economic views are supported, at least in the North, by men and organizations who have taken prominent positions against race discrimination. In Southern politics it isn't hard to tie the two roles together, in the Congress and in the public mind in the South. The great selling point of the John Birch Society in the South is the Society's support of segregation.

In the South, opposition to "strong central government" means opposition to integration. In conservative circles outside the South, the same phrase means opposition to federal spending. To accommodate the differences between these dual definitions, some interesting ideological shuffling takes place. Alexander Hamilton's philosophy of government no longer is made to rest on the importance of a strong federal power, but rather, on the importance of giving financial and business interests a major voice in running the government. (The Hamilton bicentennial commission a few years ago made some progress toward establishing this new interpretation of Hamiltonianism.) Jefferson is not revered for his dedication to individual political and civil liberties, but rather, for advocacy of state power in civil liberties matters and limited federal activity in behalf of individual citizens. The man who purchased Louisiana and embargoed shipping is pictured today as rejecting all such use of federal power in the United States.

To demonstrate how race becomes the showcase for the merchants of economic conservatism: the Southern caucus in the House of Representatives has been called together to present a united front in favor of labor legislation which proposes new federal controls over individual union members and their organizations, without regard to the obvious contradiction in terms of the traditional opposition to "federal control" as the "evil" of the civil rights proposals. The same caucus has been called to oppose public housing legislation. When some members asked why issues like this should be treated as regional policy, they soon learn that those who have been given the lead in opposing civil rights legislation want more votes for their economic philosophy. They get additional votes, too, for what comes out of the caucus for public consumption is that public housing is integrated housing and labor unions are race agitators.

Not long after I came to Congress, I asked another member how he would justify his vote on a public power issue to REA members in his area who were certain to be displeased by his stand. "I'll tell them that the Secretary of the Interior integrated the swimming pools in Washington," he declared. That kind of answer still works. The Department of Justice pushes for civil rights, consequently it should not be allowed the money to hire additional tax attorneys or any new authority to take antitrust action. All the African nations belong to the United Nations, so any money appropriated for the UN will be used to fight segregation.

The marriage between the economic conservatives and the racists has its limitations, however, and the relationship often turns out to be a bad bargain for the economics partner. Many of the business leaders in Birmingham were backers of the Dixiecrat movement and sponsors of the political element symbolized by "Bull" Connor. In the time of crisis, when the race demonstrations disrupted and threatened business stability, they found that the racism they had helped to create had become a monster which might destroy even them.

Most new members from the South come to the House of Representatives fresh from campaigns in which they have fully committed themselves to oppose all civil rights programs. The role they take in the House could be determined by their own beliefs on the issue; it is usually determined by how much they feel they must bow to political expediency. If they choose to take the racist route, the House offers an easy—and free—medium for publicity: statements for the *Congressional Record* always receive heavy play from a sympathetic press at home. This course assures them quick acceptance by their own Southern leadership, but it kills any notion they may have entertained of becoming an effective influence among other members of the House, except after the long haul to seniority. The "moderate" member who sincerely wants to make some contribution to even limited progress in the race field soon finds that he simply has no room to maneuver. The slightest deviation from complete opposition to all civil rights programs invites immediate retaliation, not so much in Washington as in his own district back home.

Today, the Southwide network of the White Citizens Councils and their allies is the primary means of communication. Normally attacks upon a fellow member are regarded as the worst breach of etiquette, or "union rules," in the House, but these unwritten rules simply don't count in racial matters. If he shows proper allegiance to the cause, the average member can then proceed to work on other legislative specialties that fit his constituency or his own interests. Even here, however, the subtle threat always exists that if he pursues that specialty too vigorously, in conflict with the economic philosophy that dominates the Southern hierarchy, he may suddenly discover that his pet legislative program has become a tool of integration in the minds of his constituents.

In late 1954, Miss Charlotte Kohler, editor of the *Virginia Quarterly Review*, asked me to contribute an article on "The Changing South" for the thirtieth-anniversary edition of that distinguished publication, the spring 1955 issue. The invitation was both exciting and fearful. I was very proud to be asked to share in a forum with such well-known Southerners as Frank Graham, V. O. Key, Jr., Harry Ashmore, Jonathan Daniels, Rupert B. Vance, and Eudora Welty. I was fearful of whether I could write an honest appraisal of the changing South without saying something that would be politically destructive for me.

Looking back on the article, I think it stands up reasonably well after ten years, considering that it was written by a politician seeking re-election in Mississippi. I was too optimistic about most of the topics I evaluated, and, of course, I handled the race issue far too gingerly. I remember deciding while writing the article that "great tragedy" was as far as I could honestly comment on the Supreme Court school decision without inviting immediate political retaliation. The great tragedy of the decision was the renewed racial bitterness among whites which it helped to unleash. The great error of my over-all optimistic concept of the South's moving into the mainstream of national life was failing to foresee fully the waves of extremism and bitterness that were about to grip so many Southerners. I mentioned the possibility, but I did not foresee the deteriorating effect that all of this would have on the quality of Southern political life and its representation in the Congress. After the article appeared, a publishing firm asked me to expand it into a book. I had to regretfully decline. The article was as far as I could go.

If the Southern congressman suffers much from the politics of race, it is the Southern electorate which suffers most. All issues save race are rendered inconsequential, and, as a result, the voter never has a chance to express a choice on any other issue. The congressman can castigate any opposition as an attempt to "purge" him because of his opposition to civil rights, no matter how shrill the opponent may be in his own avowal of segregationist views. Of course, any chink in the segregationist armor of the incumbent can be fatal, no matter how good a record of legislative effectiveness he can show on other issues. Southern congressmen usually accumulate better-than-average seniority because the Southern states have long recognized the value of that legislative commodity, but in recent years the seniority averages have risen even higher because the only characteristic essential to re-election is possession of a loud voice against civil rights.

Not all the Southern states are completely mired down in race politics; in several of them, gubernatorial and other state office campaigns are conducted much as they are in other sections of the country. But in those states which are race-dominated, the voter doesn't even get a chance to pass on the old familiar issue of graft and corruption. Malfeasance in office can be laughed at, if the candidates sweep it aside as a trumped-up side issue fomented by the NAACP. Broken promises and failure to meet vital responsibilities are ignored. The promise broken can even be the one that guaranteed the preservation of segregation, if the officeholder can make the people believe he fought hard for it. Virtually the only exceptions are in the areas where there are relatively few Negroes, and hence, where there is reasonably free Negro voting.

During the past decade the espousal of segregation by right-wing groups and causes has won them membership and support in the South far beyond their due. Alleged plans for unilateral U.S. disarmament, the "Russian colonel" who is supposed to be in charge of "all American troops under the UN"—these wild-eyed "Red" tales and many another of the same stripe—are all linked to saving the American way of life, and that boils down to saving segregation. Rabid extremism on the race issue is no respecter of caste or class in the South; it exists at every step along the economic, social, and educational ladder, and the union of conservative economics and segregation has often destroyed potential support for forward-looking economic policies among Southerners. Small white farmers in the deep South, who stand to gain the most from a progressive economy, have become the political bulwark of the segregationist extremists, and odd bedfellows though they may seem, union labor in cities like Memphis and Birmingham have joined them. The International Union of Electrical Workers, CIO, has been defeated in several small-town organization efforts by management publicity about the pro-civil rights attitudes of the national union leaders; this same line has been the basic attack on all union organization efforts for several years. Strangely enough, however, where local units of national unions like the IUE and United Automobile Workers do exist, they have been among the strongest in segregationist activities.

Because race is the beginning and the end of every issue in the deep South, the net effect of race politics is that the people of the South have disfranchised themselves. They make decisions on national and international issues on no other basis, and they are the only segment of the national electorate so irrationally circumscribed. Their representatives in the councils of the nation are necessarily treated accordingly. Thanks to determined efforts by many leaders, both in Congress and out, racism does not dictate all decisions, but there are few which are not touched by it. The effectiveness of any Southerner who attempts to shape policy in any field is sharply limited by his regional background; there may be reasons in addition to the reluctance of non-Southerners to be identified with the region, but that reluctance alone is enough to be crucial.

Thus, it is only through blindness that Southerners continue to pride themselves on the disproportionate influence they think they exercise in the Congress. The pride was once justified. Today, that influence is only a fraction of what it could be; the rest is lost because so much Southern effort is automatically suspect in the rest of the country. All too often, the Southerner working toward a worthy goal must give it up to hold some racist line. His fellow members soon become wary of him, consider him too likely not to be on hand when the chips go down. As long as all issues are debated and decided with a racist coloration, perhaps it is best for the nation that the South's influence be sharply limited, but few Southerners seem to recognize the irony of their own position: that to keep the Negro from having any political power, they have given up their own political power. The Southern Negro does not vote, the Southern white votes to no purpose—the results are the same.

Chapter IX

THE HOUSE AT
WORK

All members of Congress have a primary interest in being re-elected. Some members have no other interest. Their participation in decisions of great national import is dependent entirely upon the reaction they expect from their own district or state. When seniority pushes them to a position of influence in some special area of the government, they may begin to make decisions without regard to district reaction (because the district knows or cares little about it), but the irresponsible congressmen who reach these positions of power use them primarily for their own personal political ends.

A high percentage of the members who are indifferent to national problems, except as they sway votes in their own districts, are from the South, but there are also a large number from the urban political machines of the North and from the small-town Republican areas that are one-party to all intents and purposes. But the northern Democrats and Republicans in this category at least demonstrate a certain responsibility. They usually vote with their party leaders on controversial questions, and this at least strengthens party responsibility, however loose it may appear to the general public.

House leaders on both sides are constantly occupied with the problem of persuading members to vote in ways that will be unpopular at home. The general theme of the whips is, "Vote with us if you can, but don't vote against your district." The most successful leader is the one who brings in the votes of members who feel they are voting against majority sentiment in their districts, yet does it in such a way that the individual vote does not appear to be anomalous, and thus does not lessen the member's influence on other issues.

There are issues which come before the Congress of such overriding importance as to justify a member's losing his seat if that is the price to be paid for voting his conscience. Fortunately, there are leaders willing to take members down to this position when the legislation demands it, and there are individual members willing to take their political lives in their own hands at these times. Part of the measure of a member is where he places this point of departure from self-interest. I found that the longer my period of service, the easier the decision became. For instance, in 1951, I resolved that my seat was not worth a vote for impeachment of Dean Acheson as Secretary of State, nor a vote against sending grain to India. The Acheson impeachment vote was not taken, having been skillfully avoided by the House leadership, but the grain for India vote was. I had already faced more or less the same question when I had to comment for the newspapers on Truman's recall of MacArthur. Every other member of the

Mississippi delegation condemned it, some as "verging on treason," but I felt compelled to defend the constitutional principle of civilian supremacy over the military. One of the chief areas of congressional irresponsibility is the failure of individual members to assume responsibility for honestly and fully informing their constituents on the great issues.

There should be far more responsibility in these positions of leadership. Even those elected officials from the South who share all the prejudice of race should feel a responsibility to inform their constituents of the true facts of the civil rights picture, as both a national and international issue. This responsibility should lie the heaviest on the members of the Congress who represent the South to other areas of the country. They have a responsibility to tell their constituents how the rest of the country responds to their problems.

When I came to the House of Representatives, I wanted to be a responsible member, with both a voice and a vote in historic decisions made by the Congress. If my constituents were to give me this freedom, I felt that I had to render them special service in areas of major concern to the district. This called for specialization in flood control and water resource development, which in turn required membership on the House Public Works Committee. My predecessor, Will Whittington, had been chairman of that committee. He recommended me to the Democratic members of the Ways and Means Committee, who act as the committee on committees for the Democratic members. This was of considerable help, because Whittington had better standing with the regular Democrats in the House than any other member from Mississippi. One of my colleagues from Mississippi tried to prevent my being assigned to Public Works. Jamie Whitten foresaw the possibility of his district's merging with mine in the 1952 redistricting (as it did ten years later), and he felt it would be much better for him if I didn't have the prestige in the Delta of being on the Public Works Committee. There was one request for my views on issues before the committee. Some of the members wanted to know if I were committed to oppose the St. Lawrence Seaway, which I was not. I was elected to Public Works, the only new member named to the committee that year on the Democratic side.

The interests of my district dictated my field of specialization in the House, but the decision to specialize in some legislative field is automatic for the member who wants to exercise any influence. The members who are respected in the House are the men who do their committee chores and become able exponents of the legislative programs in which they have specialized.

Speaker Sam Rayburn liked to comment that House members had two constituencies—the voters back home and the other members of the House. There are three groups of members who either cannot or will not recognize their House constituency. The first group are the nonentities, the members who make no effort to acquire or exert influence in the House. They could be expected to have rather brief House careers, but some last a surprisingly long time. The second group are the demagogues. The term may be strong, but it is the one commonly applied in the House to the member who plays to the press gallery and the home folks on every possible occasion, in full knowledge that everything he says and does is recognized, and discounted, by his colleagues for exactly what it is. The third group who ignore the House constituency are the "pop-offs." Their behavior may occasionally be demagogic, but most of the time it is based on the sincere but greatly exaggerated notion that their colleagues and the world in general need their good advice. Their opinions are quite often sound, but because of their attitude, the "pop-offs" have no influence on the House at large. They are not good allies to have in a legislative fight, but the publicity they receive often brings them advancement. I served with several who were elected to the Senate, where they have much greater value. A talking senator has a certain influence in shaping public opinion that a House member seldom achieves.

Over the years, House members come to know how most of the other members will react to any given issue, and it is natural that the closest relationships, working and personal, are developed among those men who face common problems and have compatible points of view. The influential member is not the man who limits himself to these natural associations; he is, rather, the man who takes the time to study the problems of other groups of members, to seek among them the areas of compatible short-term interest, and who capitalizes on those interests by working with such groups in temporary alliances to mutual benefit.

Ability as a speaker is helpful to any member of the House, but it is not usually the outstanding characteristic of effective House leaders. The most talented orators, for sheer histrionic and vocal ability, were usually among the least influential during my years in the House. Perhaps one reason is that a gifted orator finds things so relatively easy in other political trials that he tends to take the easy way out when faced with the hard chores of legislative participation. With 435 members, the House learns to confine its listening to the man who has something to say, not the man who says little or nothing, though beautifully.

Integrity (or the lack of it) is one of the favorite catchwords members of the House use in assessing one another. News commentators are fond of it, too. Unfortunately, there are almost as many definitions of integrity as there are members. For some, the man of integrity is the member who votes as they vote. For others, it is the man who opposes the party leadership. The member of the opposing party who has integrity is usually the one who votes against his party. Perhaps the most valid index of integrity is the degree of reliance that can be placed on the unofficial commitments every member must make from time to time. The legislative process involves many areas of negotiation, compromise, and informal agreement which never become evident in the formal procedures through which legislation moves to enactment. On both major and minor issues, the individual member must at times enter into unofficial, unrecorded commitments to other members if progress is to be made. This kind of responsibility falls most often on the leadership, and on committee and subcommittee chairmen, of course, but it is a position in which every active member finds himself at one time or another. And it is here that his integrity counts most, and is most easily—and lastingly—assessed by his fellow members. His word is not enforceable, and he knows it is not. Can he be relied upon to honor it, regardless of pressures to the contrary? If he can, he will have the respect of his colleagues, even though they may disagree with everything he stands for; if he can't, none of them will respect him, however brilliant or able he may otherwise be.

In the years since World War II, there has been really effective majority control of the House only during the four years (1947–48 and 1953–54) when Republican Joseph W. Martin was Speaker. An exception might be made of the 81st Congress that followed Truman's election in 1948, but even then the spirit of the majority was not sufficient to carry the day on labor and education issues. This judgment appears to be a reflection on the Democratic leadership. It is not. It is simply a summation of a situation within the Democratic party that was, and still is, beyond control under existing party policy. When some thirty to sixty members, who are elected as Democrats, who vote for the Democratic Speaker, who receive their committee assignments from the Democrats, and who, at maximum strength, constitute almost two-thirds of the party's numerical majority, consistently vote against the Democratic party on every major issue, control of the House is so nominal as to be almost nonexistent. Members of a party should not be bound by virtue of affiliation alone to support any legislative program, but there should be effective sanctions against those who consistently refuse to cooperate in the basic procedural matters which must be carried if legislative proposals are to be brought to a vote.

There is every reason in the world, too, for the parties to deny the benefits of membership to those members who oppose the presidential candidates of their party and, by the same token, also oppose their party's receiving a legislative majority. The present system, which condones by its failure to condemn this absolute party disloyalty, is nothing short of suicidal. Unless the situation is remedied, and soon, Speaker Rayburn's decision in 1961 not to push for the "purge" of the Democratic members who opposed Kennedy and Johnson may turn out to have been the major mistake of his career.

In addition to some reasonable rules requiring loyalty to the party from which the members derive their positions of influence in the House, the most obvious change needed in the House rules is dilution or control of the power of the House Rules Committee. The committee majority would then, as it should, be an instrument of the House leadership for bringing the legislative program of the majority party to the floor. A responsible leadership would see to it that at least the basic items of a President's program were brought to a vote at the most propitious time, even if the leaders had no great enthusiasm for them. If the issues were not brought to a vote, the responsibility for failure would be clearly on the leadership. If this failure were thus demonstrated, public opinion in the country at large would be certain to support the President in efforts to change the leadership.

The House leadership is usually blamed when an important vote is lost. This may be an accurate estimate sometimes, but on many of the big issues the defeat comes simply because the affirmative votes are not there. During the Eisenhower administration, there were many complaints from liberal members about the lack of aggressiveness, the tendency to compromise, on the part of Rayburn and Johnson, but this criticism never approached in bitterness the attacks on these leaders and their motives made by many of the Southerners, to whom, ironically, they were accused of catering.

No theorist of republican government today would suggest that there should be no executive intervention in the legislative processes of the Congress. Enactment of programs such as reciprocal trade and foreign aid can be accomplished only with the help of massed executive pressure—on the channels of public information and opinion that influence Congress and upon the Congress itself. Massive pressure does not necessarily mean swinging a blunt instrument at a reluctant congressman. Tactics should be dependent upon both the member and the individual problem, and the successful use of executive pressure fully recognizes that fact, just as the congressional leaders do. In my twelve years in the House I voted with the Democratic leadership three-fourths of the time, yet in all those twelve years only once did Speaker Rayburn specifically ask that I support his position.

There is widespread belief that the House reflects, in miniature, the districts represented. This is a fallacy. The individual member votes many times on minor matters about which his district knows little and cares less. He frequently votes on matters on which the sentiment in his district is divided. And he occasionally votes contrary to the majority opinion of his district. Some of the members castigated today as the worst obstructionists in the Congress, for example, are more influenced by the strength of their individual prejudices than by the attitudes of their districts. These members will eventually pass from the scene, and their replacements will almost certainly be a different caliber of men. On the opposite side of the coin, the Kennedy program in the 87th Congress was supported by ten or twelve House members who, in doing so, opposed most of the normally controlling forces in their districts. Without that support, some of the most important administration measures would have failed. The votes of those particular members reflected their own political beliefs.

Lobbyists and pressure groups are a healthy part of the legislative scene when the legislators are alert to their own responsibilities, but they can become unscrupulous influences when the Congress does not exercise its duty to be fully and intelligently informed about the issues under discussion. The smartest lobbies sell their position as free enterprise, protection of the American working man, anti-spending, pro- and anti-labor, states' rights, or just plain defending the American way of life.

Most members of Congress can (and do) work closely with some special interest groups, and without any loss of integrity if the members want to maintain it. The legislative goals of the members are certain to coincide with those of some pressure or opinion-forming group. If none appears, it is useful to organize or promote one, for the pressure groups serve as valuable leverage in developing wider legislative support for special projects. Pressuring Congress has always been a major activity, but it has expanded a great deal in the past ten years, and it will continue to increase in direct proportion with the growth of the government. Many of the "organizations" operating out of Washington exist only on paper, and a lot of them have many of the characteristics of a racket. A few years ago, most of the rackets were organizations which promised to obtain for their clients the assistance of congressmen in getting financial help from the government. Today the rackets are devoted to scaring businessmen about what the big, bad government will do to them and promising protection against it, all for the price of the membership fee.

The member of Congress whose legislative aims coincide in some particular with those of legitimate lobbying groups is fortunate. He will have effective assistance in pushing his programs, both in the Congress and in his own district. He is also likely to develop important political support, and very probably an avenue to financial support outside his district.

There are several national organizations whose original purpose was to lobby in special fields, but who now cover the waterfront of legislative activity. The AFL-CIO is one, the American Farm Bureau Federation another—usually going in the opposite direction. Although neither of these groups attempts to muster any real pressure on many programs on which it takes a position, it is the general opinion in the House that these groups have weakened their influence by the dilution of their aims. It was my own experience that the Farm Bureau in more recent years devoted more time to the conservative, nonfarm issues than it did to direct farm legislation. It pays lip service to issues such as foreign trade but has not been known to work for votes in these fields.

One national organization which receives a lot of publicity but influences relatively few votes is the Americans for Democratic Action. ADA has an honorable record for giving coherence to the ideas of the anti-Communist left, but its efforts to influence legislation are greatly handicapped by the red flag it has become for many who consider themselves reasonably conservative. An ultraradical right-wing organization in Chicago distributes reprints of the ADA congressional voting record scorecard in far greater quantity than it has ever been distributed by ADA, for the purpose of defeating those members whose votes were interpreted by ADA as favorable to the liberal viewpoint. I recall one issue on which I deliberately withheld my vote until I was certain that it would not change the outcome; I was confident that that particular vote would be selected for the ADA scorecard, and I just couldn't afford the luxury of one more favorable mention. Other members have told me that they have voted contrary to their inclinations for the same reason—except that they did not take the trouble to delay their decision until they could see the outcome. ADA would be far more effective if it would resist the temptation to hang labels on everything and everybody.

Another organization—more extreme in its conservatism than ADA is in its liberalism—the Americans for Constitutional Action, seems to exist solely for the purpose of publishing its own voting tabulation. So far, the ACA has had no serious kickbacks about its scorecards from friendly conservatives, but it is probably only a matter of time until they do if the organization achieves semirespectable status.

The outright buying of votes, which existed on a large scale in another era, is a rare occurrence today. It is probable that the common is stolen from the goose more often than the goose from the common. The record of the Congress in this respect is fabulously better than that of the state legislatures of which I have direct knowledge. Approaches to this, though somewhat more subtle than those of yesteryear, are still made, however, as I found out a few years after I came to the

House. Another member came to me and said he was a director of a corporation which had just established a plant not too far from my home area. What the plant manufactured did not go directly into the consumer market, but the firm was still very much interested in good public relations over the South. My colleague said he was aware that I had been in newspaper work and therefore knew a lot of editors and publishers in the area. Had I ever done any public relations work? I told him no, never directly. He replied that it didn't matter, his firm was just interested in a general news release every month or so, and the opportunity to tell their story if the need ever arose. They could not pay much for such work, which would not involve the full time of anyone, but it probably would amount to $400 to $500 a month.

"Would I be offered this work because I'm in Congress?" I asked.

"Oh, no," was the reply. "We want somebody with a newspaper background, and I thought about you simply because of that."

It sounded interesting. I had no income except my congressional salary, and this might furnish the overhead for a business which I could employ somebody at home to handle. It might also be something I could expand if I were turned out of Congress. It developed that the president of my colleague's firm would be in town within a week or two, and we would have no trouble working out the arrangements for my to-be-organized firm to handle their Southern public relations. During the next week, my committee took its first significant vote on a major issue in which this particular congressman was intensely interested. I hadn't revealed my position on the issue before the vote, and when I voted against my colleague's position, I indicated that I would be against him all the way. I never heard from the president of the firm who was allegedly interested in my public relations talents, and fortunately I had enough caution never to ask about it, even though it took quite some time for the idea to sink in that this had been some very direct lobbying.

A common reaction of almost all congressmen to lobbying practices is disgust at the incredible amount of money that is wasted in the process. On almost any Monday morning, there are fifteen or twenty letters and brochures on every member's desk, representing several hundred thousand dollars in preparation and production costs alone. Most of these go into the wastebasket with barely a glance. Day after day, members see representatives of various organizations struggling to get their viewpoints into a hearing, people with no knowledge of how to present a case. Too many organization representatives are obviously working only to preserve their jobs rather than to give realistic advice about how to achieve the ends which will serve the businesses they represent.

The most effective lobbyists, other than constituents in general, are other members of Congress. Logrolling is a common term for this, and it is a good definition on the surface. Unless special and sectional interests work out areas of accommodation with each other, there is no way for any of them to achieve their relatively narrow goals. Just as alliances on major issues are developed by exploiting common interests, which may be temporary or shifting, effective members turn from one side to the other of the political and sectional groups. On specific projects or programs of special benefit to an individual member's district, personal friendships and personal appeals are often decisive in adding important votes in committee or on the floor. Once again, it is the active members of the House who are effective lobbyists among other members. Occasionally, a member may get support on a bill because he is a good fellow who has never asked for anything before, and therefore must need this quite badly, but this type of member rarely needs legislative help to maintain his seat.

The seniority system on which the organization of congressional committees is based is a constant target for potential reform, but nobody has yet devised an adequate substitute. Very few members are enthusiastic about the system, but every complaint about it can be set against a possible alternative that would be far more undesirable. The worst abuses of the committee system can be eliminated if the majority of the members want to end them. Procedural rules can be used to circumvent arbitrary control.

The legislative specialist accomplishes most in committee; consequently, the responsible legislator spends a great deal of time in committee work, far more than he spends on the floor. The member who can get results in committee not only accomplishes his own legislative ends in that particular field, he also greatly increases his influence among his colleagues who have axes to grind before the committee. The word committee as used here includes the subcommittees, because some of the committees are so organized that they invariably ratify, in full committee, the subcommittee decisions. The appropriations subcommittees of both houses are good examples of subcommittee power. The reports of these subcommittees are often more important than statutory law, because the agencies whose funds they appropriate often operate with those reports as a literal bible. The reports are not subject to amendment on the floor, and they frequently do not reflect majority opinion. There is no way to prove it, however, and the agency will accept the direction of the people who hand out the money, quite often in preference to any administration official's views. There is no ready solution to this problem. Improvement would come with more oversight by the responsible legislative committees and interested individual members. This would require more expert, and sometimes larger, committee staffs, and a better organized and staffed legislative research service in the Library of Congress.

Hearings are the aspect of committees that the public sees most often. They are important because they enable the individual members of the committee to obtain specific background on the more intricate provisions of the proposed bills. No matter who controls Congress, a major part of the legislation which reaches the hearing stage either originates with the administrative branch of government, or the administration's recommendations are controlling in deciding specific operating procedure under the legislation. Most congressmen soon realize that they can secure a practical estimate of how specific legislation will work only from the federal agencies operating in the field. It is customary for agencies to suggest amendments to bills to make them workable, even if they regard the legislation as unwise, or even if the official administration position is in opposition to it.

New members of Congress usually grow impatient at the long hearings when the time for questioning cabinet officers, top administration officials, and prominent national figures who appear as witnesses is all taken up by senior members of the committee. The young member may be genuinely interested in getting a specific response from a prominent witness, but he may also be interested in getting his chance to cross swords with a big name while the reporters are at the press table. (They rarely come except when the big names show up.) It may also be only the natural urge to get recognition from the prominent person testifying.

One of the first laws of congressional politics a new member learns is the great advantage of incumbency. Except for some of the "swing" districts in evenly balanced two-party areas, the general belief is that a member who fails to return has very little excuse for his defeat. This is often true. The congressman puts his best foot forward, politically, in the off-year just after he has been elected or re-elected. Plenty of publicity without obvious political motivation is available. Public appearances before civic groups can be worked out easily, and all types of personal contacts can be developed without having to ask for the constituent's vote in the same breath.

The use of mail as a means of direct communication with the voters has been developed to a fine art among the members with energetic and capable staffs. There are few members who do not encourage mail from their constituents. The most common way to promote mail on legislative issues is to distribute a questionnaire to an extensive mailing list, or sometimes to post office patrons at random. Voters apparently like this opportunity to express their opinions, even though the questions are usually stacked in their phraseology. There was one member a few years ago who made wide use of questionnaires every few months, referring to results of the polls in every debate about the issues on the House floor. One day in the cloakroom somebody asked him: "How would you vote on a bill if one of your polls showed an exact 50-50 division on it?"

"In that case I would use my own judgment," he replied, very seriously.

The questionnaire reply which I liked best was shown to me by a friend who had received it from a constituent he knew personally. The constituent had scrawled across the face of the questionnaire: "We sent you up there to answer these!"

I personally never used the questionnaire. I saw no point in inviting differences with my constituents, and I had no intention of surrendering my right to make my own judgments on legislation. The robot questionnaire device is in keeping with the current and alarming tendency to reduce all issues to the simplest terms.

A major advantage of incumbency in seeking re-election is that it reduces the cost of campaigning. The congressman in office is normally better-known than his opponent, and franked mail can remedy that situation if he feels the need for greater exposure. Questionnaires and reports can be franked out even a few weeks before the election without the outright appearance of being campaign material. Staff allowances can furnish part of the cost of campaign personnel. Even with these advantages, campaign costs can be fantastic. In my 1962 primary, cash costs came to more than $60,000 for me, even with a major part of my printing donated and many other volunteer services. Since it is easy to compare television and radio costs, plus other obviously identifiable expenses, we know that the same campaign cost my opponent at least a little bit more. Primary campaigns in the South probably cost more, on the average, than contests for the House in other sections of the country, because they usually have to carry their own weight in generating interest. Election contests in a one-party political structure demand far more in the way of advertising and similar efforts to stir up interest and get out the voters than are needed where there are other contests on the ballot.

Campaign costs are out of line everywhere, however. Obviously, some incentive is needed to bring the average citizen into the ranks of regular campaign contributors, for this not only would encourage more general participation in politics, in itself a crying need, but might also inspire the average citizen to help eliminate some of the wasteful cost of campaigning. One way of alleviating improper use of campaign contributions by special interests would be to establish a strong tradition of adequate compensation for members of Congress. Today, it is far too hard to make Congress face up to the necessity of raising its own pay. The branch of government which appropriates 100 billion dollars each year is afraid to raise the pay of its members by the few thousand necessary to bring its compensation into line with reality. Part of this fear arises from the fact that a good many newspapers devote a lot of space to vilifying Congress, just as many members of Congress devote a lot of time to general demagoguery.

One advantage of incumbency which not enough members recognize is that it offers the opportunity to educate their constituents about national problems by an explanation of the votes on these issues. So many issues which come before the Congress are so poorly defined in the newspapers that congressional explanation would (and does) attract real attention from the public. The easiest way out for most members, however, is to vote and say nothing unless they are asked, and then so to phrase their answers as to limit them to yes or no. There are sharp limits to a member's freedom of action, but many members capitalize on a reputation for independence to such an extent that it ensures their political lives.

One of the most vital elements the congressman uses to keep himself in office is his relationship with the press in his district. The metropolitan area newspapers maintain Washington correspondents, but only a limited number of the smaller papers have any special service from Washington that provides coverage of the district congressman. The paper with a special correspondent in Washington therefore becomes all-important to the member, for it is in these dispatches, rather than in the regional coverage by the wire services, that his name will be mentioned far more often and far more prominently. As an example, the Memphis *Commercial Appeal* is the newspaper of major circulation in approximately ten congressional districts, with substantial circulation in about as many more. A good working relationship with the correspondent for any newspaper of that reader-scope is vital, although in some situations it is even more important to be on close terms with the editor or publisher back home. Some of the regional Washington correspondents try to do a thorough, objective job; others are more interested in seeing that the congressional news releases are typed and double-spaced than in evaluating what they say. For the smaller papers, both daily and weekly, without Washington correspondents, the relationship varies with the paper. If the editor is friendly or at least cooperative, the congressman and his staff virtually act as special correspondents for the paper on anything that might bring favorable mention of the congressman's name.

The average House member has little contact with the big-city press unless he comes from one of the cities. He may reach a position of sufficient influence in his legislative specialty to be queried or interviewed by *The New York Times*, the *Washington Post*, the *Wall Street Journal*, or one of the few other papers that attempt thorough coverage of the Congress, but he knows that these stories don't go to his district or influence votes there. Except for a discriminating few trying to make their observations from the broadest possible base, the big-name pundits of both newspaper columns and broadcasting do not really cover the House. The gossip-type Washington columnists like Drew Pearson are an exception, and one of the reasons they give so much space to House stories is that House members are readily available sources. Despite frequent inaccuracies, the Pearson column is a valuable service to both the Congress and the general public; it uses material that often nobody else would go to the trouble to dig up. The quality of congressional reporting in Washington is low more often than it is otherwise, but its rewards are sometimes very high indeed. The most widely publicized example of this in recent years was the award of the Pulitzer Prize to a reporter, Vance Trimble, who copied and printed some payroll records which were available to the public, but which nobody had ever bothered to look at.

Personal relationships in the House transcend party divisions, but the interparty friendships seldom become close ones, unless there is some tie other than membership in the House (living in the same Washington neighborhood, friendships among wives, school or professional ties antedating congressional service, to mention a few). By common consent, it is against the rules to attack another member publicly, unless there has been extreme provocation. It is simply accepted that you have to live and work with other members on another day, and that all members of the House are honorable. A classic example of preserving the amenities came from then Majority Leader McCormack, in the face of repeated insults from a Republican gadfly: "I have a minimum high regard for the gentleman," McCormack said.

In 1959, I participated in the Brookings Institution's "Round Table on Congress," a series of informal panel discussions by some knowledgeable members of the House designed to obtain their impressions of how the House works. I agreed, in general, with the estimate of the other Democratic members of the group about the personal qualities of the members. We felt that Democratic members, on the whole, take themselves less seriously than Republicans and are generally less pompous. We thought the Democrats possess greater breadth of interest and understanding and are characteristically more independent, because they do not make themselves so subject to party discipline. Republicans, we concluded, are dour and often dull, without a sense of humor, and many times don't like either people or politics.

When Brookings published its book summarizing the round table discussions (*The Congressman: His Work As He Sees It*, by Charles L. Clapp), I found the Republican reaction summarized in a statement by one of the GOP members of the panel:

> We Republicans have a more difficult job. One reason Democrats appear to be good speakers is that they are always promoting something. It is easier to be articulate and enthusiastic when you are advocating some new service. They tell people what they are going to do *for* them, we tell them what we are keeping the government from doing *to* them. Objecting to things and trying to stop excesses is a difficult position to be in.

One of the great opportunities for conscientious members of the House to make lasting contributions to the improvement of government is through committee investigations and studies. Because the term congressional investigation has become almost synonymous with headline hunting, it is now more popular in the House to use the term "study" as a substitute for "investigation." This distinction works well. Individual members are often tempted to give their committee work a sensational flavor for publicity purposes, even after a serious tone has been set by the committee itself. Calling the work a study discourages this. It's pretty hard to find any sensational adjectives that harmonize with study. The larger studies require special funds, but adequate treatment of many important topics can be handled entirely by subcommittees and their staffs, with reasonable cooperation from the administrative agencies. Valuable assistance is available from political scientists in the universities and foundations. Some of these studies lead to no more than a compilation of long stereotyped statements, but even this can show the need for fresh

air and fresh minds in the agencies concerned with the prob
lem under consideration.

Relatively unpublicized studies and investigations seldom
garner any votes at home, but they can build prestige with
fellow members. Perhaps the greatest value of this construc
tive work, however, is the self-satisfaction that it can give the
member. The size of the House, the rules under which it
operates, the number of influential posts locked in by senior
ity, all work to limit, if not eliminate, the opportunities for
individual historic achievement. Productive committee work
alleviates the resulting feeling of frustration. That sense of
frustration is common to all members, who often wonder
what contribution they are making to the goals in which they
believe. Significant accomplishments, with their special satis
factions, may come after the member has gained the rank that
makes them possible, but in the early years his greatest con
tribution can be made in some aspect of committee work, or
in educating his constituents.

No matter how much work he actually does, on legisla
tion in Washington or on his own public relations, every
member of Congress seeks more than anything else to leave
the impression with his constituents that he is a worker. One
of the usually unavoidable chores he has to perform is attend
ing the dinners given in Washington by trade and professional
groups and national civic organizations. The congressman
who goes to one of these dinners when none of his constitu
ents will be there is a glutton for punishment, but most mem
bers show up when a voter from home is likely to be present
My favorite experience of this kind occurred at a dinner at
which three of us from Mississippi sat at a table with four or
five visitors from home. Just after dinner was served, one
congressman excused himself, saying he had to finish pre
paring a speech that night. A few minutes later, the second

member took leave, saying he had to be at his office the next morning by eight o'clock to prepare for a committee meeting. When the first after-dinner speech came to an end, I was the last congressman present, and I left too. There didn't seem to be any point in letting the visitors from home come to the conclusion that if I could afford to stay any longer, I obviously didn't have much work to do.

In the past few years, there has been a flurry of study and self-analysis of the House by both members and independent political scientists. If I may use a hoary political cliché, I suggest that it would be of great value to the students to "return to the fundamentals" and to see what our Founding Fathers said about the House. James Madison was an influential framer of the Constitution and one of the moving forces in securing its ratification. The *Federalist* papers, which Madison helped write, provided much of the basis for the early interpretation of the Constitution, but it was as a congressman himself that Madison had most to do with establishing the role of the House of Representatives in the legislative branch. He served only briefly in the House but more than any other man he cut most of the early patterns. He envisioned as represented in the Congress "A landed interest, a manufacturing interest, a mercantile interest, a moneyed interest, with many lesser interests, [which] grow up of necessity in civilized nations and divide them into different classes, actuated by different sentiments and views." Madison's idea was that the principal business of legislation would be the regulation of conflicting economic interests and that these interests would be the major influences in proposing and opposing such legislation.

It would be very refreshing if the Congress would work from this definition of its role by one of the chief Founding Fathers instead of allowing itself to be led around by empty rhetoric about alleged constitutionalism and "what made this country great." Varied economic interests fight for privilege and advantage in the Congress, and the independent regulatory force is that part of the Congress whose primary concern is the general welfare of the country and the mass of its citizens. The forces which Madison envisioned play more or less the roles that he outlined, but the representatives of these forces in Congress describe their position as defenders of "free enterprise," "the working man," "the American way of life," or some similarly vague slogan. Some members are so completely identified with one of the slogans that they blindly take positions in support of or opposition to significant issues solely on the basis of the slogans without really knowing what they mean and without regard to the effect their votes will have, if they carry, on the economy of the country or even on the special interests to which they owe their individual obligations.

Of course, Madison could not foresee the sectional economic rivalry which would become part of the congressional scene. It is actually local chamber of commerce rivalry rather than basically sectional rivalry. What it demands is that the member of Congress from almost every area has to cooperate, however unreasonable the plan or request, with every proposal for building the economy of the region he represents. This does not necessarily mean supporting programs designed to increase the growth rate of the gross national product, or even supporting programs like the Area Redevelopment Administration to help substandard regions. The demand is much narrower than that. It usually means running errands for local business interests and following their suggestions about how to vote on the issues before Congress. Almost every state in the Union, no matter what the political theories of its governor or legislature may be, today supports some agency designed to help lure new industry into the state. Congressmen and senators of necessity have to take on that type of activity as part of their chores for constituents. Even the most conservative or the most independent of them cannot afford to oppose government spending programs in their own areas. No realistic politician would risk alienating his chambers of commerce on a local issue; their local influence is far too great for that.

Our nation's position of world leadership has given the Congress many responsibilities in foreign affairs and defense that Madison could not foresee either, but most of these congressional decisions, even in these fields, are influenced by economic forces Madison did foresee. If the Congress could accept a realistic concept of its function, and devote the bulk of its energies to those forces which are decisive, rather than to those which are, at best, ephemeral and, at worst, divisive, there could be far more progress toward economic goals.

Personal abuse, constant tension, limited financial return, disorganized and dislocated personal life, and a multitude of uncertainties all serve to discourage good men from service in Congress. Sometimes it seems that certain types of congressional politicians try to make the going so rough as to shut off competition from all except their own kind, who are protected by the proverbial rhinoceros hide. Despite all the drawbacks, however, good men will seek the office, whether for the satisfaction of public service or for the glamour that is undeniably attached to it.

For the conscientious citizen who succumbs to the attractions and is elected to Congress, let him retain his courage and his conscience when the frustrations and disappointments of service set in. He will need both to avoid an overdeveloped sense of self-importance. He may also need these qualities when the temptation comes to take the easy way out in his pursuit of re-election, or to avoid the responsibility of bringing at least the minimum basic truths home to his constituents. The ideal of representative government carries with it the ideal of an informed electorate.

Few people who stay more than a term or two in the Congress willingly leave it, except in the extremities of health or age. The sense of being a part of what is making our world go has an irresistible appeal, even to those for whom the minor pomp and pageantry is not important. Let those who stay in Congress remember Immanuel Kant's dictum that a man "should treat humanity, whether in one's self or in another, always as an end, never as a means."

Chapter X

C L O U D   R I D I N G

Some of the more lasting satisfactions of service in the Congress develop from voluntary legislative work inspired solely by nonpolitical personal interests. To put it another way, members of Congress, like people in most fields, frequently find that the most gratifying work they do is the work they think should be done, not for personal or political profit to themselves but simply because the need is there. Work of this nature is seldom world-shaking, but it very often is the kind of thing that would not be done when it is done, if the individual member were not driven to the task by his own enthusiasm, push, and perseverance. Some members never get around to this sort of activity; some become so enamored of a single (and frequently, hopeless) cause that they pursue it until it becomes a weary joke; others undertake so much that they seem forever to be riding in all directions. Fortunately for the temper of the House, most members tread a middle ground, modestly and persistently working their way toward the birth of the new or reform of the old which they seek. Happily, circumstances and personal inclination made me one of this latter larger group. I tried, naturally, to exploit my projects for what political value they might have at home, but most of the time I had to be content if the sum of their political effect in Mississippi was, at worst, no more minus than plus.

Sometime in 1952 I decided that the time had come to be rid of the Buy American Act, a relic of the dying days of the depression-racked Hoover administration. Senator Hiram Johnson of California, one of the most effective isolationists of his day, had engineered its adoption as a legislative rider to an appropriation bill. Perhaps I first came across the law in reading about its pernicious effects in the comprehensive report on government matériel policy compiled by a task force headed by William S. Paley. The act provided that government agencies could not consider foreign bids for equipment or matériel unless there was an "unreasonable" difference between American and foreign costs. An executive order had defined unreasonable as a difference of 25 percent, but during World War II an amendment to that order had made some exceptions. The tariff on the imported item had to be added before the differential was computed. Late in the 1952 session, I introduced a bill to repeal the Buy American Act, and put a statement in the *Congressional Record* outlining the detrimental effects of the law. I laid at its door an unnecessary increase in government costs of more than two billion dollars a year, direct and indirect: "We lose the amount by which the foreign bid is low, plus the amount of import duty that would in some cases have been paid on the foreign supplies, plus the amount of foreign aid that may be necessary because of the inability of the foreign country to earn dollars. Our own economy loses the benefit of free competition, which we so greatly admire, inside the national economy."

In the early 1950's the dollar shortage abroad was still an acute problem. Remedying that shortage was essential to our economic growth and our foreign policy. After the 1952 election it was apparent that business voices were in the ascendancy, and I began to appeal directly to the industrial community for assistance with my Buy American repeal bill. I mailed hundreds of letters and copies of my speech to newspapers over the country and to every business or trade group leader who I assumed might favor a more liberal trade policy. Interest began to develop, and several organizations working in the foreign trade field began to endorse the bill.

Coincidence entered to implement the campaign. When I introduced the repeal bill it was referred to the Public Works Committee, probably because I was a member—the original act had not gone through any committee. I had no idea at the time that some of the most critical items of foreign manufacture then being effectively barred from sale to the United States were the turbines and transformers used in the hydroelectric dams authorized by our committee. Coincident with this, when the Republicans took over in 1953 Representative George Dondero, whose district included most of wealthy suburban Detroit, became chairman of the committee. In that same year the Detroit Chamber of Commerce was in the midst of a campaign for a liberal trade program. John S. Coleman of the Burroughs Adding Machine Company, one of Dondero's constituents, was a spearhead in the campaign. A few months later he was to lead the Committee for a National Trade Policy, a lobby group for liberal trade that I, along with people like Charles Taft and George Ball, had helped to promote. These developments gave me hope that we could get action on the bill, as business endorsements mounted.

While the liberal business groups were asking for an improved American trade policy, however, the protectionists were busily working the other side of the street. I thought that the attention my repeal bill was getting (an editorial in the Scripps-Howard chain, for example) might generate additional support in the form of similar bills introduced by other members of Congress, but the only other legislation introduced on the subject called for strengthening the act, not repealing it. On the immediate front, however, George Dondero was getting requests from home for his committee to act. There were also intimations that the Eisenhower administration would ask him to approve the bill. Then everybody got off the hook with the appointment of the Randall Commission to study the whole complex of foreign trade problems. Word came that there would be no administration report on my bill pending the Randall report.

Early in 1954 the Randall Commission reported. It did not recommend the flat repeal of the Buy American Act, but it did suggest some substantial modifications. I introduced a bill to carry out the commission's recommendations. I would gladly have yielded my sponsorship to some good Republican anxious to support Eisenhower, but none was at hand. In the meantime, my interest in Buy American thrust me into other aspects of the trade policy fight. The European and Japanese manufacturers of generators and transformers who were in a position to bid on American contracts usually had Washington representatives, and some of them began to bring me examples of the extremely high prices our taxpayers were paying for products where foreign bids were ruled out. I learned that the Corps of Engineers had refused an award to a low foreign bid on a Columbia Valley dam and that the proposed contract had been referred to Army Secretary Robert Stevens for review. I went to see Stevens, to ask him to accept the foreign bid and set a precedent which would materially reduce the cost of hydroelectric power in the years ahead. The low bidder was an English firm. Stevens said he could not approve the award to England because of national security considerations—the consideration being that he couldn't be sure England would still be part of the free world by the time the contract was completed!

"What in the world do you think General Eisenhower spent two years organizing NATO for?" I exploded to President Eisenhower's Secretary of the Army. "What are we doing with such a large part of our army in Europe today?" When Secretary Stevens went back to his textile business, he continued to oppose President Eisenhower's trade policy.

Other Republicans also failed to get the message from the White House. An editorial from the *Washington Post* tells this story of an incident in 1954:

> President Eisenhower owes another debt to House Democrats for protecting him against attacks from his own party. A week after the President urged Congress to liberalize the "Buy American" act a group of House Republicans sought to make it more restrictive. The "Buy American" Act requires the Government to favor American suppliers unless the foreign bidder can deliver the goods for a saving of 25 per cent or more. Mr. Eisenhower recommended that there be no discrimination against bidders from countries that treat American businessmen fairly.
>
> But Representative Bow and several other Republicans were not persuaded by the President. They offered an amendment to prevent the Interior Department from making any foreign purchases when there are so many as two million unemployed in the United States. The amendment, which was intended as a legislative rider on an appropriation bill, was all-inclusive. It would have prevented the Interior

Department from making purchases abroad even if it could not obtain them at home. Fortunately, Representatives Smith of Mississippi and Kirwan of Ohio—both Democrats—sprang to the President's defense, and the amendment was defeated by a vote of 44 to 38.

Despite the Randall Commission report, I never did get action on my Buy American bills in committee. President Eisenhower eventually modified the act by executive order, making use of the leeway available under the "reasonable" difference provision. Under the change, foreign bids could be accepted if they were from 6 to 10 percent lower than any domestic bid. There were too many obstacles to getting clear-cut legislative action, even though it could have been achieved if the administration had come forth with a specific recommendation in 1953 based on the then compelling demands of economy and an improved trade position. Within a few years the balance of payments picture had changed so much that there was no possibility of completely eliminating the act. I gave up my repeal efforts after President Eisenhower made the modification by administrative order, but I had one more legislative tangle with a Buy American-type maneuver. When the TVA self-financing bill was on the floor in 1959, Representative Stratton of New York, whose district included Schenectady and General Electric, offered an amendment to bar TVA's making foreign purchases. We won this fight with most of the Republican votes against us and despite an attempt by some of the Republicans to keep me from using a letter from the Eisenhower administration opposing the amendment.

The improvement in Buy American which President Eisenhower put into effect would not have come about but for my one-man congressional campaign. I discovered that attempting to repeal Buy American had no political appeal to farmers raising cotton for export, but there was some real personal satisfaction in knowing the country was deriving some direct benefits from lower procurement costs. The Tennessee Valley Authority showed the most direct results when it began to make foreign purchases. In less than four years these direct savings amounted to more than twenty million dollars. There is no way to evaluate the indirect savings in the form of reduced bids by domestic suppliers. The sharp differences between foreign and domestic prices in the electrical field, which were publicized in all the Buy American agitation, also played a role in the decision to prepare and prosecute the successful antitrust suits against American manufacturers.

Foreign trade remained one of my active interests throughout my years in the Congress. From Robert Walker in the 1840's to Pat Harrison in the 1930's, Mississippi Senators had played important roles in developing liberal trade policy, but after World War II all the other Mississippi congressmen abandoned the program. Many liberals and internationalists favored it, so they must have decided that alone made it bad, even for Mississippi cotton and soybeans.

In 1954 I introduced the first bill to provide for re-employment training where personnel hardships resulted from tariff revision. This plan was reshaped and restudied through the years, was picked up and polished by Senators Kennedy and Javits, and eventually in modified form became law as part of the Kennedy trade bill of 1961. In 1954, when the first Eisenhower trade bill passed, the Democratic members of the Ways and Means Committee gave me the privilege of offering the motion to recommit with instructions to eliminate the Republican provision, opposed by Eisenhower, which would have added an extra, and presumably protectionist, member to the Tariff Commission. The motion lost, but the Senate kept the provision out of the bill.

Speaker Rayburn asked if I would be interested in going on the Ways and Means Committee in 1955, but I couldn't afford to even think of the change. My one hope of keeping a Delta district together was the importance of my position on the Public Works Committee. I got into the 1955 debate, however, in time to be the object of some entertaining epithets by some of my more conservative colleagues. Cleve Bailey of West Virginia said I was a "cloud-rider and idealist." Henderson Lanham of Georgia expanded on this description: "I am somewhat surprised at my rotund and usually jolly friend and colleague from the South, Mr. Smith from Mississippi. I cannot understand what has got him so wrought up and excited unless he is afraid we are going to recommit this bill and provide some protection in it for our industries which are really threatened and get it in shape so we can vote for it. I think I know the trouble with him. You know he is an author. He has just written a book called *The Yazoo*. Was it the psalmist or somebody in the Old Testament who said, 'Oh, that my enemy would write a book'? Well, our friend has written a book and I understand it is a fine book. But you know he is one of these cloud riders, these idealists. You know he would ride in the clouds if he did not weigh quite so much."

At a time when spokesmen for liberal foreign trade policies in the Congress were few and far between, I became something of a Cyclops. Dick Simpson, the Republican from Pennsylvania who was the brains of the congressional protectionists, described me as the only free-trader left in Washington. "Should the United States Adopt a Freer Trade Policy?" was the subject for the 1953–54 intercollegiate debates. The Foundation on Economic Education compiled a handbook of source material, and a speech which I made on April 15, 1953, was included as the voice of members of Congress favoring a more liberal policy. The congressional speech chosen to represent the opposite side was by Senator Robert Taft. The *Congressional Digest* for January 1954 was on foreign trade. My April 15th speech was again included, along with others by Henry Ford II and then Assistant Secretary of State Thruston Morton. My experience in legislating for a liberal foreign trade policy convinced me that such programs will pass only with tremendous pressure from the Presidency and from business interests sufficiently aware of their own stake in the export market. There is simply not enough political value in this issue for the average member to devote his time to it.

My next big venture in cloud riding also had an international angle. NATO was one of my interests from its inception, along with the potentialities of Atlantic Union and other plans to promote European unity. The entire concept of American participation in NATO was threatened in 1955 when a campaign of sheer demagoguery was taken up by various newspapers and then by several right-wing groups and members of Congress. The Status of Forces Treaty with the NATO countries had been adopted by a 72 to 15 vote in the Senate in 1953, as a necessary implementation of the NATO program which involved stationing American troops in most of the participating countries. Under the treaty, those countries had jurisdiction to try U.S. servicemen charged with civilian offenses within their borders. It applied, of course, to foreign troops in the United States as well as to U.S. servicemen abroad. These treaty agreements were essential to amicable relations with the Allied countries. No sovereign nation can be expected, in peacetime, to renounce the right to arrest, try, and punish people for crimes committed against its own nationals on its own soil. Similar treaties or agreements were made with other countries outside NATO where American troops were stationed. The NATO treaty was working well, according to servicemen in the areas, until someone at home began to publicize the case of Private Richard T. Keefe of Riverdale, Maryland.

According to congressional speeches and the Idaho *Daily Statesman*, Private Keefe's offense was "joyriding." According to the *New York Daily News*, Keefe "got tanked one night and drove off in a French taxi that wasn't his." According to U.S. service records, Keefe's own admission, and the *Christian Science Monitor*:

Private Keefe and Private Scaletti arrived in Orleans together, coming from a period of confinement in a United States guardhouse in Germany. They went to the center of Orleans without permission. After drinking various alcoholic beverages, Keefe lost all but 2,000 francs of his money in a dice game. It was then after dark, and both decided to go to Paris.

They entered a taxicab with the purpose of getting out on the main highways to hitchhike a ride to Paris. About 1 mile out they had the cabdriver, Fernand Henault, stop the cab. Scaletti then got in the back seat and removed two shirts from their baggage. Scaletti placed his shirt around the driver's neck and Keefe placed his in the driver's mouth. Keefe struck the cab driver. Keefe and the driver rolled out onto the ground.

Scaletti started the cab and both got away. They then drove to Paris where they abandoned the taxi. After several days in Paris they started hitchhiking south. They were arrested at Nogent-le-Rotrou by the French police.

The victim, a 65-year-old taxicab driver, was incapacitated from work for 30 days. He had an injured nose, his false teeth were broken, and he had numerous cuts and bruises.

Keefe and Scaletti were given the minimum sentence under French law for their crime, five years imprisonment. The sentence was later reduced. Despite his sordid offense, Keefe became something of a hero in many newspapers as the poor GI that Uncle Sam wouldn't protect. Keefe must have gotten the attention instead of Scaletti because his wife tried unsuccessfully to get United States courts to take jurisdiction in his case. At any rate, the next hero of the *Chicago Tribune*, one of the newspapers crusading on the issue, was Airman Joe Montijo of Phoenix, Arizona, accused of fatally stabbing a nineteen-year-old French youth at Fontainebleau. Representative Frank Bow of Ohio described Montijo's plight as follows:

> Mr. Speaker, the French Communist press is howling for the head of an American GI.
> Airman Joe Montijo, of Phoenix, Arizona, is being held in prison in France today, denied the aid and counsel of his fellow countrymen, threatened with death on the guillotine.
> He has been left at the mercy of the French courts under the terms of a treaty which deprives him and all of his comrades of the protection of the American Government whenever they run afoul of the law in whatever foreign land they are stationed. . . .
> We may be too late to rescue Montijo. We can save other American servicemen from a similar fate.

Montijo was convicted by the French court. His sentence was six months. No announcement of the sentence was placed in the *Congressional Record*, and nobody mentioned what his sentence would have been if he had been convicted on the same charge in any one of our then 48 states.

Bow introduced a House resolution which would have repudiated the Status of Forces Treaty and agreements. Hearings were held on the resolution in the House Foreign Affairs

Committee, but it was the type of proposal committees normally bury, and the resolution died when the hearings ended. Amendments on the floor, however, are a different thing. A reserve forces bill was up for consideration in May of 1955, and Bow offered an amendment providing that no member of the Armed Forces could thereafter be stationed in any country where the Status of Forces Treaty or agreements were in effect. Before Bow's amendment was considered, Representative Adam Clayton Powell's amendment to end segregation in the National Guard was adopted with the support of an odd combination of forces, most of them more in favor of ending the reserve program rather than of ending segregation. With the Powell amendment adopted, the bill was as good as dead, if for no other reason than that the original bill's chief sponsors were Southerners. As a result, the Bow amendment did not receive full-scale debate or attention from the House leaders. It passed, 174 to 56, but the bill to which it was attached never again saw light. It was obvious that the Bow amendment or something similar would soon be up again whenever a suitable vehicle came along to which it could be attached.

The Defense Department began to get out some explanations about the agreements. Figures for a then current six-month period showed that, during that time, 1,987 American servicemen were accused of crimes over which local courts in NATO countries had jurisdiction. Of these, 1,787 were surrendered to U.S. military jurisdiction, so only 200 were retained in the local courts. Of these, only 42 were sentenced to imprisonment, and 33 of these sentences were suspended. In other words, only nine American soldiers were actually imprisoned out of nearly 2,000 charged with civilian crimes in Europe. The Richmond (Indiana) *Palladium-Item* answered back with inexorable logic:

He (Bow) is aware of would-be traitors to our country who approved a treaty nearly 2 years ago which strips our fighting men of constitutional rights. . . .

Seventy-two United States Senators voted to rob of citizenship those men we send overseas to stand guard. . . . With shame we report that only 15 United States Senators were men enough to vote against the enslaving device of treaty law. . . .

Former President Truman is not entirely to blame. The job that he started was carried out by President Eisenhower and Secretary of State Dulles.

They approved this move to please foreign allies at the expense of individual rights of the men who are thousands of miles from home helping to defend those either unable to defend themselves from Red attack, or who are too cowardly to fight for their own people.

The Bow amendment came up next on a live bill, the 1956 foreign aid authorization. It would have ended any assistance to countries with which we had Status of Forces arrangements. The defense against the amendment was better prepared this time, but it seemed to me it still lacked hard, down-to-earth answers. The members about to support the amendment were responding to slogans and newspaper headlines rather than logic or the importance of our overseas commitments. They were responding to talk about "American justice," yet they were usually leading the clamor against decisions of the U.S. Supreme Court. They were helping to make heroes out of men who were usually the bottom of our service barrel. I talked against the amendment both on the floor and in the cloakroom. I don't have a transcript of my argument, but it went something like this:

"You are asking here that GI's be tried by service courts martial rather than in civilian courts abroad. If you think you are doing the serviceman a favor, let me assure you that you are not. I am an expert on American military justice. I acted as defense counsel at special courts martial for American soldiers in my unit for about two years. I suppose I defended over a hundred men, and I never had one acquitted. If you think military courts are going to be easy on soldiers charged with these crimes, think again.

"These men who are being virtually made heroes here are often robbers, murderers, and rapists. They wouldn't be getting any attention from us if they were being charged with this same type of crime in the United States.

"Stop a minute and think how this would work in your own district. Would the people in one of your towns be willing to give up jurisdiction if a foreign soldier attached to a station in your district went berserk and committed murder, rape, or arson? Of course, they wouldn't. The Status of Forces Treaty does the same thing for our Allied countries."

The amendment failed by a tie vote. At least twenty members took the trouble to tell me that my blunt words had some effect on that vote. Even if the House had passed the amendment, the Senate would probably have disposed of it, but at least the House had for once met its responsibility in foreign affairs.

In 1956 I became a member of the House delegation to the NATO Parliamentarians' Conference and continued as a member of the group throughout the remainder of my service in Congress. There were nine NATO conference delegates from the House and nine from the Senate. Except for one session in Washington in 1959, the meetings were held each year in Paris. The very fact that the organization met in Paris gave it an automatic press classification as a congressional "junket." Those who wanted to could squeeze out junketeering side trips, but the conference sessions always involved five or six days of attendance and work for conscientious delegates, plus whatever advance preparation seemed suitable. For me it was an enjoyable experience, trying to explain American policy and American problems in parliamentary and political terms that could be understood by our Allied politicians.

There are fifteen NATO countries, and all of them were regularly represented at the parliamentary conferences. The delegates from Portugal and Turkey rarely entered into the discussions. At first I thought they might be bothered by language problems, but when I found that most of them spoke good English or French, it was obvious that their governments didn't encourage much self-expression away from home (possibly not at home, either). Each annual meeting included several briefings from various NATO commanders and occasionally other prominent figures, but the chief interest was in committee resolutions and general debate. One of the most significant purposes of the conference was to give the representatives of the other fourteen NATO countries a sense of having a greater voice and influence in determining NATO policy. There was always a feeling among the Europeans that the United States dominated NATO policy. The best answer to this, seldom stated in so many words but often implied, was to talk about the need for all member countries to meet their full commitments and obligations to NATO. My longest assignment was on the military committee, and the job there was to help our allies understand some of our own defense problems. The political considerations that influenced the other NATO governments also influenced our government, and explaining the similarities in national problems in terms of legislative problems went a long way toward bolstering support for NATO.

Fostering an amicable relationship among ordinary members of the several parliaments was a major achievement of the conferences. Language barriers were, and are, a major problem in personal contacts between members, of course, but most informal groups included some delegate able to serve as translator. The alphabetical seating arrangements and a common language made it inevitable that most of my personal ties were with delegates from the United Kingdom. Since the party in power could not spare its ministers and subministers, the big names of the Conservative party were rarely on hand, but through the years I got to know fairly well a large number of the active members of the Labor party—the Bevanites and unilateralists, of course, didn't participate in NATO affairs. The personal discussions were naturally not restricted to NATO. Hugh Gaitskell, for instance, knew more about cotton than most members of the United States Congress. He had a brother who had managed a cotton plantation in Kenya. British members grumble about their pay just as American congressmen do. Apparently pay raises lag behind for the reason that they do in our country—standard political demagoguery—plus the fact that too many influential members have, or find, additional sources of income.

In addition to showing an American interest in the problems other parliamentarians face in understanding and supporting NATO, I think the conference meetings of my service can also claim a few definable credits. I believe we convinced most of the Europeans that the American system retained full civilian control of the use of nuclear weapons. I believe that our conferences helped develop British Labor support for fully meeting Britain's share of traditional weapons and manpower, ahead of a British nuclear weapon. Our resolutions in favor of strong nuclear submarine forces, largely the work of Senator Henry Jackson, helped make this weapon a strong point in NATO defenses. I believe that if our State Department encouraged more independent discussion at these parliamentary meetings, it would help to bring a non-military emphasis to NATO affairs that would have the effect of simplifying some of the military problems. The parliamentary conferences are not likely to contribute much to NATO's present dilemma, Charles de Gaulle, for a good part of de Gaulle's problem is his contempt for parliaments.

Our 1956 meeting included what may have been Lyndon Johnson's first diplomatic crisis. We met in mid-November, while repercussions from Suez were still at their height. The American delegate to the economic committee slept on his job, and the committee brought out a report more or less demanding that the United States make up almost the entire oil shortage then being felt in Europe. This was neither U.S. policy nor Texas policy, nor good NATO policy, with the long-range economic complications it would create in the way of demands for continued high American production. Senator Johnson's explanation had to be made before the full assembly, but he did it well, and the resolution was withdrawn with a minimum of hard feelings. At this same conference I learned something of the competence of Douglas Dillon, then our Ambassador to France. Five of the top-rank former French premiers had the U.S. delegation to lunch to air their complaints about American Suez policy. Dillon acted as a flawless translator, relaying the blistering remarks about Eisenhower policy from the French and the not too comforting replies from some of the Democrats present without once yielding to the temptation to inject the official American position and perhaps letting the meeting degenerate into brawling argument.

In a day when foreign policy decisions are the daily major chore of the Presidency, every possible assistance should be provided in helping to make the Congress better informed on the subject. The Congress should help define broad objectives, but every passing year makes it more obvious that it is in no position to make the day-to-day decisions. Headline hunting is of necessity a major part of life on Capitol Hill, and that is no method of making foreign policy. The facts of political life being what they are, the one long-range solution is a better-informed general public which will restrain rash answers in the Congress. Perhaps the improved public attitude will come only when a generation has learned to live with the daily "crisis" and realizes that the world is not being made over tomorrow in the American image, or rather the image of what some particular Americans have of what the world should be.

There are few congressmen who do not harbor the natural desire to leave their names on a significant piece of legislation. I authored no Taft-Hartley law or Wagner Act, and the best-known Smith Act is named for Judge Howard Smith of Virginia, but I can claim exclusive legislative credit for a minor but important law, the Textile Fiber Products Identification Act of 1958. The Textile Labeling Act, as it is familiarly called, requires that every fabric or fiber product show on a tag or label its percentages of fiber content and that advertisements of the product contain specific information as to fiber content. My effort to achieve this started out as an attempt to help sell cotton, and it developed into a reasonably successful fight to provide protection for the consumer. This story of the long translation of an idea into a bill and then into a law is not precisely an example of cloud riding, but it does demonstrate how a narrow special interest can be broadened to serve the general public.

I knew that for several years in the late forties Senator Lister Hill of Alabama had sponsored a bill he called the "Cotton Products Identification Act." The idea had first been promoted by cotton interests who believed that a requirement to label the fiber content of fabrics would lead to customer preference for cotton over synthetic fibers like rayon. There were many differences of opinion within the cotton trade about the idea, and all sorts of resistance to it outside the trade, which explained the lack of action on the legislation. I wanted to do something for cotton that would not impair the general economy, however, and cotton labeling looked like a good way to do it. I talked to the Washington representative (lobbyist is another term) of the National Cotton Council, a personable North Carolinian named Banks Young, and asked if his group could help me with the bill. He thought they could, so I introduced my first bill on the subject in 1955. Senator Hill introduced an identical version.

Between 1955 and 1958 we rewrote the bill three times. Also in that period we wrote five lengthy explanations of the bill, made innumerable committee appearances, and mailed out hundreds of individual letters and several times that many mimeographed letters and statements. The labeling bill went to the Interstate and Foreign Commerce Committee, of which I am not a member. The whole impetus for the bill was coming from me, not from the usual committee sources, so the tedious drafting of language that would work had to be done by me and my staff. We had the important assistance of Banks Young, and soon gained that of Harvey Hannah of the Federal Trade Commission, but the bill always remained the product of Congress rather than the creation of a lobby group or a federal agency, one of which is most often the case these days. Wherever a bill originates, however, very little legislation comes out of the Congress which is not the result of close collaboration between members and their personal assistants or committee staffs. Through the years, most of my legislative work outside the Public Works Committee, and some of that as well, was the joint product of my efforts and those of my own administrative assistant, Mrs. Audrey Warren. She handled 90 percent of the technical work in changing the Textile Labeling Act from a bill into a law, for example, and added countless other invaluable contributions to the representation my office provided.

In the first year after the labeling bill was introduced, we began to get some ideas for individual improvements. The bill had to be stronger if it was to control some of the downright fraud in the advertising used to sell fabrics and fiber products. Rayon was being blended into everything from cotton towels to expensive frocks, but the consumer was being told, or led to believe, that he was buying cotton. Perhaps the worst fraud was in connection with nylon. We were shown examples of products being advertised as "miracle fabrics" and "nylon blends" that contained as little as one percent nylon—a percentage, DuPont told us, that was useless to impart nylon's qualities. There was no way a manufacturer or merchant could be charged with deceptive practices under existing law. A furniture manufacturer told me that he could not honestly compete with many other manufacturers who used a large quantity of fabric in their product and advertised a 2 and 3 percent blend as a "miracle" fiber. Dry cleaners reported that lack of information on fiber content in fabrics was becoming a major problem to them. An iron temperature necessary to press a cotton fabric is too hot to press a nylon fabric. On a nylon blend, irons set for cotton fused the nylon fibers, with resulting breaks or holes in the fabric.

When bills such as mine are introduced and pushed, the easiest way to hold them up or defeat them is to raise a scare about the difficulties of administering the law, or the increased costs it will force on the manufacturer and thus on the consumer who is supposed to be benefited. The first cry against the labeling bill was the increased cost of providing the labels. We carefully eliminated this argument in the hearings. Only three or four words, or at most another line, needed to be added to existing labels to meet our requirements. The next attack was to agree that there should be labeling, but to insist that describing the content of a fabric was not really worthwhile information. I replied that every homemaker would be grateful for performance labeling that would tell her exactly how the textile she buys would react—to water or an iron at 100 degrees, or 200 degrees, or 500 degrees—and how long it could be expected to last if properly handled—and whether the color would survive soap, or detergent, or sun, or the years. I pointed out, however, that the same apparel industry people who were making this argument had told me that the industry was unable to agree on a standard of performance characteristics or on the methods of measuring these characteristics.

We had strengthened our bill considerably from the original draft by the time it came to be "marked up" (final agreement on language) in a House Commerce subcommittee in the spring of 1957. Representative Peter Mack of Illinois, the subcommittee chairman, was very cooperative, as had been his predecessor, Representative Arthur Klein, now a New York judge. We greatly increased the power of the Federal Trade Commission to enforce the act and to restrict misleading advertisers. We had to give in without a fight and exempt automobile seat covers for fear of losing important support. The other exemptions were relatively minor, but we lost a fight to include full coverage of all fabrics used in making furniture. The widely scattered furniture manufacturers were too persuasive with too many congressmen. The exemption was written into the bill before it came out of committee, to avoid a fight over amendments on the floor of the House. The House passed the bill in August with no major opposition.

The Senate Commerce Committee had hearings on the bill in February 1958. The bill's opponents didn't really get into high gear until these hearings were called. By that time, Senator Hill had been joined in sponsoring the bill by Senator Stennis, Monroney, and Magnuson, and Senator Magnuson was chairman of the committee. More than one hundred witnesses either testified in person or submitted statements on the bill, most of them in opposition. The National Retail Federation had come to the front of the opposition, primarily fighting the requirement for identifying fibers in advertising. The retail group included some 800,000 merchants among its members, who could produce a rather large number of letters and telegrams. They paid their respects to consumer protection by supporting a bill without our advertising restrictions, introduced by Senator Goldwater of Arizona. Delay was the opponents' watchword after the Senate hearings. After a good deal of backstage maneuvering, the bill was reported by the committee in June 1958 with no really destructive amendments. The support of some labor groups was very helpful during this period. We lost no ground when it was revealed that Sherman Adams's famous call to the Federal Trade Commission in behalf of Bernard Goldfine had been made because the FTC was charging Goldfine with selling wool and vicuna fabrics containing rayon. Goldfine was charged with violating the much less restrictive fur labeling act.

The report in June left us with a tight squeeze ahead—Lyndon Johnson was driving to adjourn the 85th Congress before the end of August—and it was a struggle to get our bill scheduled for floor debate. By early August, the textile trade papers were announcing that the bill was dead, that it could not be taken up in the Senate so late in the session. The Prentice-Hall legislative tip-sheet dated August 18 announced that the bill was not likely to survive the Congress, but on the same day the bill was called up in the Senate. Senators Magnuson and Monroney were in charge of the floor debate, and

I sat with them to explain the bill's details. It developed that Senator Pastore of Rhode Island was going to offer a motion to recommit the bill to the committee, which is legislative language for "kill." I talked to Senator Goldwater on behalf of his Arizona cotton growers, but he made a speech saying he had come to the floor prepared to support the bill but believed it ought to go back to committee. Four or five votes seemed to hinge on an amendment pushed by the Armstrong Cork Company for the exemption of rug backings and related floor coverings. We agreed to hold out against that exemption, and the votes soon became essential.

When the roll call began on Pastore's motion, I stationed myself at the center doorway to try to catch any senator whose vote might be undecided. Three years later, a Department of Agriculture official, in the gallery that day to follow the bill, told me "the last time I saw you, you were on the Senate floor giving the President of the United States hell to his face." Jack Kennedy had come through another door, and I didn't catch him until after he had voted for Pastore's motion. After we talked, he agreed to change his vote if it was needed, explaining that Pastore was the man he looked to for advice on Commerce Committee bills. The vote change wasn't needed—we won, 47 to 36.

There was still the job of getting the bill through conference, but the conferees were mainly committed to the legislation and were good enough to ask our advice about the final wording. Their report did no damage to the bill, and it was adopted by both houses on the last day of the session, August 23. The last hill to climb was the President's signature. The State Department had protested a section in the bill which required that the country of origin be shown on imported fabrics. We eventually got the message across that this merely carried forward a basic requirement of the tariff act, the one label already required. Banks Young and the Cotton Council were in the best position to take our case to the White House. As our bill had evolved from cotton promotion to consumer protection, considerable opposition had developed against it in various segments of the cotton industry. Banks stayed with us throughout, despite the internal problems in his own organization. President Eisenhower eventually signed H.R. 469, "a bill to protect producers and consumers against misbranding and false advertising of the fiber content of textile products, and for other purposes," and so a significant Frank Smith act was on the books.

Eighteen months later, when the law went into effect, Federal District Judge Luther Youngdahl turned down a motion by an Alabama textile firm to enjoin the Federal Trade Commission from requiring it to label its products as rayon.

"The man of Madison Avenue has been able to emplant in the minds of the public countless slogans—sensible and otherwise," the Judge said. "They have sold shirts by depicting a man with an eye-patch; they have sold soap by advertising it to be 99 and 44/100 percent pure without bothering to add the noun; they have sold brassieres by displaying a sleep walker.

"Can it reasonably be said they are now unable to distinguish one fiber from another?" Judge Youngdahl asked.

Before passage of the Textile Labeling Act, little attention had been paid to the plight of the consumer in any field except health hazards. The Wool and Fur Labeling Acts were on the books, but they were devised primarily to protect the domestic wool growers and fur breeders against foreign competition, and the Flammable Fabrics Act was a safety measure enacted into law when indignation was aroused by the dramatic and tragic injuries resulting from the "torch sweaters" manufactured in the forties. The general principle that industry should be held accountable for its ethics in dealing with the consuming public had not been explored.

The scope of the garment industry's opposition to the labeling act, and particularly to the truth-in-advertising provisions, created an unusual amount of verbal comment around the Capitol. The comment inevitably reached the ears of some members of the House and Senate who take a dim view of so vociferous a hands-off attitude. Their discerning eyes began to scan the many ways, large and small, by which the purchasing public is misled. The careful look taken at some of these practices has inspired detailed committee investigations and has invoked such widespread public response that the President has appointed a special assistant for consumer matters, whose task it is to study the problems and recommend remedies.

The repeal of the Buy American Act and the integrity of the Status of Forces Agreements were matters of importance to the nation, but they have an abstract quality that isolates them from the personal problems of daily life. The labeling act came much closer to home, but the legislative achievement that was all heart concerned retarded children.

I had known a few families who carried the burden of a child mentally or physically unable to develop to maturity and independence. Without exception, they were cared for with patience and with love, but in most cases with quiet desperation as well. Civilized institutional care was virtually nonexistent in Mississippi for many years, and is still far from adequate, as it is in most states. Faced with the sad alternatives of intolerably crude public facilities or prohibitively expensive private ones (and even these are few and far between), most of these families tried to keep the child at home and care for him as best they could in an otherwise normal atmosphere.

Like most people, I thought about this problem when I

encountered it, but I had never given any serious consideration to its many facets, or the possible sources of help, until Fred Ellis, a young college-student cousin of mine whose personal experience gave him a deep and determined interest in the problem, came up with an idea in the winter of 1954. He pointed out that the situation, difficult at best, became even more so when the father died, leaving his widow to support and care for the helpless child. If the father had Social Security coverage, benefits would be paid to mother and child, but only until the child reached age eighteen. What then? The law held eighteen to be the age at which a child becomes an adult, capable of self-support. But the retarded child rarely reaches a mental, and frequently not even a physical, eighteen —his numerical age is a meaningless statistic. And what of the child not mentally retarded but physically incapable of becoming financially self-sustaining? Without a father, with Social Security benefits discontinued, and with a mother approaching middle years and, very probably, limited earning capacity, how is this individual to be cared for?

We explored the existing laws and drafted an amendment to the Social Security Act that would continue benefit payments to any child who was so retarded as to be incapable of self-support. The benefits were limited to children whose condition had developed before they reached age eighteen and who could not reasonably be expected to progress to a self-sustaining level. Officials of the Social Security Administration with whom we discussed the proposal informed us that its cost would be small.

The Congress, and especially the House, rarely acts on separate minor amendments to either the Social Security Act or the tax laws. I knew there was no hope for immediate action on the bill, but a general bill to amend the Social Security Act would certainly come up within the next two to four years. We began a letter-writing campaign, looking to that time, and I began talking with other members about the proposal. Introduction of the bill brought me into contact with an organization just being formed—the National Association for Retarded Children. For several months my office became something of a Washington headquarters for the group, which had an office in New York City and was working to establish chapters across the country.

Early in 1956, with a general Social Security bill coming up, one of the members of the House Ways and Means Committee with whom I had discussed the matter suggested that I revise my amendment to cover disabled children, regardless of the nature of their disability, and submit it—typed, not printed—to the committee as an informal recommendation. He didn't explain why he thought that would be the best procedure, but I followed his advice. The "informal recommendation" became law as part of the Social Security Act amendments of 1956.

Pressure was building up at the time for the broad disability coverage that was subsequently included in the Social Security Act, and it is very likely that some provision similar to ours would have been enacted within a few years without our effort. There is nothing in the record that links the amendment to me, but there doesn't need to be. This was one of those gratifying tasks I mentioned back at the beginning of this chapter—the kind of work it is satisfying to do simply because it needs to be done.

In the years after that, I always welcomed the chance to be listed among the "big spenders" when it came time to vote on appropriations for research in this field and in related fields, and I have followed with enthusiasm and profound respect the diligent work of Representative John Fogarty and

Senator Lister Hill to improve and expand the federal programs in these areas.

There is a growing national awareness of the need for federal help in meeting problems of this kind. I hope that someday some enterprising reporter will tell the story of the little-known work of that band of congressmen and senators whose definition of public interest was sensitive enough to include, and whose dedication was intense enough to secure, programs like the reading records for the blind distributed by the Library of Congress; the Library Services Act, which has carried books to nearly every crossroads and hamlet in the land; and the training of teachers for deaf children, to mention only a few. The list is long, and its congressional architects are for the most part relatively anonymous, but they are all cloud riders, one way or another.

Chapter XI

NATURAL RESOURCE

DEVELOPMENT

The political realities of representing the Delta District of Mississippi led me to the House Public Works Committee and to a legislative specialty in natural resource programs. It was a happy marriage of political convenience and personal interest. The achievements of the Public Works Committee since World War II, while far from ideal, do rank among the outstanding congressional contributions to the future development of our country. Falling within this period as they did, my twelve years on the House committee gave me a rare opportunity to participate in the formulation of national policies and the detailed planning of specific programs that was both absorbing and satisfying. The work of the committee during these years brought about another, if less well-known, improvement: it gave coherence

to the Democratic party's previously rambling policy in th
natural resources field.

Except for 1953-54, when the House majority was Re
publican, the chairman of the House Public Works Com
mittee during my service was Representative Charles A. Buck
ley of New York. Charlie Buckley has never made any secre
of the fact that the Bronx political machine, which he heads
and New York politics in general are of more concern to him
than the day-to-day workings of Congress. As in his New
York City operations, he has been more concerned with the
Public Works Committee's producing results than in con
forming to the niceties of appearance. Consequently, unde
his chairmanship, committee policy was set by a team of rank
ing Democrats working together, rather than by dictation
from the chairman or by the slow process of osmosis among
the committee membership as a whole.

The ranking Democratic members of the committee—
George Fallon of Maryland, Cliff Davis of Tennesse, John
Blatnik of Minnesota, Bob Jones of Alabama, and John Klu
czynski of Illinois—were the members most involved in the
committee decisions, but the Democratic members as a whole
worked closely and well together, all up and down the line.
Chairman Buckley usually turned over the reins to subcom
mittee chairmen on specific issues, and these men produced
unity among the teams they guided. The methods of opera
tion might not appeal to a political scientist with a predilec
tion for orderliness, but the unorthodox methods resulted in
some major legislative advances. Our bills were often passed
on the floor only after bitter controversy, but they passed
because they engendered a high percentage of Democratic
party unity. If they inspired equally united Republican op
position in almost every case, it did not matter; that very

opposition helped develop the solidarity we needed to pass the bills.

Of course, natural resource legislation is not the exclusive property of the House Public Works Committee. The committee's leading position in the field, however, helped us to influence the attitudes of the whole House on related issues. One of the great failures of our federal government through the years has been the lack of a coordinated, coherent national policy for resource conservation and development. Water programs, for instance, are the responsibility of four different cabinet departments—Interior, Army, Agriculture, and Health, Education, and Welfare. In the days of much smaller government, the Army Engineers were given the job of building government water projects, but as Congress enacted later programs, Interior was given responsibility for reclamation, Agriculture for small water control structures related to soil conservation, and HEW for antipollution work. There are still other agencies with responsibilities in the field. Ideally, they should be under one direction, but neither the agencies themselves nor their civilian constituencies (local public bodies, contractors, citizens' organizations working in the field) are willing to risk the change. As a result, there is no possibility of such legislation being approved by the Congress, and resistance has been strong even to coordination from the White House without changing the direct role of the various agencies. The Tennessee Valley Authority should be listed as a fifth federal agency with a responsibility for water programs. It is the only agency with the power to coordinate fully all water resource and conservation work, but its programs are generally limited to the Tennessee Valley.

Through the years, piecemeal congressional action probably contributed more to confusion than to coherence, until an affirmative congressional movement began to promote a more cohesive federal policy. Only hesitant steps have been taken toward the full-scale coordination which is essential to the efficiency of federal programs in this field, but these beginnings have been made with a minimum of acrimony. Future Congresses and administrations will have to continue the process we put under way.

The House Public Works Committee has responsibility for all water programs of the Corps of Engineers, the entire federal highway program, public buildings other than military, the antipollution laws and programs, large dams of the soil conservation program, the Tennessee Valley Authority, and a myriad of minor related conservation and public works activities. Because of these fields of legislative oversight, all the major congressional struggles over policy in these programs either originated in our committee or were greatly influenced by our committee policies. Some of these fights are reviewed in this chapter.

In 1951 the overriding issue before the Public Works Committee was the St. Lawrence Seaway. Before I came to Congress I knew something of the purpose of the project and that Southern ports had consistently opposed it because it might reduce the traffic they handled. It did not take long for me to discover that the real opposition came from the railroads, as far as the South was concerned, and that the railroads had at least one prominent attorney on retainer in most of the towns of my district. The committee did not have to get far into the study of the project to convince me of the value of the Seaway. It was a logical and an inevitable use of joint water resources of the United States and Canada. More than that, our resistance to building it would represent a national stand against Canadian efforts to develop their economy. From a purely political standpoint, I probably should have stayed outwardly on the fence prior to the crucial votes, and reaped the rewards of being wooed as undecided, but I never could accept that approach to the issues before our committee. As it was, I became one of the first Southern members openly to support the Seaway.

President Truman was the most powerful advocate of the Seaway in 1951, and his zeal in its behalf was of immediate benefit to me. I started out as low man in seniority among the Democrats on the committee, being the only new member assigned to Public Works. Before the end of the congressional session I had moved up four places. Truman was trying to persuade every Democrat on the committee who opposed the Seaway to switch to another committee, and he did persuade four to leave, either through personal requests or through political leaders back home. Truman's chief convert to the Seaway was Charlie Buckley, who agreed to buck the historic opposition of the port of New York. Eventually, the majority of the Democrats on the committee came around to Seaway support, but the situation was hopeless, because no headway could be made among the Republicans. In 1951 and 1952 the only Republican on the committee who supported the project was George Dondero of Detroit; Detroit was one of the major metropolitan centers which would directly benefit from it.

Eastern and Southern ports helped promote the opposition to the Seaway at the hearings, but the fight was led by the railroads, with effective assistance from the coal industry and the electric utilities. The leader of the private business interests favoring the Seaway was George Humphrey of Cleveland, president of the M. A. Hanna Company, which planned to develop the newly discovered iron ore deposits in Labrador. The Seaway project didn't come to a vote in the 82nd Congress because its defeat, then, was a foregone conclusion, but the controversy brought another change on the committee that moved me up another seniority notch. Representative Tom Pickett of Texas made such an impression on the coal companies in leading the fight against the Seaway from the Democratic side that they persuaded him to resign from Congress and take over as manager of the Washington office of the National Coal Producers Association.

In 1953, George Humphrey left the Hanna Company to become Secretary of the Treasury. Thanks in part to him, President Eisenhower was also an advocate of the Seaway. Secretary Humphrey had considerably more success with the Republicans on our committee than had Businessman Humphrey, and the project finally cleared the committee. It took 41 years of study and debate, consideration and reconsideration, pleading, persuading and battering to overcome the obstructionists and enact the Seaway legislation. (It took just five years to build it.) The financing plan was hobbled by restrictions that would prove burdensome to the Seaway, and the program for distribution of the power produced by the Seaway dams was far from the traditional public power concept, but even with its obvious flaws, the project as enacted was infinitely better than continued refusal to approve it at all.

One of the by-products of joining the fight for the Seaway was my association with Lieutenant General Lewis Pick, the Chief of Engineers under President Truman. He had a vision of what resource development could mean to the country and was not afraid to talk about it. He was aware of political realities, but he believed in an expanding economy based on new opportunity. It has been fashionable for many years to refer to the Corps of Engineers as a "pork barrel" agency, allegedly reflecting the narrow interests of special groups opposed to all other types of conservation development. The general criticism has at times been justified, but it has never been true of the most able of the Corps's officers and civilian employees. Much of the conservation energy of the New Deal days was wasted in purely bureaucratic power struggles that reflect no particular credit upon any of the agencies concerned. For instance, it is now apparent that Secretary of the Interior Harold Ickes was probably more interested in preventing the Corps of Engineers from building some projects than he was in having them built. It is also probable that the Corps during this period planned some projects to appeal to the opponents of public power in the Congress. The Kings River project in the Central Valley of California is an example of work long-delayed as a result of the struggle between the agencies and the various interest groups supporting them. More vigorous administration leadership in the field, or more intelligent congressional policy, could have avoided the wasteful rivalry which resulted in long delays on much-needed work, without sacrifice of conservation principles.

During my years on the House Public Works Committee, no consideration was ever given to the proposals for a Columbia Valley Authority or a Missouri River Authority. The basin authority concept, patterned after the TVA, would have worked well in many river valleys of the country, but the last opportunity to achieve basinwide programs was probably lost during the first two years of the Truman administration, when a fight was made for both the Columbia and the Missouri Valley Authorities. In both cases the attempt was made in the relatively favorable atmosphere of the Senate, but the massed opponents of public power stopped them cold. Ideally, these and other river valleys could still benefit from a coordinated regional development of their resources, in the TVA pattern, administered by officials in the region itself rather than by the agencies in Washington. Regional development of the river basins would not have to change the present patterns of power production and distribution, for it is not in that area that the major waste and inefficiency arises. In the political climate of today, there is no hope that the Congress will approve any basin development program that bears a noticeable resemblance to TVA.

Politics or no, however, the responsibility is still on Congress to provide for the full development of our resource potential. This chapter tells the story of how congressional policy did give impetus to a trend toward coordinated development during the past decade. The congressional policy grew up haphazardly, without real step-by-step planning, but it did grow, and it offers well-laid ground for fertile and expanding administrative and congressional policy in the years ahead.

Use of the power potential of Niagara Falls was another long-dormant proposal with which the House Public Works Committee wrestled for five or six years. There were plans for federal development sponsored in the Congress by Senator Herbert Lehman and Representative Franklin D. Roosevelt, Jr., plans for state development pushed by Governor Thomas E. Dewey with no support from the Republican House members from New York, and plans to hand the power production over to the private power companies in the area, largely supported by the upstate New York House members. The plan for federal development was the only one which recognized the national interest in an international boundary like the Niagara, and it clearly should have been accepted. Unfortunately, it had very little committee support and a lot of opposition. For a while I considered supporting, as an alternative that might pass, the plan for the power to go to the New York State Power Authority. Dewey and Robert Moses had worked out a state program which had its antecedents in proposals by Al Smith and Franklin Roosevelt when each was governor, but none of them was able to get any help from the Republicans.

When the Republicans took over the House in 1953, the private power plan for Niagara came out of our committee over the opposition of the majority of the Democrats, and passed the House by a heavy margin. Fortunately, the Senate did not approve it. Nature ended the stalemate in 1957, when an avalanche of rocks destroyed most of the hydroelectric generating facilities of the Niagara-Mohawk Company. In the resulting emergency the power company settled for a portion of the power generated by the New York State Power Authority under a federal license, with the remainder to be distributed under regular government power policy. It was by no means an ideal arrangement, but it was better than allowing a wasteful impasse to continue indefinitely. The bitter-end opponents of all public power opposed even this bill, decrying an "opportunistic sellout" by Niagara Mohawk and the New Yorkers. A by-product of all this activity was the rehabilitation and beautification of the Falls by the Corps of Engineers. An efficient system is now in use for storing water for power at night and maintaining the full beauty of the Falls during the daylight hours.

In the years following World War II, the inadequacy of the nation's highway system was obvious, but there were few signs that the states would improve the situation. In the Roads Subcommittee we were offering some incentives to the interstate highway system, but the progress was mostly on paper. During the first years of the Eisenhower administration, the only attention given the problem was contained in a suggestion by Sherman Adams that the states be encouraged to solve their traffic problems with toll roads like the Pennsylvania and New Jersey turnpikes. The automobile industry itself began to wake up about this time. There had to be some additional driving space if the market for new cars was not to die of driver frustration in traffic jams. The result was the gigantic new Interstate Highway Program, to be paid for 90 percent by the federal government.

In line with established Eisenhower policy, the administration proposed that the highway program be financed by the issuance of bonds based on future gasoline tax revenues. The bond idea would have increased the cost of the program enormously, and it would have jeopardized approval of improvements to the system in future years. Democrats on our committee had been the most outspoken in favor of an expanded federal highway program, but their reaction to the bond financing scheme was immediate and adverse. (Any kind of program to avoid immediate increases in government appropriations was popular in the Eisenhower administration, even if the result would be long-term greater costs to the government. Another example handled by our committee was the lease-purchase scheme for financing public buildings, which greatly increased the long-term costs for the buildings by interest rates higher than that paid for normal government obligations.) That proposal unified the Democrats on the committee for the first time since I had joined it. Two or three Democrats liked the bond issue proposal at first, but they turned against the idea as we explored it and as the opposition of other party members was explained.

The highway program took most of the time of the committee for two years. The first bill we reported out lost on the floor of the House, but we eventually came up with a plan that both Republicans and Democrats largely accepted. Theoretically, the Interstate System is to be completed in 1972. I am confident, however, that the ever-expanding demands of our mobile society will make it mandatory that the program, in modified form, continue as a permanent part of federal participation in highway construction. I hope that by then the Congress will be ready to consider the road program in concert with conservation activities and economic and natural resource development needs.

The interstate road program may eventually become the chief monument to President Eisenhower's administration. It was a massive federal attack on the traffic problem to prevent a crippling of the entire automotive industry. It was good for the country, and it was also good for General Motors, Ford, American Motors, and Chrysler. Whether because of this coincidence or not, the National Association of Manufacturers did not denounce the plan as a plot leading to either socialism or bankruptcy, which is the line the NAM usually takes against federal programs. The road program set an example for future attacks on resource crises. If we can convince the Congress and the public that such crises have to be solved in the interest of American business, as was done in this case, perhaps the remedies required by emergent situations will have smoother sailing in the future.

By long tradition, the Public Works Committee generally ignored national politics in preparing the authorizations for flood control projects, rivers and harbors development, and highway legislation. Members scratched each other's backs in working out specific provisions, but guidance as to the merits of the projects and programs was accepted only from the administrative agency concerned. This custom was abrogated in 1954, when the Republican majority on our committee refused to approve projects which did not have the prior approval of the Bureau of the Budget. The resentment which this built up spilled over outside the committee and helped spark a floor revolt against the Appropriations Committee in 1955. The budget that year was sharply limited in its allowances for natural resource items, and the Appropriations

Committee carried the reductions even further. The day the committee report came out, I sent a letter of protest to all Democratic members and arranged for Representative Overton Brooks of Louisiana, in his role as president of the National Rivers and Harbors Congress, to call a bipartisan meeting of House members to discuss strategy. The meeting designated me floor manager to prepare amendments to the bill and select the people to introduce them.

House rules are designed to protect appropriation bills. Once a figure has been amended, it cannot be amended again, and specific projects cannot be added to a bill except by amending the total figure for the major sections of the appropriation. New projects could be added, in a successful amendment, only by three stages—the original amendment, an amendment to the amendment, and a substitute for the amendment. Consequently, I had to plan our amendments with this limitation "to the third degree" in mind; I also had to have some assurance that the members who were to introduce amendments would get recognition from the chair. Recognition is given first to members of the committee handling the bill and then to members at large on a basis of seniority, persistence in seeking recognition, or the individual whim of the presiding member (chairman of the committee of the whole House). Jere Cooper of Tennessee was chairman for this bill. With him I went over the list of members who would offer our amendments, and then began to prepare them.

Our strategy was to make our original amendments conform to the original Bureau of the Budget requests, thereby restoring the cuts made by the Appropriations Committee. We were confident that the Senate would raise these figures, but we had to take the first step ourselves. Of course, the two amendments to our original amendment put the total above the budget, but this was essential in maintaining the strength of our coalition. Our amendments were parceled out among Republicans, liberal Democrats, Southern Democrats, and just plain Democrats. On the first test we won by about thirty votes. As the afternoon dragged on we won each vote, and eventually the opposition quit demanding counts. Those who had failed to join our coalition either lost their amendments or did not even get a chance to offer them because of the parliamentary situation we controlled. The members who offered our amendments did not tarry long at the microphone. I did not talk at all. Our victory was the first time the Appropriations Committee had ever sustained wholesale defeats on public works issues. No more fights were necessary in the succeeding years, because the committee refashioned its tactics to meet the mood of the House.

"Pork barrel" is the derisive term usually applied to public works projects by newspapers in areas which are not seeking a public works project of their own at the time. This convenient sarcasm had not been coined when George Clinton was pushing the Erie Canal, but similar attacks were made upon that pioneer project. The lock at Sault Sainte Marie opening up Lake Superior to navigation is probably the most famous "pork barrel" item in congressional lore, and the speech ridiculing the industrial potential of Duluth is often cited today as the best example of a congressman's folly in putting his foot in his mouth about water projects. Opponents are more careful now, but newspapers and TV commentators still like the flavor of the term "pork barrel." Nobody who knows the field would deny that there has been waste in water control programs through the years, but what the people who don't bother to know the field do not recognize is that the waste has not been in the projects themselves but in the failure to develop related projects on a broadly coordinated basis.

Natural resources development is probably the most poorly reported and least understood of all major governmental activities, and out of the resulting ignorance has come much of the obstruction to a coherent, well-planned, and truly productive governmental policy. Our national press is entitled to a good share of the blame. Like politicians, newspapers relish doing battle with government spending, and to do it, they need a straw man to knock down. Next to "wasteful bureaucrats" in general, "pork-barrelling politicians and government agencies" are the handiest victims to have around. For example: flood control programs in the Mississippi Delta can be made to look like maniac extravagance to the people in unwisely water-complacent or dangerously water-starved areas, but what is never said is that the cost of those flood control programs in the Mississippi Delta has been more than equaled by the increased federal income taxes which have been collected in the region—an increase far out of proportion to the increase in the national average, and one directly traceable to the benefits the flood control projects have brought to the economy of the area. These benefits are not confined to the Delta alone, either; they inevitably extend to the regional and thence to the national economy, but the spread of benefits through the channels of commerce is impossible to measure.

There have been wasteful federal public works projects, of course, but they are isolated cases. The waste which concerns us most is the long-lived kind that results when a project is built or put into operation without linking it to every related regional resource available for development and use. The Tennessee Valley Authority is the closest approach to full, nonwasteful development that the federal government has ever devised. Politics overwhelmed national interest and made it impossible to breathe life into the vision of similar farsighted undertakings during my years on the House Public Works Committee, but the goals toward which the committee worked between 1954 and 1962 were the opposite of "pork barrel." We tried to eliminate as much waste as possible and still fulfill as much of the legislative responsibility for resource development as could be brought within the committee's jurisdiction.

When our committee began to write an omnibus flood control bill in 1955 and 1956, we found that most of the Republican members merely wanted to rubber-stamp the projects submitted to the committee as approved by the Bureau of the Budget. Bureau policy included across-the-board rules for local cash contributions that would have killed most of the projects. More important, the Bureau would have effectively barred any new public power construction by arbitrarily changing the criteria by which power benefits were computed. Other projects were denied clearance by the Bureau for a wide miscellany of reasons, even when the power benefits could not be obscured. As the Republicans hardened in support of the Bureau, the Democrats solidified in opposition to the dictation from downtown. Most of the controversial projects were added. The bill passed late in the 1956 session, but President Eisenhower vetoed it after Congress had adjourned. There were loud cries that the veto would have been overridden if Congress had still been in session, but there is no way of being sure. The President got a good national press reaction to his veto—he was acting "boldly" to stamp out "pork barrel."

In the new 86th Congress of 1957, the lines of political division in our committee had hardened as never before. In the spring of 1958, the Congress passed a new bill, which originated in the Senate, with virtually all the 1956 projects included plus a few more. One of those added was an eight-million-dollar harbor improvement project for the port of Greenville, Mississippi. The most important amendment was one which established federal policy to anticipate future water needs and to plan for them in water resource projects. Offered by Bob Jones of Alabama, the amendment also provided for controls to maintain downstream water flow and for extensive studies of future water needs. President Eisenhower vetoed the new bill. Faced with this stalemate, the White House and Senator Bob Kerr began to exchange signals. The White House didn't want the congressional backlash which would result from another veto, and it also didn't want to run the risks of a veto override fight. Senator Kerr wanted assurance of approval for certain Senate projects. Senator Kerr and Robert Merriam, a former Republican white hope in Chicago who was then assistant director of the Budget Bureau, rewrote the bill to the minimum specifications for the President's signature. Most of the House bill was retained in the rewriting, but the Jones water resource planning amendment was lost, and the Greenville harbor was modified to cost the local people more. Several power projects in the West were again put aside. Few of us on the House side cared for the compromise, and all of us looked forward to renewing the battle.

We didn't have to wait long. The President handed us another veto the next year. The Congress approved a public works appropriation which went slightly above the President's budget in money appropriated, but, more important, included a dozen or so "new starts" opposed by the Bureau of the Budget. Most of these, including Greenville harbor, were projects forced upon the unwilling President in our 1958 authorization bill. He vetoed the 1959 appropriation. The bill was called up for a vote to override, but we lost by three or four votes. Back in the Appropriations Subcommittee on Public Works, Mike Kirwan, the veteran Democratic leader from Ohio, moved that a new bill be reported retaining every item but reducing the appropriation for each by 2½ percent. This was a concession to the President to the extent of holding the total appropriation down to his budget level, but it yielded not a bit on "new starts." Kirwan's motion failed by a tie vote.

When the full Appropriations Committee met next day, another committee was meeting in the Public Works Committee room. I had been made chairman of an *ad hoc* group of 28 members to lead the fight to beat the veto. We had talked and worked through the night, and we kept a telephone line open to the Appropriations Committee in session. We asked our allies on the committee to relay the polite ultimatum that, unless the appropriations group approved the Kirwan plan, we would offer it on the floor of the House, with a certainty of enough votes for passage. Jamie Whitten offered the Kirwan motion in full committee, and it carried, 19 to 17. The new bill passed the Congress and President Eisenhower vetoed it. We were nearing the end of the session, and the fight had been going around the clock for three or four days. The absentees and the potential vote-switchers from the first override vote were being pressured from home and by their House colleagues. The big job, however, was to persuade Speaker Rayburn to give his approval to our fight. His fingers were burned from the first defeat, and the easiest thing to do was to settle for the President's bill. Four of us—Hale Boggs of Louisiana, B. F. Sisk of California, Ed Edmondson of Oklahoma, and I—bearded Mr. Sam at the Speaker's chair while he presided over the full House just a few minutes before a vote. The argument was loud and fast for a long time. The Speaker made it clear that he was with us but afraid of losing the fight.

"If we lose again, the damn Republicans will all make speeches about how they and Eisenhower saved the country from going bankrupt," he said. Our chief argument was that he would be letting the rank-and-file members down if they didn't get a chance to make this fight for new starts one more time. He relented as this argument bore home, and the override vote was scheduled again. Most of the speeches were superfluous, and our *ad hoc* committee made none. When Whitten rose to speak for the second time, the hall was filled with cries of "Vote!" The vote came, and we overrode by a margin of five. It was a pleasant moment for the Speaker. He had been carrying a lot of burdens for President Eisenhower for seven years, but this was a clean-cut partisan victory on a good Democratic domestic issue, the first Eisenhower veto overridden.

The Democratic unity on our committee during the four-year fight over new starts made it possible to bring out and pass a workable bill for self-financing the power program of the Tennessee Valley Authority. Rapid growth after World War II made it necessary for TVA to turn to steam-generating plants as the major source of new energy, but the power companies and their allies—the coal producers and the United Mine Workers—fought the appropriations for each new facility. The first postwar steam plant at New Johnsonville, Tennessee, was approved only because there was a large Democratic majority in the 81st Congress. Others were approved without major controversy because of defense needs during the Korean War, but the Dixon-Yates scheme was the signal that the Eisenhower administration would not approve new generating power for TVA even for atomic energy purposes. TVA and its congressional supporters turned to the idea of self-financing by taxable bonds sold through normal commercial channels. The idea had been endorsed a few years before by even the U.S. Chamber of Commerce as a means for TVA to meet its normal load growth without the intervention of a special subsidy. The Budget Bureau approved a self-financing plan, but made it so restrictive that TVA could not have lived with it. Cliff Davis and Bob Jones on our committee introduced a plan prepared by the TVA staff, modified in the hope of a presidential signature but still workable from a TVA viewpoint.

At one point in the hearings, I had a chance to deflate one balloon. A few months before I had bought a thousand dollars' worth of Middle South Utility stock. This holding company owns the Mississippi Power and Light Company, which operates next door to TVA. When the president of Mississippi Power and Light was testifying about what a terrible threat the TVA bill would be to his company, I asked him if I should dispose of my stock before it became worthless. He assured me that it would still be very good investment even if the bill passed. (It was, but unfortunately I could not afford to hold my shares long enough to realize much of its increase in value.)

My interest in TVA was not a requirement of service to my district. None of the old Third District was in the TVA power service area, although most of northeast Mississippi was supplied by TVA electricity. As the financing bill was being considered, the power companies opened a full-scale campaign against it among Southern Democrats outside the TVA area. Even with the heavy Democratic majority in the 86th Congress, there was real doubt that the bill would pass, with almost solid Republican opposition plus the defection of Democrats influenced by the coal operators and United Mine Workers. Some concession had to be made to secure the votes of the Democrats feeling the power company pressure, and the price was an amendment forbidding any expansion of TVA territory. TVA had not expanded its service area since before World War II, but the possibilities for expansion had always been a bargaining weapon for municipalities and co-operatives making contracts for the purchase of wholesale power from the private power companies. All of the Delta was virtually on TVA's boundary, and I now had to vote to establish a permanent barrier against any future sale of TVA power beyond its existing service area. That barrier would end any hope of the Delta's ever being able to benefit directly from TVA, but approval of the financing plan was absolutely essential to TVA. The amendment had to prevail; without it, TVA would not be able to generate enough power to supply even its old territory. Democratic opposition collapsed with the adoption of the amendment, and the bill passed.

One of the first legislative tasks undertaken by the Democrats after they regained control of the committee in 1955 was amendment of the Water Pollution Control Act to provide grants to cities and communities for construction of sewage-treatment plants. This program was passed in 1956, under the leadership of subcommittee chairman John Blatnik. A wealth of information was developed between 1956 and 1960 that made it obvious the 1956 program would barely scratch the surface of the acute national problem, and the entire water pollution program was given renewed impetus in 1961. (The 1961 bill was preceded by a similar measure vetoed by President Eisenhower in 1960.)

The 1961 law was one of President Kennedy's first major program achievements. The Kennedy-Johnson Natural Resources Advisory Committee report had given it top priority for legislative action. It stepped up the pollution research program, increased the sewage-treatment grants, and served as the vehicle for a water quality-control amendment which directed all federal agencies to include this factor in reservoir planning. The antipollution programs established under these two laws are still inadequate to meet the rapidly mounting problem, but we passed them through the House only after struggles so bitter that we resorted at times to implied threats to push or bury other committee legislation in which recalcitrant members were particularly interested. The bills were attacked as "reckless big spending," and they never would have cleared our committee without the Democratic unity that had been built up in the partisan fights over Bureau of the Budget domination and TVA and highway financing. Once resource development programs are successfully under way, they are given general nonpartisan support, but while they are in the legislative mill an unremitting battle must be waged to overcome the familiar attacks of "pork barrel" and waste.

The lands still under the worst flood threat in the Delta are those that lie to the east of the Yazoo and its tributaries, in the narrow strip between the river and the adjacent hill ridge from Memphis to Vicksburg. Seeking some program to protect this land, I found that adequate protection against flash floods from the hills would be almost impossible in some areas because of the terrific costs of the massive levees that would be necessary. The tons of red clay and sand that washed down from the eroded hill lands could destroy the value of any channel improvements on the creeks and bayous. Obviously, an effective program had to be a joint undertaking by the Soil Conservation Service in the hill lands and the Corps of Engineers on the larger streams in the Delta. The ideal situation would have charged one government agency with responsibility for the work, but the ideal situation didn't exist and there wasn't the remotest chance of creating it. Hoping to get the earliest possible relief, I persuaded the Mississippi offices of the two agencies to work out a coordinated program, which they did in very good fashion. These flood and soil conservation problems might not be exactly duplicated anywhere else in the country, but there are similar critical needs in every area.

At the beginning of the 1959 session, the Public Works Committee set up a permanent subcommittee on watershed development, and I was named chairman. Our first responsibility was to oversee the larger projects built by the Department of Agriculture under the Small Watershed Projects Act, all subject to authorization by our committee. A broader task was to explore the whole field of problems in coordination of watershed development among the Corps of Engineers, the Soil Conservation Service, the Bureau of Reclamation, the Fish and Wildlife Service, and any other agency having responsibilities in the field. Our hearings were planned so as to make it clear that the Congress was looking toward a comprehensive program of interagency cooperation and that we expected the executive agencies to take the same approach. We wrote and passed into law one bill specifically spelling out the authority for joint surveys and studies by the Corps of Engineers and the Soil Conservation Service. In the ten years since the Small Watershed Act became law, the SCS has made remarkable progress in improving the planning and development of these projects, but I did not discover the ultimate in coordination until I explored the TVA tributary area development program. In addition to the obviously needed coordination of the water resource aspects of its watersheds, the TVA program attempts to weld together all the local efforts toward economic development, working out individual projects so that they will be related parts of one greater, general goal—balanced and complementary economic opportunity for all citizens of the watershed.

My service on the Public Works Committee, which had begun with the battle for the St. Lawrence Seaway in 1951, ended with the intense struggle for the Public Works Acceleration Act in 1962. President Kennedy was determined to stop the recession that was gathering momentum in 1961 and early 1962, and this goal encompassed the Public Works Acceleration Act. It was aimed primarily at injecting renewed life into the chronically depressed areas in the economy. The plan was simple: it authorized an appropriation of $900 million for construction of public works projects, either by local governments or by the federal government. This made it possible for many local governments to undertake needed civic improvements without first having to raise funds to cover the local matching share usually required for such projects. Raising the local funds in the depressed areas is a long and weary business; they simply don't have the tax base from which the revenue can be drawn. The new program would eliminate the time lag, partly by direct grants to cover part of the local cost and partly by financing long-term loans for the remaining local contribution.

The eligible projects included water and sewer systems; hospitals, streets, and public buildings; watershed, river and harbor, and flood control projects; soil conservation and reforestation; and improvements in national parks and forests. It was an effective program, designed not only to alleviate the immediate economic situation but to do it with projects that would ensure permanent returns on the investment. The fight for its approval got under way with the traditional attacks on public works programs arrayed against us. The early votes in committee followed party lines. We had to have a reasonable bloc of Republican votes to win, however, and some of these switched over when we agreed on an amendment to liberalize the direct grants to the depressed areas. The sponsor of this amendment was freshman Republican Representative William Scranton of Pennsylvania.

The Accelerated Public Works Act was the first bill the committee had ever handled which covered the whole field of public works in one piece of legislation. The experience that will be gained in the administration of this program will be invaluable in mounting future government attacks on recessions or threatened recessions. The federal government will have to underwrite the basic measures to stem the tide when recession looms, but permanent assets which will remain productive well into the future are a far wiser investment than transitory, down-the-drain type relief measures that may bolster the immediate economy but make no lasting contribution to economic stability. Luckily, in 1961 we had a roster of authorized projects on which preliminary planning had already been done but for which no funds had previously been available. The importance of having just such a reserve of projects ready to be put under construction was demonstrated in the accelerated program, and it is a lesson that should not be forgotten.

Most of the bills we haggled and stewed about in the Public Works Committee, and then struggled mightily to pass over the stubborn conservatism of the House, have already demonstrated their value to the national economy and to national resource productivity. They have given some small but significant pushes toward improved coordination of all federal activity in the resource and conservation field. For me, the committee's achievements have a special significance. They made it possible for me to make a worthwhile contribution in a specialized field of national import, and in doing so, to offset the frustration of being politically precluded from participation, as a legislator, in the field of human relations.

Chapter XII

NOW THE TRUMPET

SUMMONS

John F. Kennedy was entering his third
and last term in the House of Representatives when I came to
Congress. I met him on the House floor, but my first memory
of him is in the center of a bustling group pouring out of the
old House Office Building one evening, tossing a football
around. During those two years in the House, Jack was devoting his time almost exclusively to running for the Senate.
Senator Henry Cabot Lodge was spending most of his time
arranging General Eisenhower's entry into the presidential
race, which left the field in Massachusetts open to the steadily
developing Kennedy campaign.

A strong part of the Kennedy program for Massachusetts was the promise to bring new vitality to the New England economy. The postwar textile revolution, with its shift

from cotton and wool to the new synthetic fabrics, the urgent need for costly modern equipment, and the large number of plant relocations in the South, all had contributed to the acres of empty factories in Massachusetts and the other New England states.

Candidate Kennedy thought he had found a ready-made scapegoat, and he issued a blast at the use of TVA "cheap power" to lure away New England industries. His complaint was poorly researched. The textile mills that had moved South had all gone into the Carolina-Georgia textile region, entirely outside the TVA area. Even apart from the textile field there wasn't a runaway New England mill of any description in the TVA area. The plants had moved because they were primarily interested in cheap labor, and the general consensus was that they could best get it—and keep it—in those sections of the South outside the TVA influence. Some of the members of Congress from the Tennessee Valley fired back at the Kennedy charges broadside. Their answers might very easily have backfired into his campaign had he been opposing a Republican whose supporters recognized the fallacy in Kennedy's campaign charge, but he wasn't.

I hoped Kennedy would be successful, but I wanted him pointed in the right direction in the Senate. Jim Silver, from Ole Miss, was spending a year at Harvard under a Ford Foundation grant, and I made my first visit to Harvard during the Easter congressional recess. Jim introduced me to Arthur Schlesinger, Sr., who at that time was chairman of the Massachusetts branch of Americans for Democratic Action. Kennedy had been campaigning among the university community in Boston with great success, and the ADA was about to come out in his favor against one of the established Republican liberals.

"Get Kennedy straightened out on TVA and public

power," I told Schlesinger. "The ADA shouldn't be supporting a man who doesn't understand something so basic to
American economic liberalism." Taking advice on sticking to
liberal policy from a representative of benighted Mississippi
must have been a novel experience for Mr. Schlesinger. In the
two years that followed, I never remembered to ask Jack
whether this advice got back to him. I do know that he found
other themes for his campaign, and in the Senate he was a loyal
supporter of TVA and other natural resource development
programs.

In the four years between 1952 and 1956, my contacts
with Senator Kennedy were slight. I was impressed with his
pragmatic approach to liberal issues. He was obviously more
interested in achieving results than in espousing causes or be-
laboring issues. As I was trying to conduct my own political
career on that basis, I naturally approved of the trait in somebody else. Kennedy reaped a greater harvest of publicity than
most senators do, but because he dug deep into history for
some of his speeches and some of his ideas, the publicity
seemed to reflect more of the characteristics of a statesman
than those of a showman.

Profiles in Courage is a masterpiece of historical interpretation, but it appealed to me most because I have always been
convinced that an effective legislator must also be a serious
student of history. As a legislator and would-be historian
myself, the conflict between conscience and constituents was
one I was living daily. I was also pleased, of course, that
historian Kennedy had dipped into Mississippi for one of his
portraits—Lucius Quintus Cincinnatus Lamar was the Mississippian of grand stature that I admired most. Lamar was a
rarity among Mississippi politicians, a student and intellectual
who won victories at the polls.

Some of us at the 1956 Democratic convention had high

hopes that Stevenson could defeat Eisenhower, in spite of the discouraging polls and predictions. The only road to victory lay in taking the big cities by a wide enough margin to carry the big states. These, added to the South, could perhaps provide the necessary strength. Several of us believed that among possible vice-presidential candidates, Jack Kennedy could best help pull that city vote, but not enough of the effective leaders, save the New Englanders, were thinking that way. In Chicago, I went to Kennedy and offered my help. We learned that, although Stevenson would ask Kennedy to place him in nomination, he had given no indication of his vice-presidential choice. Stevenson and his advisers would have to be persuaded that Kennedy was his best bet, so my first three or four days at Chicago were spent telling the Stevenson people how much Kennedy would help the ticket in the South, and taking Southern delegates up to the Merchandise Mart suite at the Hilton to meet Jack. When Jack wasn't around, we met with Bobby Kennedy and Ted Sorensen. They were making a good impression, but everyone was waiting for Stevenson to make his choice.

The out-of-the-blue announcement that the choice would be left up to the convention took us all by surprise. Before the Stevenson announcement, I worked over the convention floor. Too many Midwestern liberals, true-blue to their doctrine on things like civil rights but apparently unable to extend the doctrine beyond color to religion, just couldn't tolerate the idea of a Catholic on the ticket. "The Lutherans wouldn't stand for it," was the most common reaction. What was worse, some of the congressmen among them said it would make it harder for them to get re-elected. Most of the militant liberals were opposing Kennedy. In the New York delegation I talked with Charlie Buckley and Carmine De Sapio. They were officially for Mayor Wagner for Vice-

President, but they knew it would take more than ADA to swing a large enough New York City margin to carry the rest of the state for Stevenson.

When Stevenson opened up the vice-presidential free-for-all in his acceptance speech, a meeting was called immediately at the Kennedy headquarters uptown. The crowd collected about 1 a.m. It was predominantly from New England, with two or three from the Midwest. Camille Gravelle, national committeeman from Louisiana, was the only Southerner other than me. Chores were sorted out, and calls were begun. Nobody in the room knew any of the delegates from many of the Western states. The meeting eventually became a "I know somebody who may know him" sort of thing as we thumbed through delegate lists and divided up assignments. Governor Abe Ribicoff of Connecticut joked about the inefficiency of smoke-filled rooms, and in a few minutes we proved it.

We were meeting in one of the smaller rooms of the hotel suite. The big reception room was filled with a mixture of people, most of whom seemed to be the college students who always gather around a convention headquarters. At about 3 a.m. my assistant, Audrey Warren, who had come along to handle some of the telephoning, told me that she thought one of the visitors sitting quietly—and just as quietly being ignored—in the partly darkened reception room was Carmine De Sapio.

"There's a man outside who has 86 votes in his pocket," I announced. John Bailey, then the Connecticut state chairman, took De Sapio under his wing at once. Kennedy got the New York votes on the second ballot.

When morning came, my job was to visit Southern delegations with one of the Kennedy sisters, Eunice Shriver, and make talks before their caucuses whenever possible. Before the first talk, we were buttonholing delegates in one of the hotel lobbies. One man asked Eunice point-blank, "Just why should I vote for your brother?" It was obviously the first time she had ever had to summarize any reasons.

"He's terribly smart. He's got three college degrees and has visited Europe nine times," Eunice began. I managed to shift the conversation to political considerations more practical in the eyes of a delegate from South Carolina. We talked about the common interests of Carolina and Massachusetts in the textile business. As soon as we could pull away, I gave Eunice a rundown on the points more likely to appeal to the people with whom we would be talking, and the degrees and trips to Europe didn't come up again. She spoke of the dedication to public service for which her brother had been prepared, and it made a very appealing talk. We met that morning with the South Carolina, Florida, and Alabama delegations and spoke to many other delegates individually. The most discouraging notes still came from the Midwest delegates. In the voting that Friday afternoon, the Southern delegates assigned to me came through with a sizable Kennedy majority, but the story of that fortunate loss to Estes Kefauver is well-known.

When the Congress convened in January 1957, most of the Kennedy supporters—including his fellow New Englanders—were thinking in terms of the vice-presidency for 1960. For some reason, probably a combination of the atmosphere and experiences during those five days in Chicago, I didn't believe that Kennedy would try for second place the next time round. While others suggested that he should—and would—settle for the vice-presidency, I was confident that he would—and should—try for the presidential nomination, and said so.

I hoped the people of Mississippi could be persuaded that John Kennedy would be the most desirable candidate for

President. There was no hope of bringing most of the state's political leaders into his camp—they weren't very likely to be in any nationally acceptable Democrat's camp—but if the rank-and-file citizen could be sold, the leaders would have to support Kennedy in 1960 whether they liked it or not. In falling victim to this specious reasoning, I had forgotten how often a convention delegation has been ruled by one man, or has found it expedient to vote its own choice without regard to the preference within the state.

I knew it would be a long, hard climb; that I believed it could be done at all is perhaps a good measure of my tendency to see Mississippi politics as I would like it to be rather than as it is. I grossly underestimated the obstacles, the yawning chasm that lay between Mississippi and John Fitzgerald Kennedy: an absolute rejection of civil rights on the one hand, support of it on the other; a preponderance of militant Protestantism on the one hand, a Catholic on the other; an antipathy to intellectual outsiders on the one hand, a Harvard Yankee on the other. The chasm was to prove too wide and too deep, but in the summer of 1957 I honestly thought it could be bridged.

The logical first step was for the people of Mississippi to see and hear Kennedy firsthand, and with that in mind we asked him to address the state convention of Young Democrats at Jackson in October 1957. A very able young man who was later to work for me, Gray Evans, was scheduled to become president of the Young Democrats, and he made the arrangements. September came, and with September came Little Rock. Any presidential candidate making a speech in Mississippi that October had to refer to school integration, and I couldn't see anything but lost votes in the forthcoming speech. Ted Sorensen and I talked it over, and we came to the conclusion that canceling the speech would leave a worse impression than making it.

We met the Kennedy party at the Memphis airport and made an aerial inspection of flood control works in north Mississippi before flying on to Jackson. On the way, I showed Jack a copy of that afternoon's Memphis *Press-Scimitar*, which contained a story about a statement by Wirt Yerger, the Mississippi Republican chairman in Jackson, demanding that Senator Kennedy give his position on the Supreme Court school integration decision. That was the only talking we did about Little Rock and the speech that night.

A man from *Time*'s Washington bureau had been on the plane to Memphis with Jack and Ted, and they were convinced that he was covering the Jackson speech in the belief that Kennedy would imply some sympathy with Southern segregationists. Jack expressed the hope that he could avoid being photographed with Senator Eastland. He wasn't photographed with Eastland, but we had to bend and break the reception line several times to prevent it. The only picture of Eastland and Kennedy together that *Time* made was one of the entire speaker's table at the dinner that night. It included not only Eastland, but Senator Stennis, Governor Coleman, and other state officials as well. (The other House members from Mississippi refused to come to the dinner.)

When Jack was being taken to his room at the hotel, the Negro girl who operated the elevator handed him a note. It read something like this: "Mr. President, I'm proud to have had you on my elevator. Please give me your autograph." There was no signature. There were two elevators, so obviously the girl had prepared the note on the 50-50 chance that Senator Kennedy would use her elevator. Jack didn't get a chance to read it until later, and he then gave me a note in reply, with instructions to make sure that it was delivered. By the time I got a chance to do this, a new shift was on the elevator, and we didn't have the girl's name. I had to leave the note for someone to try to find her the next day. I hope, whoever she is, that she still has that special note from John F. Kennedy. It was an incident that could not be publicized, and it showed a humanity in Jack Kennedy that was heartfelt beyond all politics or public images.

The reception preceding the dinner that night was a wild success, greater than anything similar ever held in Mississippi. The biggest turnout was among young people, who even then identified themselves with him. These young Mississippians were also responding, of course, to the fact that for the first time in a century, a national political figure seeking the presidential nomination had seen fit to visit their state as part of his quest. With my usual optimism, my hopes for the future of Mississippi rose with this turnout of her youth. The young people who came to Jackson for that meeting thought of themselves as a new force in Mississippi politics, but perhaps they were too young, and so they lacked the economic and social strength to stand against the force of their know-nothing elders when the heavy pressures of prejudice were brought to bear on them.

The Kennedy speech that night was devoted to his concern about the gap in our defense preparations at home and abroad (this was just a few weeks before Sputnik I punctured national complacency). Jack also found time to pay his respects to our Mr. Yerger, however.

"Let me say that I believe the Supreme Court decision is the law of the land, in Boston as well as Little Rock, and I ask Mr. Yerger to tell us what Mr. Eisenhower's and Mr. Nixon's views are on that." The audience clapped and cheered for this statement approving the desegregation decision as the law of the land! Jack Kennedy had put his affirmation of support of the decision into the same sentence that dared the local Republicans to say that their leaders had a different view. *Time* had to describe the Mississippi visit as a triumph.

Early in 1958, with actual campaign plans developing rapidly, Kennedy asked me to join with Hale Boggs in heading up his campaign in the South. I was willing to do anything that would help, but it seemed to me that members of Congress were not the ones who should be out in front. Governors traditionally swing convention votes in Southern states, and 1960 was not likely to be an exception. The plan was put aside for later development. In 1958, it seemed likely that Hubert Humphrey or Mennen Williams would be Kennedy's chief rival for the nomination. No broad-scale campaign for delegates in the South was tried when it became apparent one would not be worthwhile because of Lyndon Johnson's strength there.

Through 1958 and 1959, most of my meetings or telephone conversations with Kennedy concerned aspects of the nomination drive as they would influence the South or various members of the House; running for President involves countless approaches to potential electoral votes. As the nomination campaign moved into high gear, I began to move out of it. Mississippi elected Ross Barnett governor in 1959, and the issue became not who Mississippi would support at the convention, but whether the state would support anybody, at the convention or after it. The only hope of forcing the governor into a position where he would have to support the party's candidate was to persuade him that he should openly support one of the candidates for the nomination. Our two senators were backing Lyndon Johnson, and I had no compunction about joining their effort to swing the Mississippi votes to Johnson under the unit rule. I told Bob Kennedy this was the only course even faintly in our favor, and the Kennedy forces wasted no energy on the Mississippi delegation at Los Angeles.

I was a delegate in 1960 only because, by long-standing custom, Mississippi names all its congressmen as national convention delegates. It was a Barnett delegation, dominated by the faction opposed to any national candidate. At the Mississippi caucus in Los Angeles, Senators Stennis and Eastland tried to persuade the delegation to vote for Johnson, but they didn't try to force a vote on the issue against the combined opposition of the governor and the other five congressmen. Mississippi offered the nation Ross Barnett for President.

On the morning before the balloting for the presidential nomination, Jack Kennedy visited the motel where the Mississippi, Maine, and Wyoming delegations were housed. He called on the delegation leaders of Maine and Wyoming, and was emerging from one of those meetings when he called me over to a whispered session on the motel's inner balcony. The usual few dozen reporters and cameramen were following him. He told me about his visits that morning and asked whether there would be any point in looking up Governor Barnett. I told him that there was no need to waste the time; that Barnett was fully committed to oppose him in November. As a gesture, if he had time, he might telephone Barnett, but I could see nothing to be gained by it.

"How does it look for November?" Jack asked.

"It looks real rough," was my reply. "The only thing that can save the South is some really dramatic appeal for support."

"Well, we'll have to see," he said. If he thought that putting Lyndon Johnson on the ticket might be the answer, he didn't say so, and neither did I.

When the radio flash first came that Johnson would accept second place on the ticket, I heard it in a taxi riding to the convention hall with one of Barnett's delegation leaders. He groaned in anticipation of the threat it meant to the independent elector scheme. Actually, the Citizens Councils spokesmen in Mississippi attacked Lyndon Johnson more savagely during the campaign than they did Jack Kennedy. Johnson was the "renegade," and there was no abuse too petty to be heaped upon him.

Most of my work during the campaign was in my Washington office as director of the Kennedy-Johnson Natural Resources Advisory Committee, but in my only discussion with Kennedy we talked briefly about the situation at home. Ever optimistic, I believed he had a chance to carry Mississippi, on the theory that the Republican campaign in the state—which was a duplicate of the race prejudice line of the Barnett independents—might divide the opposition vote enough to squeak Kennedy through. Jack, however, had written the state off and was not much interested in my suggestion that he revise his speaking schedule to include Mississippi. When the vote came in, Kennedy lost Mississippi by a little more than 7,000 votes. My district went heavily against him—except for Washington County, the home of Greenville, the *Delta Democrat-Times*, and my own strongest support.

In every conversation I had with him after the election, his first question was how my political fortunes were going. He knew that my support of him had brought into the open the attack on me that the Citizens Council leaders had long been pushing. Each time he asked, "Do you want to come with us?" And each time I told him that I would like to, but that I thought I owed it to myself and Mississippi to make the fight against the forces that were out to get me in 1962.

"Well, we'll keep a light in the window," was always his

answer. I was the optimist and he the realist when it came to Mississippi politics.

The memories we cherish most are often the little ones. One such incident involved the appointment of the civilian member of the Mississippi River Commission, the Corps of Engineers agency in charge of the flood control work on the lower Mississippi river. Harold Council of Greenville was an obvious choice to replace the Republican appointee. He was a close personal friend, and I recommended him. When I learned that a man from Arkansas, with potent backing, apparently had an earlier commitment for the appointment, I went to see the President and explained that while Harold's appointment would be no particular political gain for me, it did have personal significance. He agreed to check into the commitment to the Arkansas man, and promised that Harold would get the appointment if the commitment to the other man could be otherwise satisfied.

"If we can't give the appointment to Mr. Council, I'll phone him and tell him why," he said, and I relayed that promise to Harold. The appointment came through, but Mrs. Council told me that during the interval of waiting she wasn't sure which kept Harold more in suspense, the appointment or the possibility of getting a phone call from the President.

Another time, I was in his office when Mrs. Kennedy came in, carrying John-John and leading Caroline and her kindergarten classmates. The President stopped everything to compare the spelling abilities of Caroline and several of the other children, telling her how smart each playmate was. Afterwards he said that his quiz might not be the best psychology, but, like politics, "everything shouldn't always be done the best way."

My 1962 election was the first chance to defeat the know-nothings in Mississippi since the rise of the Citizens Councils, and I had convinced myself that it was an all-important battle, but breaking with Kennedy as a means of winning it never occurred to me. Some of my chief supporters must have thought a break might simplify their problems, but I am proud of the fact that they were good enough friends not to ask me to do it. The build-up of the forces that took me out of the Congress in 1962 had been under way since I was first elected in 1950, and, in retrospect, they would probably have been successful no matter who was President in 1962. Since "the Kennedys" were the chief issue in my campaign, however, my defeat made me the only member of Congress turned out of office because he supported Jack Kennedy during the three years of his administration. It is not a bad distinction.

The confrontation over the Cuba missile sites marked both his courage and his mastery of the power of his office, and there are examples from almost every day he spent in the office of the grace and verve he brought to the Presidency, and of the new respect for intellect and for ideas and ideals that was the greatest since the time of Thomas Jefferson. I believe, however, history will give its highest praise to John Kennedy for two unparalleled contributions to the future of the world in which we live.

He brought a real flexibility to the cold war, symbolized by the test-ban treaty but evident in a dozen other policy precepts, that offers for the first time a path we can follow with hope for the future rather than in fear of inevitable total war and destruction. And he fully committed the powers of the United States government to the elimination of racial discrimination and injustice, a commitment upon which no future President can turn his back. Even if neither of these goals is fully achieved, the course he set toward them will rank him among the great Presidents of the United States. However, if they are achieved, his brief three years as President will rank him among the great leaders, not alone of his own country but of mankind as well.

No politician from Mississippi since John Sharp Williams has had any significant role in the resolution of great national issues or played any positive part in the choice of our national leaders. In the years since World War II, our state political leaders have deliberately turned their backs on participation in national decisions. With this background, rare good fortune allowed me to help make John Kennedy President and then to be part of his support in the Congress. A novelist's skill and a poet's words would be needed to express it, but surely everyone who had any part, however large or small, in his rise to triumphant championship of peace among men must share the pride I feel.

Chapter XIII

DEVELOPING

RESOURCES FOR

KENNEDY

One of the most frequently heard charges against the average American citizen is that he has only himself to blame for the sorry state into which politics has fallen (if, indeed, it has), that he deserves what he gets because he does not take an active part in the political affairs of his country. This is probably a just criticism insofar as local and state politics are concerned, but for many years it has been growing less and less valid as applied to presidential politics. The development of mass communications media has lifted the presidential campaign out of the old preserve of the professional politician and put it on the breakfast table and in the living room of almost every home in the country.

For this reason, among others, presidential campaigns are much more complex than they used to be. The candidate can no longer depend upon making a few key personal appearances in each area and then leaving the bulk of the work to the standing local party organizations. He must find ways of reaching not only every locality but every special interest group in the country, or at least as many of them as he possibly can. One of the ways in which the candidate does this is by organizing the specialized campaign committee which directs its appeal entirely to the people known or presumed to be interested in that particular field. Ideally, these committees are composed, at the top level, of highly qualified people who have both the respect and the personal confidence of the candidate and upon whom he can and will rely for guidance as to the positions he should take on the issues with which the committee is identified. Down the line, it is their function to get across to the public in general, and to their potential allies in particular, the candidate's philosophy and policies. All of this, of course, is designed for the primary purpose of getting votes. The committee, as such, rarely survives election day, but the strength and influence of the successful ones do carry over into the elected candidate's administration, in the persons of committee members who are placed in key executive or advisory positions within the government departments. Some of these committees are purely paper organizations; others are active. My own view is that if they are worth putting on paper, they are worth using to the maximum, for both vote promotion and long-term policy counsel.

The idea of a natural resources campaign committee had been proposed to Adlai Stevenson in 1956, and tentative steps were taken toward organization, but the proposal never got beyond the talking stage. The Democratic Advisory Committee, a more or less peacetime (noncampaign year) arm of the National Committee, included a natural resources group which had done some sounding-off on resource issues and had made some good policy suggestions, but it was not set up to operate as a moving force in a presidential campaign.

The idea came up again in 1960, during the postconvention session of Congress. Bob Jones of Alabama presented the suggestion to Jack Kennedy and sold him on the value of a natural resources committee as a campaign tool. In addition to the obvious vote potential, the proposal had some other attractive features: The heavy guns of the campaign would not be aimed at the deep South, and this would give us one more not entirely political inroad in that area; as a Mississippian, my usefulness on a broad scale was limited, and this would give us a chance to capitalize on the nationwide standing I had acquired among natural resources groups through my work on the Public Works Committee; and, probably equally persuasive, the information and staff were already at our command, so the cost would not be great.

I am sure that few presidential campaign operations were ever as autonomous from the main campaign, or less bother to the high command, or less drain on finances. Sargent Shriver was Kennedy's personal liaison with and supervisor of the various advisory committee activities, but we worked more closely with Ralph Dungan and Mike Feldman, brought into the campaign headquarters from Kennedy's Senate staff.

Jack Kennedy and I talked about the natural resources committee only once, when we met at his Georgetown home the day the committee's formation was announced. The plan we had in mind included a big-name advisory council, with committee membership to be drawn cross-country from individuals of local, sectional and national prominence in the natural resources field who would lend their names and commit their support to the Kennedy-Johnson candidacy. We discussed how the committee would operate and the various groups we should be able to arouse. He interrupted my sketch of a possible approach to one group with, "I get it, we're for everything," but he agreed that what we were working toward was a broad picture of what his administration's natural resources philosophy would be, with outlines drawn in by specific stands on selected individual issues during the campaign. We were both convinced that in this way we could get some real help from the people who were more concerned about resource programs than about anything else the government might do.

Averell Harriman had been waiting with me to see Kennedy that morning, and to report on a foreign policy mission that was also part of the campaign, so our meeting was necessarily short. Jack Kennedy had never had a broad political grounding in the natural resource field, but those of us who had were satisfied and pleased with his instinctively sound reactions to the issues after his Massachusetts campaign. His support of the St. Lawrence Seaway soon after coming to the Senate, in opposition to long-standing Massachusetts prejudice against the plan, plus the active fight against it by the New England private power interests, had been the first sign of a broad national outlook. The people he turned to for advice in the field were those who believed in conserving and developing our natural resource heritage in the interests of the general public. That Kennedy viewpoint was the test we used, and it was a good working basis, for setting committee policy.

Every political campaign activity starts out with a lot of optimistic talk about the amount of enthusiastic and valuable volunteer help that's going to be available, and ours was no exception. We were going to have offices downtown; we were going to have a full team of people working on the professional level; we could count on volunteers from other congressional offices; and we would have some stenographers on loan from the National Committee. Talk is one thing, reality another. As it turned out, we used my congressional office—it didn't require any rent, and it was a lot more convenient for me and my staff than any of the downtown possibilities. That team of professionals and the stenographers never did materialize. One thing we did get—a monumental amount of help, professional and clerical, from other congressional staffs. And to my great personal satisfaction, the most dedicated and tireless volunteers were my own staff, who worked as if the Kennedy-Johnson campaign were our own. Before it was over, my wife and her friends and the husbands of my staff had joined the force for the night half of the shift. And for one brief hectic period, we even had our children licking labels and envelopes (they were all to do it again, just as faithfully, two years later, for me).

The bulk of the operating costs of the Kennedy-Johnson Natural Resources Advisory Committee were for printing, postage, and telephone calls. Steve Smith was Kennedy's personal comptroller of expenditures, and he told me to have a separate line installed, to be billed direct to the Democratic National Committee. I protested the added complication, but his answer was strictly business: "The telephone company is more likely to wait on the massive total of the entire National Committee bill than they would be for yours." He squeezed out a budget for our operation, realistically setting a tentative figure somewhat higher than my estimate but explaining its limitations in terms of the mounting deficit for the whole campaign. "If we lose this election," Steve joked, "Papa Joe will have to go to Timbuktu and I'll have to go to Africa." Our committee operation, happily, added little to the deficit. The total costs came to better than $10,000, but our own committee members contributed more than half of that directly through the committee.

The operating procedure for the committee was simple. The Advisory Council lent their names and led us to other groups and potential committee members. They were chosen primarily for their publicity value and the vote-getting power that would have. The proposed committee members had to be selected and persuaded to use their influence and to allow us to use their names all within a few days' time. We inevitably ran into some problems, acute at the moment but amusing to us later. One conservationist in Pennsylvania was unhappy because Democratic Senator Kerr had ridiculed supporters of an amendment to give a financial incentive to antibillboard measures in the states. I pointed out to him that some of the rest of us on the committee had been among the chief supporters of the amendment, and that helped. One lady who was outstanding among garden club and League of Women Voters groups never did make the committee, because she was hiking or mountain climbing in California all during the period we were trying to reach her. All my advisers agreed there should be a man on the committee to represent mineral resources of the West, and we began a frantic search for a person who met the description and was also willing to admit being a Kennedy supporter. After long efforts on long distance, I found such a man in Rodney DeVilliers of Albuquerque, New Mexico. Several prominent Westerners recommended him to me as an expert on mining and a good name for the Advisory Council. Within a few hours after the committee was named, we learned that many other good Democrats had different views. DeVilliers had allegedly been involved in some sort of mining operation that had overtones of financial scandal. There was nothing to do but sit tight and let the DeVilliers storm blow over. It did, and New Mexico was one of the few Western states that the Kennedy-Johnson ticket carried.

The statement Senator Kennedy released on September 20, when the resource committee was announced, is a good explanation of the committee's purpose; it also defined the political orientation we gave the subject for campaign purposes. Here are some excerpts:

> Vigorous action is needed if we are to conserve and develop America's natural resources. An aggressive, affirmative policy in this field will be one of the major goals of my administration. I am, accordingly, very pleased to announce the establishment of a Natural Resources Advisory Committee to aid me in the presidential campaign and to submit plans for action by my administration.
>
> Preservation of our natural resources is an investment in America's future that has been disastrously neglected by the present administration. A revitalized resources program will be needed in the years ahead to make up for the shortcomings of the past few years.
>
> The total demand for water in the United States is increasing rapidly, while the available supply is decreasing at an alarming rate, due to heavy usage, continued waste, depletion, pollution, and inadequate development. The conjunction of these two trends, if allowed to happen, spells crisis—a crisis characterized by extreme scarcity, widespread hardships and economic stagnation.
>
> Happily, the means are available to avert this crisis if we muster the courage and intelligence to use them. The keys to the solution of the nation's water problems are capital, technology, organization, and a proper concern for the public welfare. We possess the first three in abundance, but for 8 years the Republican administration has refused to use them for the general good.

The committee job broke down into three distinct campaign tasks. We were to enlist as many people as possible as members of the committee. We were to prepare and mail a series of brochures on the principal natural resources issues. We were to write letters and statements for Kennedy's signature about individual local projects and problems in the field. Naturally, we also answered general mail on resources and helped congressional candidates with publicity on local issues.

By telephone and letter we extended invitations to people in every state to join the committee. Any person active in conservation, flood control, public power, or water development programs was asked to support Kennedy and Kennedy's programs. At the height of our activity we completed an average of thirty to fifty long-distance calls every day. For six weeks, lunch in my office consisted of sandwiches and milk at our desks. Too many calls came through that couldn't be picked up again for hours if we left the office. The committee members were asked to publicize their appointment in the local newspapers, TV, and radio. A press release with local variations was prepared for each appointment, or occasionally for a group in the same area. We usually asked the committee members to distribute the release, but we sent it direct to the newspapers if they thought that would be best.

Use of the release publicly identified our committee member with the Kennedy-Johnson ticket, and it necessarily pointed up Kennedy's interest in conservation or resource projects or problems in that individual area. This local identification, basic to any political campaign, cost us relatively little, but the investment brought us some very healthy extra dividends through the work of many committee members over the country.

The Kennedy statements on resource policy were printed as brochures suitable for both personal distribution and mailing, and we used them both ways. When the individual committee members were in a position to put them into the hands of interested voters and local organizations, we sent them large blocks of the brochures for that purpose. In addition, we mailed thousands of them ourselves to special mailing lists. The most harassing problem was obtaining mailing lists that adequately covered the many natural resource groups we knew existed. We were fighting time as well as Nixon, and delay could materially lessen the effectiveness of what we were trying to do. Even with the delays, however, we had encouraging and productive cooperation from the conservation clubs, sportsmen and garden club groups, public power advocates, regional development associations, water resource groups, and allied trade associations all over the country.

The actual writing of the statements was left to me, with the help of a dozen or so public and private sources, chief among them Ben Stong and Phineas Indritz, two long-time congressional committee staff members, and my own administrative assistant, Audrey Warren, who also handled coordination of the whole printing, publicity, and clerical operation so that I could be free to handle the personal contacts with the committee members. The texts of the statements were cleared downtown, but the only editing they did was to insist that "Republican" be substituted for "Eisenhower" in the negative references, a politically astute requirement certainly.

Putting out the political brush fires that developed along the way was another part of the committee's job. One flared up early from the TVA territory, obviously a smolder from the days of Jack Kennedy's senatorial campaign. We mailed out a comparison of the voting record of Kennedy-Johnson *vs.* Nixon-Lodge on TVA issues during the years they were in the Congress. Kennedy's Senate record included one vote against funds for transmission lines, and some absences. The two Republicans had never voted favorably on a TVA issue, yet the Republicans and anti-Kennedy Democrats apparently made great headway in the TVA territory by harping on that Kennedy vote in 1954 against funds for transmission lines.

The response from the general public often reflected confusion about responsibility for natural resource policies. A lady from Ford City, Pennsylvania, wrote:

> I have received a political pamphlet on natural resources. It is for John Kennedy's campaign.
>
> I am inclosing a copy to you, and have marked the part where he says he favors Indian homeland rights. If he does this, he is different from our Democratic Governor, who has been the biggest instigator of taking the Indian Reservation in our state to build a dam on Kinzua. Also this work and the politicians have broken a treaty (forever) made by George Washington. There is much inconsistency here. Signed by a Republican.

The Kinzua Dam authorization had been sponsored in our committee long before Dave Lawrence was governor of Pennsylvania. I thanked the lady and pointed out that funds for the Kinzua Dam and the decision to build it over the objections of the Indians all came under the present Republican national administration.

Fortunately, most of our responses were like that of the lady from Connecticut who sent us a list of people who should get the statement and included this note:

> Thank you for leaflet on Senator Kennedy's position regarding matters of conservation. I have been hoping to hear him *speak* on this subject. Several of the situations mentioned I have written to Washington about. I should have voted for Mr. Kennedy anyway, but I shall do so with even greater enthusiasm.

One of the most critical aspects of the committee's work arose from requests for pledges to support individual public works or conservation projects. These were usually to members of Congress or candidates for Congress, and they went out over John Kennedy's signature. Most of them could be couched in general terms that made no specific commitment for funds or administration approval, but some of them had to be direct pledges of support.

There is no way to measure the impact of an operation such as the Kennedy-Johnson Natural Resources Advisory Committee on a total campaign effort. We blanketed the country, hoping to gather in the pockets of voter interest in our particular field. Presidential campaign tactics have to be measured in terms of voter response in the states which turn out to be crucially close. I believe our committee efforts were important in carrying Illinois and Texas, to mention two of the big states that were very close. In addition to helping elect a President, we demonstrated that conservation policy is dependent upon political policy. One of the major reasons for the lags and stretches in our national conservation policy through the years has been the attitude of many naive conservationists that it should be divorced from politics. Theoretically perhaps it should be, but for practical purposes, positive politics is the only way to overcome the obstacles that shortsighted economic interests have always used to block progress in conservation.

The advisory committee held its formal meeting, to make its report to the President, on January 17, 1961. More than 400 of the committee members attended. Over a hundred of them were members of the House and Senate already in Washington, but the rest had traveled from all parts of the country for the meeting. The theme of the report, which was based on the campaign commitments and the selected advice of fifty or sixty of the committee members, was the "full development" of all natural resources. We also recommended a Council of Resource and Conservation advisers as an instrument for coordinating resource programs. We asked immediate priority on a stronger stream pollution control program, recommended a Youth Conservation Corps, asked for inclusion of recreation and other public benefits in measuring the value of water projects, and spoke out against any form of tolls on inland water transportation. These recommendations were in addition to the basic demand for expansion of flood control, watershed, power, forestry, and waterway development programs.

I had discussed the proposed report with President-elect Kennedy in December. Aside from the general commitments, he was interested in projects in the public works field that could be implemented in the first days of his administration with the smallest cost in appropriations. There were significant policy changes which could be made without materially changing any early spending commitments, and the President had the new Director of the Budget, David Bell, come to my office to review these possibilities and other ideas. The most urgent long-range reform in resource development, the adoption of some form of permanent capitalization program, was eliminated from discussion on pragmatic grounds—the practical impossibility of the new administration's asking for it in the face of the "big spending" attacks which it would invite, with resulting damage in other fields of domestic policy. I had high hopes that the second Kennedy administration would come to grips with the issue and, at least, begin the educational campaign necessary to a receptive Congressional climate. Resource development will never receive the attention it demands until it is financed by a separate capital improvements budget in much the same way that private business finances this type of expansion.

I think the Kennedy administration made a good record in fulfilling its campaign commitments in the resource field.

Our batting average on getting committee recommendations adopted was fairly high. The Council of Resource and Conservation advisers we recommended was not established, but several appointments looking in that direction have been made. Although there has been considerable improvement in coordinating policy, formally and informally, there is still vast room for improvement. Perhaps our biggest failure was on the issue of waterway user charges and taxes. Here the committee commitments and recommendations ran head-on into transportation policy recommendations. Most of the differences were resolved in favor of the transportation side, although there was no final resolution by either the administration or the Congress during the three years Kennedy was President.

Although we will never know how many votes we accounted for, there was considerable satisfaction in knowing that the committee made a distinct contribution toward winning the election and that our efforts pleased the man we were working for. Months later, the President was talking to one of our mutual friends when the subject came up, and he is said to have remarked: "Frank knows more about water than anybody else." This comment may merely illustrate the point made earlier in this chapter, that President Kennedy was not the most knowledgeable man in the country on the subject of natural resources. I'm proud of what he said, anyway.

His public display of confidence in me was to come when I badly needed it. A few days before the primary in which I was defeated for renomination, one of the White House staff members called a friend of mine to tell him that Herbert Vogel was resigning from the Board of Directors of the Tennessee Valley Authority. They agreed to withhold any announcement of the resignation until after the outcome of my primary was known. TVA was the agency that exemplified

to me, more than any other, the potential of full natural resource development that had become my gospel in twelve
years of congressional work in the field. There was nothing I
could do better suited to my background and experience. The
President appointed me to the TVA Board and gave me the
chance to keep on working for development of the nation's
natural and human resources.

Chapter XIV

STAYING AHEAD

One afternoon, the phone rang at my residence in Fairfax County, Virginia. It was an alcoholic veteran in Mississippi. After long conversation about his many problems, it developed that the most pressing one was his plan to kill himself that Sunday afternoon. He was sitting with a pistol beside the phone, and would use it unless I had him admitted to a VA hospital for alcoholics that day. I persuaded him to promise to wait until I called back. While I was trying to get his doctor, his wife called from another phone. The doctor confirmed what both the man and his wife had told me about his condition. The VA hospital director heard the story from me and promised to admit the man when he arrived. I called the alcoholic back and told him when and where to go. I don't know anything about his present condition, but he at least survived that round.

In many areas of the country, VA alcoholic wards are the only facilities available for adequate treatment for alcoholics, and I have helped place many a veteran in one. Most of the time I've had to spend with alcoholics on the phone, though, has not been with people seeking treatment but with people who wanted to tell me how to vote or otherwise conduct my affairs as a congressman. Few congressmen declare themselves unavailable to listen, whatever the request, and I was insecure enough to have to listen to virtually all callers.

My congressional office was organized originally on the basis of my two years' experience as a Senate employee. I was convinced that constituent service—prompt and courteous handling of mail and telephone requests—was a key to popularity with the voters back home. A reputation for successful action on a reasonable percentage of the requests would be a major asset. Over the years, we acquired that reputation. I use the pronoun "we" even though the reputation was acquired in my name. Most of the work was actually done as a joint effort with my persistent and energetic staff, and any reference to results has to be in the plural. I believe the constituent service we stressed was an important factor in holding off opposition until 1962, and it brought support in the final test. Some of the worst disappointments in the campaign, however, came when people who had literally used up hundreds of hours of our time turned up among the opposition. Some of these might have believed they were putting principle above selfish interest, but for most of them it was merely another case of "what have you done for me lately?"

The congressman from the old Delta district of Mississippi was elected by fewer voters than any other member of the House of Representatives, which made every voter that much more important. A little more than 11,000 people had put me in the office in the primary tantamount to election,

and every one of those voters learned to expect prompt attention to his requests.

Constituent requests can be divided into three categories.
First come personal requests for things like government publications, expediting a passport, getting a pension approved,
being admitted to a VA hospital, obtaining a farm or small-
business loan, getting in or out of military service, finding a
job. Some of the requests seemed insignificant, but I operated
on the theory that they must have been important to the
constituents or they never would have taken the trouble to
contact us. I know that some of the pension and insurance
claims which were approved meant the difference between
security and the ragged edge of starvation. One request involved a tax refund of more than a quarter of a million dollars;
that constituent would eventually have had his refund without our help, but he would have waited a lot longer for it. I
don't know what the refund meant to him, but I know it
didn't mean enough to inspire a campaign contribution.

Some of these requests were entertaining, of course. An
otherwise drab winter day was considerably lightened by a
letter, a very serious letter, requesting government publications, any publications but preferably bound ones, in sufficient quantity to fill 22 linear feet of shelf space. The staff
turned the request into a personal circus, selecting books in
compatible colors and in volumes that measured down to the
last inch. They also used the request to needle me about my
own motives in lining my office with bookshelves and
whether the books I bought were selected for content or
space consumption.

The case that required the most painstaking preparation
called for a thirty-page legal brief upholding a Negro
woman's common-law marriage to a veteran, which brought
an award of his insurance. I'm not an attorney, my executive

secretary was not an attorney, and it was a grinding task. Cases like this don't usually require such strictly "legal" handling, but it is a standing staff joke around the Capitol that congressional offices practice law for some of the best legal firms in the country.

The most dramatic case was probably the one outlined at the start of this chapter, but the most heart-rending one started when a county school superintendent called to tell me that the daughters of one of his Negro teachers had been kidnapped off a school bus. The teacher didn't want to press charges, because the girls' father had taken them. He was an Air Force master sergeant and had been divorced from the mother for several years; she had complete legal custody of the children, which was why the charge would have to be kidnapping. As far as they knew, he had taken the children to his home near Washington. We traced the sergeant and had no difficulty confirming that he had the children with him. Arrangements were made to bring the youngsters into the office to be turned over to their mother, who came to Washington for them.

The sergeant and his second wife apparently agreed to come to the office in the hope that some last-minute miracle would let them keep the children. The new wife was a nurse in a Washington hospital, obviously intelligent and educated. It was clear that she and her husband believed that his children faced a dead-end and, possibly, nameless terrors as Negroes in Mississippi. He was about to be assigned to Europe, and they had hoped to start a life with the daughters there. I've sometimes wondered what course I would have followed had there been a choice, but there was no choice. The divorced wife had legal custody of the children, and she was insistent that they be returned. I will always hope that their future will be better than their father feared.

A good many newspaper and magazine articles have been written in recent years deploring the fact that the congressman and his staff spend a substantial amount of time on this kind of work, and that, in requiring them to do so, the voters turn their representatives into "errand boys" instead of the legislators they are supposed to be. To an extent, of course, this is true. Some of the requests are unreasonable; some of them are downright outrageous; some of them concern matters which have already been rightly disapproved at every executive level and on which the decision could not properly be reversed no matter how many congressmen intervened or how often the problem was reconsidered. But—and to me this "but" was the determining factor—for every half a hundred requests like this, there is the one that legitimately cries out for attention, and until you check them all out, you don't know which one will turn out to be that kind. Government agencies are not exempt from error, or delay, or just plain poor judgment. A negative decision that looks sound on the surface sometimes, upon investigation, proves to be an unnecessarily narrow construction of facts and law that could just as properly, and far more humanely, have been interpreted the other way.

One such case concerned an application for veterans' benefits for the daughter of a deceased World War II Air Force officer. The child's mother insisted that her husband's death resulted from a condition that he already had when he was released from the Air Force. The Veterans Administration insisted just as vehemently that the cause of death had not developed until more than two years after his discharge, when it was first diagnosed. The man's GI insurance had been paid to his parents, and the wife was left to support the child on her own. Her letters were well written, patient but determined. She had been trying to get a favorable decision on her application for years. We had the case reviewed by the Veterans Administration on two different occasions, and my executive secretary and I went over the VA file ourselves trying to reconcile the opposing sets of facts. If, as the VA said, the illness had not shown up within two years of the man's discharge, the law was clear—the child was not eligible for benefits. As far as we could determine, the evidence supported the VA's position. We wrote the mother that there seemed to be no way to pursue the matter, and closed the file.

More than a year later, my secretary walked into my office one morning and remarked that the man had died in a VA hospital but that the VA medical files we had reviewed had not included an autopsy report; one must have been performed—where was the report, and what did it show? We asked for the autopsy report. It took the VA three months to find it, stored in archives down in southern Virginia. It had never been read by the VA officials who made the repeated decisions on the mother's application for benefits. The VA had diagnosed the man's condition as multiple sclerosis and that was what appeared on the records as the cause of death. The autopsy, performed by a VA physician, flatly ascribed the cause of death to a brain tumor that had begun to develop "probably as far back as 1943." We located the private physician who had treated the man before he went to the VA hospital; he was one of the VA's top consultants. After about six more months of telephone calls, personal conferences, three-page letters, and some just plain brawling over that autopsy report, the VA conceded "administrative error" and approved the payment of monthly benefits to the child.

I'm sure the number of errors like this, particularly when considered in relation to the number of claims the VA handles over the years, is not high, but to the individual who is the victim of the error, the relative percentages aren't much comfort. About once a year, one of the staff would drop a request back on my desk with an airy wave and a cheerful "If you think you should have a yes answer to this one, you make the phone calls." This kind of seeming insubordination didn't bother me very much; my staff had long since proved that they would work just as hard as I did on the reasonable ones.

Case work is not all blood, sweat, and tears. I suppose every congressional office has a group of constituents whose problems, even on Monday, have a fascination and appeal all their own. For us, these were our Chinese constituents. People are frequently surprised to learn that we have a fair-sized Chinese-descent population in the Delta—an industrious, provident, unfailingly gracious people who, because of their numerous and close family ties, are forever embroiled in one immigration problem after another. My secretary once observed that it might be cheaper to assign a staff member to Hong Kong than to keep on paying the airmail postage for our steady stream of letters requesting consular reports on the progress of immigrant visa applications. But it wasn't a bitter observation; we never performed even the most routine service for a Chinese constituent without receiving a charmingly worded "thank you" in return (a habit some of our more anglicized citizenry could well acquire), and even if we had, there was always Frank Smith Chow.

I don't remember, any more, what Frank Smith Chow's original name was, but I know exactly what he looked like, and his sister as well. His parents are a young couple in Greenville who wanted to adopt two children, and being Chinese-Americans, they wanted the children to come from China. Over a period of many months, we contacted welfare agencies, church missions, government agencies, and consular officials, and eventually two children were located who were suitable for Mr. and Mrs. Chow. It's a long way from Hong

Kong to Greenville, and not in miles alone. You could almost see "Hurray" hanging in the air the day we received the snapshot of the two little children stepping off the plane with their new parents, and things got downright hilarious when we learned that boy had been named Frank Smith Chow. The Founding Fathers may not have had this kind of satisfaction in mind when they set up the House of Representatives, but I don't think they would object very strenuously.

The most common constituent request, of course, and the kind even the first members of the House must have had to handle, was to vote one way or another on some piece of legislation, or to work and vote for a general program outlined by the letter writer. I tried to have a clear-cut answer for most specific legislative mail, unless the bill in question was developing so obscurely as to rule out an advance position on its possible provisions. Form letters were used on issues which inspired large quantities of mail. If my position was different from that of the writer, I tried to explain my reasons in the light of local understanding of the issue. If the bill was not likely to come to a vote and my opinion was different from the writer's, I tried to avoid taking a positive position on it. The soft answer to divergent views became a practice which I had to develop into a fine art, for there was very often complete disagreement between me and my correspondents.

The third request category was projects. This was my label for requests for government action on something sought by a town, a county, an organization, or a group of citizens working together for some special reason. Project requests ran the gamut, from a flood control program involving several million dollars to approval of house-to-house mail delivery for a growing town. Sometimes these projects originated entirely with the local group, sometimes they developed entirely from an idea which I picked up and transplanted because it would bring specific economic benefits to my district. Some of the projects involved working with government agencies to persuade them to take action for which they already had both authority and funds; others involved seeking both legislation and appropriations in the Congress and then follow-up action by the executive departments.

One project, still spreading over other areas of the nation, began when a farmer asked me in all seriousness why the government didn't do something about the weather. Delta farmers invested twenty to thirty million dollars a year in insecticides which they applied to cotton and other crops, knowing that rain a few hours later could destroy all their value. They planted cotton without any knowledge of soil temperature and only a guess about the weather for the next few weeks, and consequently averaged two or three replantings a year. The weather forecasts they received were read several times a day over local radio stations, but they were brief generalities prepared 24 to 36 hours before they were read.

I started off by asking the Weather Bureau what they could do in the way of localized agricultural forecasting. They had some men with ideas but with limited experience in the field, and no money. The chairman of the House subcommittee which approves funds for the Weather Bureau was a good friend of mine, well aware of my need to provide special service for the Delta. I testified before his subcommittee and talked to some of the other members. When the committee made its report, it included a paragraph directing the bureau to experiment with agricultural weather service in the Mississippi Delta. The work during the first year required an allocation of only $25,000, which mainly financed research activities by Jack Riley, one of the bright young scientists in the bureau. He found that cotton farmers not only could use detailed forecasts, revised throughout the day, but that long-range forecasts would be valuable, from planting through all phases to harvesting. Today, this special agricultural weather service is operating in a dozen states ranging from New Jersey to Oregon, and it will eventually cover the whole country, wherever agricultural communities need it. Research will continue to increase the value of the service.

Another project developed from a long series of requests to help individual landowners obtain clear titles to lands which had been ceded to the United States under the treaties with the Choctaws and the Chickasaws in 1820 and 1830. The Mississippi State Land Commissioner, Walter McGahey, who brought some of these cases to me, wondered why it was necessary that Congress pass a private bill every time we needed to validate a title. The Land Office in the Department of the Interior agreed with us and helped draft a general bill giving it authority to grant the titles; the bill eventually became law. There was no question that in most of these cases the titles were cloudy with good reason. The land had simply been stolen from Indian titleholders in the years immediately after the treaty cession, either stolen outright or taken in some semilegal fashion. Under the Mississippi Indian cessions, Indians who decided to remain in the state—instead of joining their tribes in the trek to the Oklahoma Indian territory—were given title to some of the tribal holdings ceded to the government. Land pirates eliminated most of them within a few years, more often than not with the connivance of corrupt government Indian agents. After more than a hundred years, however, there was no way to find the heirs of the original Indian owners of the land in question.

The Delta district had fewer voters, but I am sure that it

had more special problems with the Congress, and the government in general, than any other. We faced an annual fight, for example, to prevent the Congress's placing a limitation on the value of cotton that could be put under Commodity Credit Corporation loan. Members opposed to "wasteful farm programs" were always attracted by the idea of limiting the "subsidy" any farmer could receive. Ever since the federal farm programs began, the subsidy and the loan have been confused. Most people, including a surprising number of congressmen and a startling array of newspapers, think they are the same thing. They are not. A subsidy results only if the farmer gets a loan on his crop at the support price, yields title to the government, and the price which the government eventually receives in selling the crop turns out to be less than the loan to the farmer.

It was common practice in the Delta to attack the loan limitation proposal as a depraved invention of the left-wing Democrats. As a Democrat, I tried to explain that it was Republicans who usually proposed it in the Congress, and that the principal sponsor of the idea in the beginning had been Senator Harry Byrd of Virginia, a popular idol in Mississippi. One year, I persuaded members of the House Banking Committee to reject the limitation in a conference report by telling the Democrats that the idea came from Senator Byrd and Senator Williams of Delaware, and by telling the Republicans, just as correctly, that Secretary of Agriculture Brannan had once proposed it.

The biggest project, however, and the one that required unceasing work on one of its aspects or another, was to keep a major flood control program always moving forward in the Delta. Title to a good part of the Delta had originally been ceded to the state by the federal government as useless swampland. The great saga of the Delta's first hundred years was its struggle to turn back the flood waters of the Mississippi, a fight in which the river kept the upper hand until the federal government assumed full responsibility for the job in the Flood Control Act of 1928. The Mississippi itself had been pretty well tamed by the time I came to Congress, but her tributaries had taken up where she left off, and the urgent need during my years in the Congress was flood protection from the Yazoo and its tributary streams. Originally, the lower Mississippi program had been authorized with a minimum requirement of local contribution toward the cost, and it was a running battle to keep the Yazoo program on the same basis. "We should call a halt to the special treatment heretofore accorded local interests in the lower Mississippi Valley area," was the way the Republican members of the Public Works Committee expressed it in a 1958 minority report. Beyond the authorizations, which set the scope and cost of the work, I had to press for funds for anywhere from five to a dozen Delta flood control projects every year, with annual appropriations ranging up to ten million dollars. Delta voters got attention to their needs.

The fact that the largest town in my district was Greenville, the most urbane and progressive city in Mississippi, was an invaluable asset to me as a congressman. The business leadership of the community understood the role federal programs could play in the town's economic development, and we worked closely together to build new business and new jobs. Some of the results are evident; others will show up as the years go by. Greenville became the Delta's metropolis of approximately 40,000, instead of just another Delta town. My closest association was with the waterways industry of Greenville, which grew up from very small beginnings in the years I was in Congress. Barge building and barge operating are stimulants to economic growth, and congressional programs in waterway development gave me many opportunities to help the city's growth.

More than anything else, however, Greenville was an oasis in the racial strife and obsession that smothered the rest of Mississippi. Negroes voted here more freely than anywhere else in the Delta. Strict segregation prevailed, but there was an atmosphere of harmony and respect for basic rights that did not exist elsewhere. It was a main ingredient of the economic progress of the town. The moving force behind the spirit of Greenville was Hodding Carter, and his newspaper the *Delta Democrat-Times*, but its base went far back to the quality of leadership in older generations. In the 1920's and 1930's, it was best exemplified by men like the poet-lawyer William Alexander Percy, who wrote "Lanterns on the Levee." Some dozen Greenvillians were published authors, if you counted both those who had strayed away, like the late David Cohn, as well as those who stayed at home, like Ellen Douglas. The staunch support I received through the years from the *Democrat-Times* could easily be converted into a liability—as in the end it was—in the rest of the district, but I was proud and pleased to have that support. It was a good buffer for the slings and arrows that were so often ranged against what I considered conscientious service.

Many congressmen and senators keep a steady stream of TV and radio recordings going back home at all times, except for campaign periods when the stations can't use them as "public service" features. I tried the radio tapes during my first year but found that the effort cost far more than it was worth, so far as I could judge from the visible response. I gave up the radio tapes and never did try the TV. I was told later that business and labor groups often underwrote this expense for members, but nobody ever volunteered to assume the burden for me. The recording is done at nominal cost in studios subsidized by the Congress. Some of our more liberal House members may be surprised to learn that through this service they subsidized a weekly series of shows sponsored by the Citizens Councils of America for more than four years.

My medium for a direct message to the voters was a regular newsletter. I started with a weekly mimeographed letter in 1951, mailed under my frank to the newspapers in the district and to several hundred key supporters from the previous year's campaign. For two or three years, there were regular requests from people to be added to the list, or to add their friends. When the list grew to more than 2,000, the office staff and I decided to add comprehensive coverage of every county in the district, and by 1960 the mailing list covered the white residents of the Delta fairly well, going to about 7,000 families. The newsletter started as a weekly, then became semimonthly, and eventually was put out every three or four weeks.

Rather than trying to cover the waterfront, I made the newsletters 500- to 700-word essays on some legislative issue of the hour, or a report on some legislative activity of my own. I chose the subjects and tried to write the newsletter as a means of persuading the constituents to accept my point of view. Occasionally someone got mad and refused to accept them in the mail, but on the average, each one provoked about fifteen to twenty personal letters, most of them in approval. A review of the entire twelve-year output reveals that more than half were on foreign affairs or directly related military security issues. The next most frequently covered subjects were public works and agriculture. Once or twice a year I paid my respects to civil rights. In 1951, when every mail brought two or three dozen letters or Fulton Lewis–inspired postcards demanding the impeachment of Truman and Acheson, I sent out a newsletter explaining why I could not vote to do so. The letter writers gave up. At first I tried to avoid commenting on Senator Joe McCarthy, but felt that I had to speak up after some of my colleagues made statements that sided with the senator. My words were cautious, but they at least identified McCarthy as a "Frankenstein." In March 1956, I reported my belief that the armed services were not doing enough on missile development. In 1958, I based my letter in criticism of the Supreme Court on quotations from Edward Corwin of Princeton and Judge Learned Hand.

My civil rights newsletters were designed to make it clear that I was opposing specific civil rights bills. This was the comment when the House was about to act, in 1959, on a civil rights bill which became law in 1960: "Paternal morals encored by the judgment and choices of the central authority at Washington do not and cannot create vital habits or methods of life unless sustained by local opinion and purpose, local prejudice and convenience, and only communities capable of taking care of themselves will, taken together, constitute a nation capable of vital action and control." It was hard to find language that would satisfy my constituents and still not stir up hate. About the only hate I ever earned credit for was directed entirely at me by the people who became more and more embittered by my moderate position.

After the demise of the old *Morning Star*, there were three daily newspapers in the Delta—at Greenville, Clarksdale, and Greenwood. The Greenville *Delta Democrat-Times* has been, for nearly twenty years, one of the outstanding small-city newspapers in the country. The Clarksdale *Press-Register* does a good job, far above the average for a small town. The Greenwood *Commonwealth* gave up being an active force in the community when I was a child, but it cooperated with me through the years in publicizing all the programs I worked on in behalf of the Greenwood area. The local newspapers were more than fair with my efforts, and they tried to be fair to their communities in resisting racial agitation. Their great problem was their proximity to Jackson and Memphis. The Jackson papers were hopeless from the start, but they had relatively small circulation in the district. The important paper was always the Memphis *Commercial Appeal.*

In the first year or two after the Supreme Court school desegregation decision made race agitation a popular and respectable activity in Mississippi, the *Commercial Appeal* tried to maintain a responsible news policy. Representative John Bell Williams denounced the paper in the House as unfit for good Mississippians to read, and the Citizens Councils repeatedly attacked it. I recall one doctor in my district who paid for an advertisement in the *Commercial* pleading for the paper to become a good Mississippi segregationist again. One night in Washington, I was a guest at a dinner along with Frank Ahlgren, the editor of the *Commercial.* I decided it was time somebody in Mississippi spoke up to commend his position.

"I want to tell you how much I appreciate what you are doing on the race issue with the—" I started off. Ahlgren interrupted before I could finish.

"Thank you," he said, "we're opening up all the way now." I've forgotten the rest of his exact words, but what they amounted to was that the *Commercial* was no longer holding out against Mississippi extremism; it was joining the fray as a chief spokesman. I was afraid to correct Ahlgren's misconception of what I had started to say. I still thought I could avoid his paper's opening up on me.

The change in the *Commercial Appeal's* policy was virulent. Southern resistance to integration became the paper's big running story. It was a big story everywhere, but there is a difference between telling a story and promoting a story. The thing that made this rabid policy in the *Commercial*'s Mississippi edition so vicious was that in the news columns of its Tennessee edition the paper was an angel of moderation. Where Memphis itself was concerned, the *Commercial* joined the Memphis business and political community in helping to bring about peaceful integration of the local school system and full acceptance of Negroes into the political life of the city. Thus, Memphis arrived at reality in the handling of race relations, while the Mississippi edition of its leading newspaper was daily refueling the race hatred in the surrounding countryside.

The fact that there were two sets of signals operating in the editorial rooms in Memphis didn't mean much to the paper's Washington correspondent, Morris Cunningham, either. Cunningham did some good work shortly after he first came to Washington on the Dixon-Yates story, which was centered in Memphis and Washington. After that issue died, however, the race story was the only one he watched closely. The trails he followed were those of the congressional racists, every report of Negro crime or immorality in Washington, and every appeal to the Negro vote by Democratic politicians. As the *Commercial* correspondent, the daily stories he filed provided the measure of my political life for most of the voters in my district. Nobody stood higher on my priority list, and there were few favors I didn't try to render him. I wasn't a good source of race stories for him, but I did constantly go out of my way to give him tips about other stories that should have been newsworthy and that had nothing to do with publicity for me. As the time grew closer for the 1962 showdown I faced, it became more and more obvious that all my approaches had failed. My stories didn't make the

Mississippi edition, and the emphasis was all on Whitten when we were mentioned in the same article. On one occasion when one of my projects was approved in an appropriations subcommittee, Whitten was written up as the man who made the motion, even though he was not a member of the subcommittee and its members approved the item as a favor to me, knowing I faced a potential campaign with Whitten. On another occasion, while I was persuading the White House to revise cotton acreage figures to protect my district from a loss, Whitten was featured as the man who controlled the decisions.

If there were a Pulitzer Prize for partisan reporting, Cunningham would have won it for the story he filed in the *Commercial* on January 18, 1961, two days before President Kennedy's inauguration. A Cunningham story announced that Congressman Whitten had met Orville Freeman, the newly designated Secretary of Agriculture, at a reception on the night of the 17th. He undoubtedly did—a lot of people met Freeman that evening. On the morning of the 17th, however, I had presided at the meeting of the Kennedy-Johnson Natural Resources Advisory Committee. More than 400 people from every state in the Union attended, including more than 100 congressmen and senators. Secretaries-designate Freeman and Udall were the only speakers beside myself. Some thirty reporters covered the meeting, which was given page-one coverage in *The New York Times* the next day, along with an editorial and a digest of our report. There were members of the committee at that meeting from every state in the *Commercial*'s circulation territory. Our report dealt with subjects rated top priority in the paper's editorial columns— flood control, navigation, public power, soil conservation, and reforestation. Cunningham didn't file a line about the meeting, and not a word on it appeared in the *Commercial* on the 18th.

That conspicuous void convinced me that my kind of politics would never fit the *Commercial*'s concept of news coverage.

Memphis does have a second newspaper, the afternoon *Press-Scimitar*. It is a standard Scripps-Howard paper, but its editor was an able man named Edward J. Meeman, who made significant and enduring contributions to the progress of Memphis and Tennessee. The *Press-Scimitar*'s Washington correspondent, Milton Britten, was an able reporter who took the ethics of his profession seriously and covered his territory thoroughly and objectively. Unfortunately for me, the *Press-Scimitar* has a very limited circulation in Mississippi, with a relative handful of readers in my congressional district.

Much of my legislative work for the Delta could not be publicized at home, because in many instances the publicity would have made it impossible for the people who helped me to be of assistance in future fights. I was content to believe that enough of the responsible leadership in the Delta would understand the tactics I was using and underwrite them when the chips were down. One such instance occurred in 1959. All through the early months of that year, I nursed through the House Agriculture Committee a bill which would allow counties not using their full cotton acreage allotment to surrender it to the state allocation committee, which could then reassign it to counties that needed more acreage. Many hill counties were not using their allotments, and all of my Delta counties could use more.

The bill came to the House floor under suspension, which meant that it had to have a two-thirds vote to pass. What was worse, it came on a Monday in August when I had to be at home to vote in the primary against Ross Barnett. The Agriculture Committee members had anticipated no difficulty, but they did not foresee the opposition of a California member who decided that the bill would eventually harm Western cotton growers. Against a combination of Republican and big-city members who were in the mood to vote against anything labeled "farm" or "cotton," the bill had no hope of a two-thirds majority. Arrangements were made to put off the roll-call vote until Wednesday.

I called several members from Greenwood, and then flew to Washington Tuesday night. Until the House met the next morning, I stayed on the telephone. At noon, I stood by the main entrance as members came in to vote. On the phone and the floor, I had personally asked more than 200 members to vote for the bill. Before the roll call was over, we managed to get the votes of even the majority of the California delegation, and the bill passed and became law. One of my strongest supporters in this operation was Frank Thompson of New Jersey, a leader in the Democratic Study Group, the organization of House liberals. As a result of this change in the law, every county in the Delta district received additional cotton acreage the following year. We estimated that it meant extra cotton income of ten million dollars that year, an increase that would be magnified with each succeeding year. A fair number of my cotton-growing constituents believed that they owed their added acres to Congressman Whitten.

My publicity problems were never important to me in relation to my civil rights stand. Even if I had wanted to, I could not have competed with the other members of my state delegation, who were past masters of the art of making headlines out of race issues. If I registered my position and made it clear that my votes were with the other Mississippi members, that was as much as I could accomplish. My most serious problem, which was to show up in 1962, lay in a field where my votes were almost always at variance with my state colleagues—foreign relations. Even Senator Jefferson Davis of Mississippi had spoken out against the anti-immigration policies of the Know-Nothings of the 1850's. John Sharp Williams of Mississippi had probably been Woodrow Wilson's most fervent internationalist supporter, and he quit the Senate in disgust when it rejected the League of Nations. When I came to the House, the Mississippians sounded more like the political descendants of Henry Cabot Lodge than of John Sharp Williams (while young Lodge was sounding more like Williams than like his grandfather). They were all-out isolationists, automatically opposed to anything even remotely related to the United Nations (John Rankin always referred to it in his speeches as the "Jew-nited Nations"), foreign aid, or any other international involvement. Jim Eastland, who had run for re-election in 1948 on a combination platform of the Marshall Plan and the Dixiecrat movement, and John Stennis, elected in 1947 as a fervent UN supporter, joined them a few years later on a path that was to include solid opposition to foreign aid, support of the Bricker amendment, and opposition to the test-ban treaty.

I believed that the people of my district could be persuaded to my viewpoint, and I took pains to explain my position in my newsletters and in my speeches at home. Through the years, I must have received thousands of letters in opposition to foreign aid, and never more than three or four in support of it. I had a problem, but it did not reach momentous proportions until internationalism in any form became synonymous, in Mississippi, with socialism, communism, one-world-ism, or (worst of all) integration. The actions of the DAR ladies should have warned me. In most sections of the country the Daughters of the American Revolution are considered something of a political joke, but in mine they were—and are—a moving force. The average member was a nice lady, like club ladies everywhere, but a half dozen or so of the leaders were rabid activists who responded with alarm to every breeze that shook a branch. One of these patriots more or less severed relations with me when I wouldn't volunteer to keep her son out of military service (it would associate him with too many lower-class people), and most of them had been confirmed opponents since a day in May 1951 when it fell my lot to introduce Benjamin Cohen, Assistant Secretary-General of the United Nations, to a Delta Council meeting. One year, the resolution writers at the DAR national convention dropped the perennial resolution condemning the UN, perhaps in an attempt to improve the never very flattering publicity the convention received each year in Washington. Two DAR leaders from my district remedied this shocking mistake by offering the anti-UN resolution from the floor and getting it adopted, one of the few times a resolution was ever adopted from the floor at a DAR convention.

In Greenwood, a group of church ladies organized the young people of several churches to collect funds for the United Nations Children's Fund on Halloween night. Some of the DAR people went after them, so I made a ten-dollar contribution and saw to it that my enthusiastic support of the children's effort was used in the publicity for next year's campaign. From that time on, the UNICEF opponents widened their attack to include me. The collections seemed to go up each year, but so did the critical letters I received.

I spoke out against some of the Dulles brinkmanship theories and some other aspects of the Eisenhower foreign policy, but throughout this period, when foreign policy issues came to a vote in the House they were always characterized as "support of the President's internationalism" on the one hand or as "voting for anarchistic isolationism" on the other. I was with the "pro-Eisenhower" side each time, along with the Democratic leadership, but that didn't keep Wirt Yerger, the Mississippi Republican front man, from joining the DAR leaders and the John Birchers in attacking my internationalist record. Not long before he left office, Eisenhower sent me a letter of thanks for my support on some of these issues. One of the regrets of leaving office was that I would not be around to use it in reply to a Republican attack.

When 1962 arrived, UN bonds and other issues easily susceptible to demagoguery both in Congress and at home were coming up. I decided I might as well fight with my internationalist flags at full mast. My first newsletter that year was a defense of internationalist policy, and an attempt to explain some of the difficulties the nation faced—"World leadership does not mean that the United States can control the actions of the rest of the world. The UN has through the years become the symbol of all hopes of survival of the human race. It can remain that symbol if we do not yield to the folly of trying to make it our instrument of national policy."

After I had been in the House two weeks, in January 1951, I wrote a friend at home that ". . . I've been alternately impressed and dejected by some of the situations I find here. Impressed by the sincerity of people from all sides in regard to our present (world) situation, and dejected by so many others who can only see the political angles in the matter. The worst offenders are probably my colleagues from Mississippi. I'm getting along with all of them, but sometimes it is a chore. Their negative reaction to anything that doesn't have political significance in Mississippi is sometimes the hardest thing to understand. . . ."

After twelve years, I still didn't understand it, and I probably never will. All things considered, I suppose I was lucky to last the twelve years without losing the sense of proportion and responsibility the office demands. That's what "staying ahead" really means.

Chapter XV

THE BUILDING

BONFIRE

          In 1952, a friend of mine returned to Mississippi after a year spent in Winthrop, Massachusetts. He was convinced that his neighbors in Winthrop would react to most racial strife in the same way similar people would react in Mississippi. Over the years, the succeeding immigration waves, first of the Irish, then Jews and Italians, had brought a sizable measure of race conflict to the Boston area. My friend felt that the continual preaching of the gospel of tolerance in the schools, churches, and press of the Boston area was an absolute necessity to maintenance of peace in so heterogeneous a population. He was also a little irritated at those in the East who incessantly demanded racial justice in the South but were willing to make no concession toward the economic equality which he considered essential to freedom. In a day when the Negro's lot in Mississippi had begun to improve, if only economically, it was easy to accept gradualism as the solution to the race problems.

The fatal flaw in this argument was that the political and economic power structure in the South refused to admit that racial equality was a reality, not just an idea. The outlook then was certainly improving in the South, and even in Mississippi, but without basic adherence to a national philosophy, the growing harmony could be torn asunder in a few days' time.

The Supreme Court decision on school desegregation in 1954 ended any hope for gradual elimination of racial injustice in the South. It demonstrated to the Negro that progress did not have to come with glacial slowness, and it roused the white extremists to all-out resistance to any change. If the decision had been followed by a prompt and concerted effort to win acceptance for an intensified but graduated pace, the story would have been different, but the lack of leadership from the White House on down killed any chance for calm, if slow, compliance. The contrasting reactions in Mississippi were depicted in a story in *The New York Times* the day following the decision. After ten years, the story makes clear my incurable optimism, or my failure to recognize the absence of leadership, or perhaps simply that there were far too few on my side:

MISSISSIPPI REPRESENTATIVE HOPES FOR CALM, BUT EASTLAND SEES STRIFE

Washington, May 17—Hope for a peaceful solution of problems raised by the Supreme Court's decision against segregation in public schools was voiced today by Representative Frank E. Smith, Democrat of Mississippi.

Mr. Smith's views attracted attention because, as a former newspaper editor, he is an experienced observer and because Negroes outnumber whites by more than 2 to 1 in the Yazoo country he represents.

No other district in the South has a more preponderant Negro population. Of the 990,282 Negroes in the state, 286,000 live in Mr. Smith's Third District. There are only 135,000 whites in the district, which embraces eleven counties in the northwestern part of Mississippi.

"I disapprove of the decision," Mr. Smith said, "but, as long as it has been made, the court seemingly followed the best course it could in seeking advice from all quarters on how to put it into effect.

"I am hopeful that the situation can be handled in such a way that there will be no incitement to violence or anything to break down the good relationship that has developed between the Negroes and whites in my district."

Representative Smith declared that there was less bigotry in his district than there was in many other areas. He noted that the district "never was a stronghold for the Ku Klux Klan."

Other Mississippians took a gloomier view of the decision. Senator James O. Eastland, for example, asserted that the South "will not abide by nor obey this legislative decision by a political court." He said an attempt to integrate schools in the South "would cause great strife and turmoil."

"A state has the police power to take those steps necessary to prevent disorder and riots," he declared. . . .

Mr. Smith asserted there was in Mississippi "no important sentiment among either Negroes or whites for the elimination of segregation," but he predicted that the situation "will work out pretty well."

He noted that the Mississippi legislature at its recent session had set up new school districts, one to a county. These new boards, elected last week, will assign children to schools. Mr. Smith indicated that something that "might be called segregation by place" may result. The legislature sought without success to initiate a constitutional amendment making it possible to scrap the public school system.

(© 1954 by *The New York Times Company. Reprinted by permission.*)

For a few months following the Supreme Court decision the situation in Mississippi gave no outward evidence of change. The change was developing, however. For many years the NAACP had been the legendary cause of all Negro unrest and the symbol of the alleged control Negroes had over Northern politicians. Most discussions about the NAACP ended with the joking comment: "What we need is a white man's organization."

The jest came to life when white men began forming one at Indianola in the summer of 1954. It was called the Citizens Council, and that summer and fall it spread rapidly over the Delta and north-central Mississippi. (The word "White" in the title has never been widely used in Mississippi; it did become popular in Alabama, where Council membership was second-highest after Mississippi's.) A young farmer who had been one of the original members at Indianola, Robert Patterson, took on a full-time organizing job. At first, the state (and Southern) headquarters were established farther east—in the hills at Winona—to avoid the appearance of a "Delta organization." There was more interest and money in Greenwood, however, so the permanent headquarters were finally established there.

Patterson's intellectual guidance to the Councils included mailing to members a list of some thirty hate organizations and publications over the country, including filth-sheets like the *American Nationalist* of Los Angeles and *Common Sense*, the anti-Semitic publication edited by Conde McGinley which was cited by the House Un-American Activities Committee. Patterson recommended that Council members subscribe to the hate sheets. Some of the members who took this advice wrote me letters and enclosed the publications as proof of their argument. A few who did this were too embarrassed to send the whole publication and clipped away the masthead of the *American Nationalist*, apparently reluctant to let anyone know they received it.

According to a friend at home, the Council once reported me as one of only ten white men in town who were not members. This was an exaggeration, of course, but it was still uncomfortably close to the truth. Most of the members were simply average citizens, swept along by the passionate assertions that the Council would save them from the holocaust. During the first membership drives, the cry had been raised that Armageddon was at hand. There was all sorts of talk about secret caucus ballots and other schemes to defeat the impending horde of Negro voters. No hordes appeared, and there was no other activity on the part of the local Negroes. Council members began to wonder whether it was worth all the effort and the endless harangues. One night at a meeting, somebody asked "Tut" Patterson just what the Council had accomplished. Patterson asked the members to stop and think a minute. Hadn't they been carefully watching every move the Negroes made, hadn't they become suspicious of every activity, hadn't everybody in Greenwood become aware of the necessity of putting every nigger in his place?

This was a revealing statement of the true purpose of the Council, in terms of what its professional leaders considered to be the role of the average members. For the diehard leaders, the Council was designed to stir up hatred and suspicion between black and white, and setting the pot to boil began to pay all sorts of dividends, expected or not. One of them was Emmett Till. This twelve-year-old Negro boy from Chicago had been visiting relatives on a farm near Money, just north of Greenwood. He was accused of whistling at a woman clerk in a store. In the night, two white men came and took him from the tenant cabin of his relatives, drove him over the countryside, murdered him, and threw the body into a river, weighted with a gin flywheel.

The day the first news of the Till case broke, I was at a

meeting with Congressman John Bell Williams. "I'd like the chance to prosecute and hang the men who did that," Williams said. His remark was indicative of a popular feeling all over the state. There was genuine indignation at the brutal murder of a child, and widespread fear of how the crime would reflect on Mississippi in the opinion of the people across the country. In a few weeks, everything was different. Negro organizations in Chicago naturally used the Till murder to bolster their efforts to fight Southern injustice. The mood of Mississippi changed from shock and humiliation to defiant defense of Mississippi and her customs, even if that included murder of Negroes who transgressed them in any way. Late one Sunday night, I drove into Greenwood and found hundreds of people milling in the streets. The wild rumor had spread that "hundreds of cars of Chicago niggers" were en route to take the accused killers out of jail and lynch them. The two men were tried for murder but promptly acquitted. In October I landed at Genoa, Italy, on my way to a meeting of the International Roads Federation. I picked up a local newspaper and on the front page was the news that a Leflore County grand jury had even refused to indict the pair for the kidnapping which preceded the murder. "Till" and "Greenwood" made it easy for me roughly to translate the Italian.

The Emmett Till murder was only the most spectacular in a long series of acts of violence and physical intimidation against Negroes which broke out as the Councils spread. There is no purpose in reciting them here. From my knowledge of how some incidents are publicized and others are not, it seems very likely that some of the cases were exaggerated in their reporting from Negro sources, but it is even more certain that many cases were never reported at all. For Mississippi, the great black mark on the record is not so much the crimes, which seem to occur wherever and whenever men's passions and fears are aroused, but the abysmal failure to be able to exact retribution from the criminals. Not too long after the Till murder, a white man who had been an associate of the accused killers in the Till case shot and killed a Negro filling station attendant in a nearby plantation village. The local Lions' Club, obviously in deep shock, passed a resolution of abject apology that such a crime could take place in their community, but that killer wasn't convicted either.

The Mississippi delegation in Congress had no higher duty than opposing civil rights legislation, but back in Mississippi their constituents, in the Till case, gave the strongest single push to enactment of the 1957 civil rights bill. The lynching of Mack Parker in Pearl River County had an even more important part in the passage of the 1960 Act. The Parker lynching, in 1959, was a lynching with all the traditional trappings—a prisoner was taken out of jail and brutally executed by a mob; no one was convicted of the murder. Most of the local politicians were more intent upon protecting the alleged mob members from an invasion of their rights by the FBI than anything else, and one of them sought to make capital of Governor J. P. Coleman's full cooperation with the FBI. In response to an inquiry from Mississippi, the United Press called me for a statement about the charges against Coleman. "Somebody's trying to use you to help them play politics with a lynching," I answered angrily, and hung up on the reporter. Within an hour one of J. Edgar Hoover's assistants was in my office to thank me for the support. The comment from Mississippi was different.

A good example of local Council activity occurred in Holmes County. The cooperative farm at Providence Plantation that I had visited with Lillian Smith back in 1939 was still in existence. It was in such a remote part of Holmes County that I wasn't even aware it was still there, but the Council was. I learned about its problems when A. E. Cox, the manager, came to my office and asked if I knew of any way he could prove he was not a Communist. I told him there wasn't any government agency in the business of certifying nonsubversives. The only solution I could think of was to ask the House Un-American Activities Committee for a report. What I got from the committee was a letter stating that its files contained no information about Cox or his farm. Two mass meetings of protest against the farm were held at the nearby town of Tchula, and Cox read my letter at one of them. The Lexington lawyer who was acting as prosecutor at the kangaroo court commented, "I do not say these men are Communists, but I do say they are following the communist line." Cox and the farm physician, Dr. David Minter, held out for a few more months, but the pressures were too great to make it worthwhile. A pastor who spoke a word in their defense was voted out of his job. When Cox and Minter left, they made this statement: "Only two members of our church wrote to us. A few others have voiced their faith in us, but above these small voices is the frightening SILENCE. It is frightening— not only for us, but for any Christian and American who may wake up some morning to find himself persecuted because of his beliefs, or for unfounded rumors and 'guilt by association.' "

The Council had a small hand in the Mississippi elections of 1955, and in the succeeding four years it worked its way to complete domination of the state and local elections in 1959. It moved into national politics in 1956 when it attempted to control the selection of delegates to the Democratic convention. I was told that I would be opposed as a delegate unless I pledged myself to oppose any nominee for President or Vice-President who did not hold the Supreme Court desegregation decision unconstitutional. The Council plan carried the Third District convention, and I was the only congressman in the state not chosen as a delegate by his constituents. The Council failed to dominate the state convention, however, and I was made a delegate at large.

Another propaganda move was a play on Mississippi's inferiority complex. Virtually every filling station began to sell front license plates bearing the legend, "Mississippi—The Most Lied About State In The Union." My constituents apparently didn't appreciate the inconsistency between those front license plates and their letters to me asking how they could avoid being abused when they traveled out of state, or how to keep their cars from being damaged or destroyed by people out to "get" Mississippians. They probably didn't get much comfort, either, from my explanation that through all my years in Washington I parked my car, with its regular Mississippi tag, on the streets of a solidly Negro section of Washington when I went to baseball games at Griffith Stadium, and never had the slightest indication of reaction to the Mississippi identification.

Over the years, various boycotts have been attempted against Hodding Carter and the *Delta Democrat-Times* at Greenville. When Hodding attacked the Councils, a boycott was organized against him and an attempt was made to start another newspaper in Greenville. The tolerant attitude in Greenville even before Hodding came, plus the strength that he had built, rendered the attacks ineffective and killed off the abortive attempt to invade his newspaper monopoly. The attacks did, however, block what would have been a natural expansion in the *Democrat*'s circulation to cover the entire mid-Delta. Boycotts became something of an unofficial way of life for the Council. In addition to selected newspapers, there were large-scale attacks on Ford cars, Phillip Morris and

Marlboro cigarettes, Falstaff beer, and a dozen other lesser-known products. A conspicuous consumer had trouble consuming without violating Council doctrine. Ford, Phillip Morris, and Falstaff survived, but some individual merchants lost out, and more than one Council merchant or dealer thereby emerged on top in his local community.

The Clarksdale Negro leadership decided to use the boycott as a weapon in a local campaign to secure downtown employment and other concessions. The leaders were promptly arrested and fined—for leading a boycott. And while this incident was in progress, the Mississippi legislature was passing a resolution urging good Mississippians to boycott the city of Memphis, because Memphis was failing to hold the line for segregation. The Citizens Council also carried on a campaign of boycott and threat against Memphis, but north Mississippians still flock to Memphis in great droves. Facetious as it sounds, there may be a ray of hope in this fact. If the head of the house, so vehemently segregationist in public, cannot summon the persuasion or power to override m'lady's shopping habits, his position may not be so irreparably adamant after all.

There is a newspaper boycott still going on in Holmes County. Hazel Brannon Smith was the prosperous owner of the two newspapers in the county when I first met her. That first meeting was in 1951, when she raked me over the coals for upholding President Truman's firing of General MacArthur. The next year, she was one of President Eisenhower's chief supporters in Mississippi, making a statewide radio network speech for the Eisencrat ticket. Then Hazel published an account of the shooting of a Negro by the local sheriff which very plainly indicated that more than resisting arrest was involved. The sheriff sued, and a local jury gave him a $10,000 libel award. The state supreme court threw out the judgment. Instead of letting it go at that, Hazel decided to fight the pressures she knew were constricting local opinion. A lady fighting the Southern gentlemen who lead the Lexington Citizens Council does not necessarily choose the most judicious weapons, but she is still fighting back after ten years. Instead of closing the columns of the Lexington *Advertiser* to racial news, the paper has become complete in its coverage of all race controversy in Holmes County, and in many other parts of the state as well. The Council still controls nearly everything related to the race question in Holmes County, but the story of that control is fully reported in Hazel Smith's paper. That she is a formidable opponent is evidenced by the fact that the *Holmes County Herald* was established in 1958 as an opposition paper. There was a lot of fanfare about the "popular stock subscription" by which it was financed, but in actuality its support was assumed by a few local businessmen. The *Herald* has run through three or four editors and a lot of the investment of its original founders, but the persistence of the Council's campaign against Hazel Smith has probably assured the *Herald* a long life.

In 1962, an automobile dealer who had helped underwrite the *Herald* told me that "a lot of old ladies and people like that still read Hazel's paper." She still has the readers, but some issues contain not a line of local advertising, and almost none from outside. The *Lexington Advertiser* was founded in 1837, and Hazel promises her readers that it will still be around to publish their obituaries, but it will survive only with outside help. In the meantime, as Hazel Smith describes it: "Today we live in fear in Holmes County and in Mississippi. It hangs like a dark cloud over us, dominating every facet of public and private life. None speaks freely without being afraid of being misunderstood. Almost every man and woman is afraid to try to do anything to promote good will and harmony between the races, afraid he or she will be taken as a mixer, as an integrationist or worse, if there is anything worse by Southern standards."

Hodding Carter was much better known in the state, and consequently he drew most of the barbs of the Council leaders and the political figures looking for the publicity to be gained by attacking someone on the race issue. The awesome majesty of the Mississippi legislature's "censuring" editor Carter, and his rebuttal censure of the legislators, has its comic aspects. Hodding handles most of these attacks by ridiculing them, and he is probably wise to do so. The trouble with viewing the Mississippi legislature through the lens of levity, however, is that one is apt to overlook the fact that the legislature takes itself very seriously, and that too many citizens of Mississippi take it seriously, too.

The Citizens Council didn't have to initiate the attempt to purge Mississippi's schoolbooks of everything the Council hierarchy considered inappropriate for young Mississippi minds. The DAR, the Farm Bureau, and the American Legion were all officially listed as backers of a campaign to remove a long list of standard textbooks from the state school system. A legislative committee was prevailed upon to hire a professional book-banner, E. Merrill Root, to establish the depravity of Mississippi textbooks. Unfortunately for them, Mr. Root's book-banning business operates all over the United States, and he could not afford to be as strong against intimations of integration as his Mississippi clients would have liked. The Mississippi purifiers would also have been very unhappy had they known that Root was a slavish admirer of the novelist Ayn Rand. Miss Rand is a well-known intellectual opponent of brotherhood and other democratic fetishes, but she is also well-known as an outspoken atheist. The book-purging campaign created great furor in the newspapers and in the legislature, but it has failed to make as much headway as might have been expected in the present Mississippi atmosphere. One reason is that the textbooks are innocuous, and another is that the school teachers have fought back vigorously against the purge, which they rightly sense as an indirect attack upon their own integrity.

One of the principal "educational" activities of the Citizens Council, however, has been a concentrated effort to get its viewpoint over to the students. Schools are encouraged to hold an annual essay contest on anti-integration topics, and a vast assortment of supplementary literature is made available to the students so they may "prove" their points. Many schools actually teach the Citizens Council pamphlets on race relations. This is for the third and fourth grades:

> God wanted the white people to live alone. And He wanted colored people to live alone. The white men built America for you. White men built the United States so they could make their rules. George Washington was a brave and honest white man. It is not easy to build a new country. The white men cut away big forests. The white man has always been kind to the negro. We must keep things as God made them. We do not believe that God wants us to live together. Negro people like to live by themselves. They like to go to negro doctors. They like to go to negro schools. Negroes use their own bathrooms. They do not use the white people's bathroom. The negro has his own part of town to live in. This is called our Southern Way of Life. Do you know that some people want the negroes to live with the white people? These people want us to be unhappy. They say we must go to school together. They say we must swim together and use the bathrooms together. God has made us different. And God knows best. They want to make our country weak. Did you know that our country will grow weak if we mix the races? It will. White men worked hard to build our country. We want to keep it strong and free.

Having established itself as an expert on the racial aspects of both hygiene and theology, the Council expanded at length on the latter subject. It published pamphlets like "A Christian View of Segregation," "A Jewish View of Segregation," and "Is Segregation Unchristian?" The Jewish pamphlet was anonymous; I've often thought its author would be an interesting person to meet, at least once. The Council was the chief proponent of a bill before the legislature to allow local church congregations to take title to church property if they withdrew from national affiliation with the parent church. The bill, now law, was specifically aimed at the Methodist Church, but it has implications for most others, including the Catholic. Its chief supporters included legislators who have spoken out vigorously against violation of the traditional separation of church and state. The Mississippi Baptist Convention, composed of churchmen always loudest in their protestations on this issue, was very prominently silent as the church bill rolled through the legislature.

As the Citizens Council grew in Mississippi, there simply was not enough room for two top employees in the same echelon of professional staff. Bob "Tut" Patterson, a former football star at Mississippi State, was a farmer. He was good for the hard-hitting organizational work in the first years, but his presence at the head of the paid staff left no room at the top for William J. Simmons, the rising egghead of the segregationist movement. Eventually, a plan was worked out to keep the official headquarters of the Citizens Councils of America at Greenwood, as well as the Mississippi office, with Patterson as executive secretary. Simmons was established at Jackson, where he is editor of *The Citizen*, official journal of the Citizens Councils of America. The Jackson Citizens Council came to be known as the main voice of the Councils in Mississippi, and most groups over the state took their cues from Simmons through this medium. Most of the decisions on segregationist doctrine and political action have come through Simmons and probably will continue to do so in the future.

Simmons has not bothered too much with the original Council doctrine, that it was a movement designed to preserve segregation by legal and peaceful means. He frankly concedes that the present conflict is a war between the races, but in spite of his admiration for programs in South Africa and other parts of the world, he would not yield Mississippi's place of leadership. The standard expression is that Mississippi is out to save the country from self-destruction, but sometimes this position becomes confused with an admitted interest in saving segregation above all else. Mississippi moderates joke, behind closed doors, that both Simmons and Patterson are leaders of the "White Muslim" branch of the Citizens Council.

Simmons is generally credited with originating the Jackson Citizens Council plan for a door-to-door census of the views of individual citizens on segregation and related issues. Under this plan, Council volunteers would, like census takers, call on every white residence, with a questionnaire about race issues. They would also solicit memberships in the Citizens Council. It was a skillful plan to search out anyone who deviated in the slightest and to bludgeon into silence those who had any differing ideas. Annnouncements were made from time to time that Jackson and other towns were 99.9 percent pure, but none of the opinion enumerations were apparently ever completed. Even the Council found it impossible to inspire enough volunteers for such an ambitious program.

The 1958 election gave the Democrats their largest majority in the House for many years, and Washington pundits talked of the new strength of liberalism. The election gave cold chills to Southern moderates in the House, however; the big news for them was the defeat in Little Rock of Brooks

Hays, who thus reaped his reward for trying to avoid violence when Central High School at Little Rock was integrated. Mississippians paid for ads in the Little Rock newspapers, urging the Arkansans to stand with them in repudiating Hays, and others jumped on the bandwagon when it happened. Jamie Whitten told a Rotary Club at New Albany that the defeat of Hays was "the best thing that has happened to the South in a long time," and went on to attack Hays's record. "You're either for or against integration, because there is no middle ground," he said.

Many right-wing Republicans had participated in the congressionally subsidized Citizens Council TV forums, and the economic and political doctrine expressed there was against the existence of labor unions. In Mississippi, however, the Council found it very worthwhile to move into labor union activity. Two labor officials at Jackson who joined a Negro in a suit to test the constitutionality of the donation of state funds to the Citizens Councils were practically hounded out of their CIO union, and they quickly withdrew from the suit. Various local union members were constantly encouraged to protest integration stands taken by their national unions and officers. During my 1962 campaign I was denounced by my opposition as being "too friendly to labor," but union members were more interested in being told that Kennedy and I were "too soft on integration."

In 1959, the Citizens Council assumed a strong control over state politics, electing Governor Ross Barnett and a legislature ready to do his bidding—if he could move fast enough to stay out in front of them. The plan to underwrite the Council's "educational" program, mentioned above, won approval from the governor on down, and Mississippi taxpayers' funds were added to those used to keep electoral votes from John Kennedy in 1960. A later session of the legislature approved a bill to allow counties and cities to donate funds to the Council. When a member questioned the constitutionality of the bill from the floor, he was answered by being told that the president of the American Bar Association, John C. Satterfield, had drafted the bill. Membership in the Councils has fluctuated through the years, but the income from taxpayers' money has been the steadiest and surest. Under Barnett, the Council was given virtual control of the State Sovereignty Commission, a state agency created to propagandize the segregationist position over the country. Outwardly, the major function of the commission appeared to be paying the expenses of local politicians when they made speeches defending segregation before Northern Rotary clubs and the like. Mississippi papers always carried long releases on the speeches, usually much longer than those carried in the Northern city, if any. In 1962, Erle Johnston of Forest, who was public relations director of the Sovereignty Commission by virtue of having been Barnett's public relations director during the 1959 campaign, brought a dispute within the commission out into the open, declaring that the main purpose of the Council leaders "now appears to be making white people hate each other."

Mr. Johnston had finally spoken a truth obvious to observers of the Councils for a long time. The first purpose had been to stir the antagonisms of white and black people. To gain and hold political power, however, there had to be enemies closer to home. It was all very well to hate the Kennedys, and anybody else in national life conveniently open to attack, but there were white people in Mississippi who had to be hated if local power was to be grasped by the right hands. These were not only the people who believed that the Negro was entitled to some measure of justice, but anyone so presumptuous as to think Mississippi had anything to gain by making concessions to national opinion, or even some who were simply going to vote wrong in the next election.

The admission of the incitement to hate each other indicated also that our state's hate mongers had reached the saturation point on selling hatred to outsiders. Politicians and editors had no corner on writing hate. A crop of letter writers, huge in comparison with the literacy rate, seemed to jump at every chance to write bitter and often vicious letters in response to any statement from outside that could be interpreted as criticism of Mississippi. This was partly the offspring of another Council project, but it caught on spontaneously. I first became aware of the intensity of the effort when Representative Edith Green of Oregon recounted her experience. While driving from Portland to Washington, she was delayed in Jackson for a few days, having her automobile repaired. In the hotel one day, she talked with a Negro maid about conditions in Jackson. For the maid it was probably her first contact with a sympathetic outsider, and for Mrs. Green it was probably her first contact with a Southern Negro on the scene. She wrote a newsletter to her constituents about her experience, and the report naturally criticized the Jackson caste structure. The news about the comment in the Jackson papers resulted in a flood of abusive mail to Mrs. Green. A good part of it was obscene. Other members of Congress told me of similar experiences. Two conservative members who had made comments interpreted as friendly to Mississippi were also embarrassed by the resulting letters. Too many of the writers had welcomed them with open arms as 100-percent subscribers to the Mississippi philosophy. "Don't let any of that stuff get back to my district," the congressman told me.

All Mississippians, from the time the state first emerged from the frontier, have grown up and lived with the race issue. During the Civil War and for two or three generations thereafter, it was talked about as the war for Southern independence. In the years since World War II, it has been called the defense of states' rights, the Southern way of life, the duty of all brave and patriotic Americans to save their country from destruction from within. Because Mississippi was fighting to save America, the state was persecuted by the Communist-controlled national press, radio and TV, and the people of the United States did not know of the fight for freedom being made by her heroic leaders and their followers. Those who did know the story were enthusiastic for Mississippi. The national political parties were prisoners of the NAACP, but the Democrats were willing prisoners. The Negroes were satisfied and happy with segregation everywhere, more especially in Mississippi, and the only complaints were stirred up by the Kennedys to get votes, or at the request of Khrushchev or Castro, who controlled the President. Whatever the rest of the country wanted, under states' rights a state had a right to decide how to run its own affairs, no matter what anybody said. Only the states were strong enough to resist communist domination. The Mississippians who were courageous and independent were those not afraid to stand up and say "No!" to the President, or the Supreme Court, or anybody else. The only hope of saving the United States from communism was for Mississippi leadership to prevail. And when you got right down to it, Barnett had saved segregation by standing up to everybody, and that is more important than anything.

Confusing as all that may be, it accurately reflects the minds of Mississippi leadership, symbolized in Governor Ross Barnett. The youth of the state has been taught that only the Mississippi way is right, and that anyone who accepts anything else is cowardly. Vast numbers believe that any Mississippian who differs has either sold out for cash or has been a Communist all the time.

Mississippi had been organizing massive resistance against integration in any form for eight years. Unless the leadership symbolized by Governor Barnett was willing to make a concession and stand behind it, the first crack in the segregation wall was going to set off an explosion so violent it could not be contained. Looking back, it is easy to say that the political leadership, headed by Governor Barnett and the Citizens Councils, was so weak in moral fiber and so corrupt in spirit that it could not meet the challenge. But while the kindling was piling up, there was nothing to do but hope that by some miracle the crack in the wall would not detonate the explosion.

Chapter XVI

THE LAST EFFORT

During my 1950 campaign for Congress, Jackson editor Fred Sullens had observed that the outcome of the contest was immaterial, since the Third District would be abolished in the 1952 redistricting of the state and made the preserve of Congressman Jamie Whitten of the nearby Second District. Whitten's home county of Tallahatchie—part Delta, part hills—bordered on my home county of Leflore, and as a state senator my district had consisted of Tallahatchie and Leflore. Whitten was preparing for the possibility of his home county's being added to the Delta district when he tried to block my assignment to the House Public Works Committee in 1951.

The Delta district was preserved intact in 1952, thanks to a fortunate combination of favorable circumstances. Whitten preferred no contest to a campaign with me, and my own enemies in the Delta had not yet been convinced that it was worth destroying the Delta district to get rid of me. Mississippi's representation was reduced from seven to six, and the senior member of the delegation, John Rankin, turned out to be the man who lost his seat. Even in 1952, however, it was fairly obvious that Mississippi would probably lose another seat in 1962, and that sword hung over everybody for ten years. During that time, I sought to build up the Delta's interest in maintaining its identity as a separate congressional district, and Jamie Whitten sought to convince the Delta people that he would make a good congressman for them.

As the years went by in Washington and the differences between my attitudes and votes and the attitudes and votes of the other House members from Mississippi became more apparent, I convinced myself that the traditional Delta power in the Mississippi legislature would save the Delta congressional seat. I failed to realize that more and more influential Delta leaders were being persuaded that it was more important to get rid of me than to preserve a voice for the Delta in Congress. They were afraid to challenge me in a primary within the Delta itself, but they were willing to turn the job over to another member of the congressional delegation, with the cards stacked in his favor.

The man who typified this Delta-based opposition was Walter Sillers, a legislator from Bolivar County since 1916 and Speaker of the State House of Representatives since 1944. Under our state constitution, Mississippi has a "weak governor" system. The governor has considerable power during the first year of his four-year term, but the power tends to pass to a legislative oligarchy during the following three years. Sillers has been head of that legislative group during his 21 years as Speaker.

The disastrous mutation in Mississippi's political character in the last forty years is probably as forcefully demonstrated by the difference between Walter Sillers and his father as by any other example I know. Sillers' father was the leader of the Populist (pro-silver) wing of the Democratic party in the Delta sixty years ago; Sillers himself is an arch-conservative, whose views on national issues make the John Birch Society look like a branch of the ADA. He was active in all the ramifications of the Dixiecrat movement well before 1948, and is said to have boasted that he has not voted for a Democratic nominee for President since 1932. In 1922, he led a successful fight to take control of the Delta levee boards away from the governor, but any forward-looking legislation he has sponsored since that time has been largely accidental. Through the years, Walter Sillers has come to be known as "Mr. Delta" in state politics. He has defended Delta interests in the legislature, and has been proud to serve each year as chairman of the Delta Council's resolutions committee, strongly in favor of federal economy everywhere but in the Delta. He lives in Rosedale, a town of about 2,000, but his law practice includes retainers from some of the largest corporations doing business in the state. Through the years, my personal contacts with Mr. Sillers have been limited to those he considered essential to projects of direct financial benefit to the Sillers interests.

When the Citizens Council elected Ross Barnett to the governorship in 1959, it also helped elect a legislature subservient to a Council-controlled oligarchy. The talk of reprisal against me did not come out in the open until the presidential campaign of 1960, but it had been common enough through several earlier legislative sessions. My hope in 1962 was that Walter Sillers would be proud enough of being "Mr. Delta" to use his overriding power to save the Delta district.

From the standpoint of population and geography, the Delta's case was strong enough. The 1960 census gave us a population of 378,000. The Delta counties were all similar physically and economically, with special legislative interests and needs in the Congress. Whitten's district, with a population of 231,000, was the logical target for dismemberment, and the obvious similarities should have put his home county in an expended Delta district. Not surprisingly, logic played no part in the redistricting.

It was decided, after a number of conferences among Citizens Council leaders and Barnett's legislative henchmen, that the simplest plan that could be sold to the legislature and at the same time ensure my defeat was a straight combination of the Second and Third Districts. This had the beauty of guaranteeing the support of the other Mississippi congressmen; it left them home free with their districts intact. On the surface, it was made to look like an advantage to the Delta because of the large difference in population between the two districts. Voters, not people, are what count in an election, however. The average total primary vote in the Second District was 10,000 more than in the Third. The Second District contained a number of part-Delta counties, but most of it was in the hills, where the white population far exceeded the Negro. And always in the background was that determined, if minority, opposition to me in the Delta.

The new district established by the legislature covered 24 counties and a population of 608,000. Thirteen of the counties were from Whitten's old district and eleven from mine. It was approximately twice as big as two of the four remaining districts in the state. It was the largest district ever newly created by a state legislature.

Before this plan passed the legislature, Walter Sillers made a token speech against it, but his tacit support had already been announced. Even in his so-called opposition speech he made it clear that he would support Whitten in the coming vote. The legislature did not complete the redistricting until the end of March, with the primary due in early June, but the campaigning had been going on, one way or another, since 1952. Whitten had accomplished most of the effective work in those ten years. Most of my time had necessarily been concentrated on staying ahead in the Delta.

One example of Whitten's precampaign tactics is worth mentioning. Jim Silver, the professor of history at Ole Miss who gained national attention in 1963 as one of the few speaking out against Mississippi's "closed" society, had been a target of the right-wing extremists in the state for more than twenty years. We have been good friends since I first knew him at Ole Miss in 1940. Despite Jim's readiness to speak out on controversial issues, he has always been an influential citizen of Oxford, in Whitten's old district. In 1954–55, Jim's son Billy was a senior in high school and wanted to be a congressional page. I had never appointed pages, preferring patronage assignments helpful to boys working their way through college, so I could be of no help to the Silvers. They applied to Whitten, who had a well-known system of rotating pageships every month.

Shortly before the new session started in January 1955, Jamie called to tell me that he would appoint Billy Silver as a page for the month of January if I could help him overcome any problems about the appointment in Oxford. "You know Jim is pretty controversial in Oxford," Whitten said. "If any questions come up about the appointment at Oxford, I need to be able to tell the people that you appointed Billy. If anybody asks any questions about it in the Delta, you can tell them I did it."

I agreed, glad to help Billy become a page. During the

congressional recess that year, I learned that Whitten's friends had passed the word all over the Delta that my congressional page was the son of that integrationist professor at Ole Miss.

Probably the most disheartening incident of the campaign occurred in 1962, before the legislature acted. For five or six years the Delta Council, with my help, had been trying to work out a training program for tractor drivers. It was envisioned as part of the state vocational education program, and it was the most important technical training Negroes in the Delta could use. Operating the mechanical equipment on cotton plantations is literally the only semiskilled job open to Delta Negroes. Tractor drivers as a whole are known to be notoriously unskilled, causing millions of dollars' damage to equipment each year from sheer lack of training in how to use it. The opportunity for improved skills like this, which would benefit both the tractor driver and his employer, had been one of the reasons I supported the area redevelopment program, with its job training provisions.

Under the sponsorship of the Delta Council, the Mississippi Department of Education and the state Agricultural and Industrial Board, both controlled by Governor Barnett, worked out a crash program of tractor driver training to be handled by state agencies but financed by the Area Redevelopment Administration. The tractor drivers would be paid during their training period by the ARA. The program would cost more than a million dollars and was the most ambitious approved by the ARA up to that time.

When the program was approved in Washington, I issued a statement announcing it, carefully pointing out the local sponsorship and the economic advancement it would bring the Delta. The announcement story in the *Commercial Appeal*, however, was built around a statement by Representative Whitten attacking the program as a weapon of the CIO, the NAACP, and Secretary Goldberg in an attempt to take control of Delta plantations. Some of the chief Whitten supporters in the Delta began a telephone campaign among farmers about this plot to "unionize" their labor. The state Farm Bureau's Delta organizer, in the process of transferring to Whitten's payroll, organized a protest meeting at Cleveland. The Delta Council backed away from the plan, and the most ambitious single effort in the entire country to upgrade Negro workers was allowed to die by default.

From the 1960 election on, it was fairly clear that Whitten would label me "the Kennedy candidate" and that I would label him "the Barnett candidate." Since the association was to be used against me, I set out to pick up whatever benefit could be gained from my support of the President. The four Mississippi congressmen who had fought the election of Kennedy and Johnson had been denied post office patronage, and the appointments in Whitten's district were turned over to me. Some of these appointments proved really helpful; others were of no help whatever. I tried to take advantage of my position as the only member from Mississippi supporting the administration by promoting projects that might have political benefit in the new district. President Kennedy gave some specific instructions in this regard, and the projects were moved along, but at the critical stage—announcement of their approval—Whitten was often notified even earlier than I was. I discovered the truth in the age-old congressional adage that a member of the Appropriations Committee is more important to many bureaucrats than the President or the secretary of any particular agency. As an example, I was the only member from Mississippi who supported the 1961 Housing Act. For months I worked on a college housing application for Ole Miss. It was finally approved in 1962. Whitten was given the announcement and its attendant publicity.

The Whitten-Smith campaign started out with no openly clear-cut issues. By the Whitten definition, it was a fight between a conservative and a liberal, and an attempt by the Kennedys to purge a conservative who was a bulwark against their plans to establish a dictatorship. In another vein, it was a fight between internationalism as typified by my record and Americanism as typified by his. Good Mississippi conservatism was the only thing that could save the country from self-destruction, and only his re-election would ensure the strength of that conservatism.

My own approach was to ask the people of the district to reject provincialism, to help put Mississippi into the mainstream of American political life. One man whom I ran into in the course of a handshaking tour put it succinctly: "Whitten is against the United States, you are for it."

In more practical terms, I pointed out the advantages in having a congressman who was a friend of the President of the United States. I discussed my achievements in behalf of the Delta, and explained why they could not have been accomplished had I, like Whitten, been an obstructionist in Congress, and I promised to achieve more in behalf of the new district. I appealed to the small farmers and the working people of the new area by demonstrating how a real Democrat would be of more benefit to them. I tried to convince the segregationists that I could be more effective in preventing integration than the Whittens and the Barnetts, but I could not promise them that they would win, and that was what they wanted; it was, apparently, all they wanted.

As I have mentioned earlier, the campaign was fantastically expensive. I had decided at the outset to avoid putting myself in debt again in the face of a losing cause. Inevitably, at the height of the campaign, commitments were made that did not show up until long after it was over, and in the end I became one of my major contributors. Good friends were overwhelmingly generous, however, and met the basic campaign obligations. One of the opposition tactics was the direct assertion that my campaign expenses were being underwritten by the Kennedy family fortune, occasionally referred to as mysterious Northern money. We tried hard to get unobligated contributions from inside and outside the state, but the money simply wasn't there. I made no attempt to assess the sources of Whitten's funds, but it would have been politically naïve to suppose that a man who controlled an annual appropriation of seven billion dollars for the Department of Agriculture would have trouble finding willing contributors. As the campaign developed, the reports of the alleged Kennedy contribution to my campaign ranged all the way up to a million dollars. Many of our friends began to think it must be true, and some of them were naturally reluctant to put in their own money when so much was available. To set the record straight, I received $2,000 from President Kennedy. My campaign cost more than $60,000.

Whitten's chairmanship of the Agriculture Appropriations Subcommittee, with all the influence on agricultural policy which this implied, was simply unexplainable to the people of the district. Here was a man who had fought the President and the Democrats in Congress, yet they gave him a job in the Congress that he painted as the most important a Mississippian could have. It was easy to see why they believed Whitten's version—that the Northern Democrats either were afraid to touch him or secretly agreed with his position. Tolerance of party disloyalty by the congressional leadership makes untenable the position of a loyal member in the same state.

Campaign tactics in 1962 were necessarily different from those in 1950. I had the advantage of being only twelve years from a campaign, while Whitten had never had one, but it didn't pay off after the Whitten people learned they were in trouble. Even in the sixty-day campaign that we had, the opposition was able to organize and strike out all the weaknesses in their otherwise strong points. In the first days of working over the old Whitten district, I was highly encouraged. In more than half the counties I uncovered people who promised strong support for wide varieties of reasons—they regarded themselves as loyal Democrats, they had grievances against Whitten or Barnett, they thought I could help them get a federal job or that I could work out some beneficial federal program for their county or community. More and more, I found people who said they were tired of politicians who talked nothing but race as the reason for votes.

I spent the first three weeks of the campaign almost entirely in Whitten's old district, calling on the influential people we believed might come over to our side. The first reactions seemed good in at least half the counties. Apparently a lot of people were interested in supporting me, and others were keeping the door open to see how the campaign developed. A candidate can look at any picture and uncover signs favorable to him, and I was finding them. Had I looked a little deeper, I could have seen the favorable reaction being choked off. For instance, I had done some special work with one of the veterans' groups to improve the operation of the state VA hospital, and had established a fine relationship with one of the leaders. He agreed to take over organization of veterans' groups in half a dozen counties. We had several meetings to get things under way, and then he didn't show up any more. A few days before the primary we learned that his employer in Jackson had told him to stay away from Frank Smith.

Whitten's campaign opened on a dual theme and stayed that way throughout—an attack on my voting record and my support of the Democratic party and the President, and emphasis on the importance of his assignment by the Democrats as chairman of the House Agricultural Appropriations Subcommittee. He said Mississippi had made progress "despite national policies and not because of them." At the same time, he was careful to explain that his Appropriations Subcommittee supplied the funds to pay for price support programs and other aspects of federal assistance to agriculture. After this explanation, he would wind up his description of his powers as a member of Congress by saying, "As a member of the Appropriations Committee and as chairman of its subcommittee on Agriculture, I firmly believe this is the most powerful weapon we have against measures that are contrary to our beliefs and our way of life here in Mississippi." Apparently, nobody ever asked for any elucidation.

The voting record attack was entirely generalized during the first month of his talks. Taking his figures from a Congressional Quarterly table, he said, "During the 86th Congress I have voted with a majority of Southerners 25 out of 26 times, while Smith has gone along with the Southerners only 14 out of 25 times."

In my newspaper releases for the next few days I demanded details about the bills instead of numbers. The only specific he ever got down to was a daily attack on foreign aid, which he castigated as costing a lot of money and as being responsible for Cuba, integration, the United Nations, the Congo, and most other national ailments. He favored withdrawal from the UN, stopping all foreign aid, and reduction of military expenditures. Eventually, the answer came to my

demand for specifics about the voting record. The opening
gun was fired in a full-page advertisement in the Greenwood
Commonwealth, signed by "Leflore County Friends of Jamie
Whitten," who invited you "if you are interested in preserving
the MISSISSIPPI WAY OF LIFE" to write them in care of
General Delivery. The ad was addressed to the "73% of the
Leflore County voters in 1960 who voted for candidates other
than John F. Kennedy." (The biggest portion had voted for
the unpledged electors.) It read:

> We are now faced with a clear-cut choice between a Con-
> gressman who truly represents Mississippi, Jamie Whitten;
> and Frank Smith, a supporter of the New Frontier, who was
> the *only* Mississippi Congressman to vote for such Kennedy
> Administration measures as:
>> Foreign Aid
>> Special UN Appropriation (including Congo operation)
>> Increase Debt Ceiling
>> Peace Corps
>> Travel and Tourism

A week or so later, the whole district was flooded with
newspaper ads and circulars headed "How Does Your Congressman Vote?" It listed the last four items and showed how
the other five Mississippi House members had voted against
each bill while I voted for them. "Information" about each
bill was offered. Representative James Harvey of Michigan
was quoted on the evils of foreign aid. Representative August
E. Johansen was quoted on the Peace Corps, which he described as an effort to socialize missionary movements, as the
bureaucrat's dream, taxpayer's nightmare, and an ideal target
for penetration and infiltration by members of the communist
conspiracy. The UN appropriation was described as a means
of financing many of the communist activities around the
world. The travel and tourism bill, which established American policy to encourage foreign travel to the United States,

was described as "this bill put the Federal Government in direct competition with private owned airlines, steamship companies, travel agencies and others in the field of tourism." The debt ceiling increase was described as intended to lower the purchasing power of your dollar and increase taxes in later years.

Another Whitten advertisement stated, "Senator James O. Eastland and Rep. Jamie L. Whitten, both of Mississippi, are among the twelve most important men in Congress." The other ten who made this exclusive list were Senators Ellender of Louisiana, Holland of Florida, Aiken of Vermont, Hickenlooper of Iowa, and Talmadge of Georgia; and Representatives Cooley of North Carolina, Belcher of Oklahoma, Beerman of Nebraska, Hoeven of Iowa, and Poage of Texas. Other ads totaled up the various millions in appropriations which Whitten claimed he had brought to Mississippi while saving the country from bankruptcy.

Some of the members of the Kent Courtney branch of the John Birch Society distributed a voting record comparison based on a tabulation put out by Courtney's *Independent American*, published in New Orleans. By coincidence, one of the so-called socialistic subversive bills listed by Courtney was the agriculture appropriation bill of which Whitten was the author.

The advertising turned repeatedly to the race theme, however. The worst racial attacks were unsigned handbills printed by the same firm which turned out large orders for the Citizens Council. Quotations from some of them are worth repeating for the general flavor:

YOUNG NEGRO STUDENT IS FIRST
GREENVILLIAN IN PEACE CORPS

Walter Lewis, Jr., 22-year-old Negro, is the first Greenvillian to be accepted for service in the U.S. Peace Corps.

. . . Lewis is the son of Mrs. and Mrs. Walter Lewis, Sr., 446 N. Ninth. A native of Greenville, he is a graduate of Sacred Heart High School.

The above appeared on the front (first) page of Hodding Carter's Greenville *Democrat-Times*, Sunday, May 13, 1962.

It is difficult to subdue the suspicion that the prominence given this story was because in Greenville there are a great many negro voters and no appointment in the District is likely to be made without the approval of Frank Smith—in other words, a subtle try for the negro vote.

Frank Smith was the *only* Mississippi Congressman to vote *for* the Peace Corps Bill. Jamie Whitten is *against* the Peace Corps.

KEEP JAMIE WHITTEN IN CONGRESS

The Peace Corps ad must have been considered very effective, because it was used repeatedly, at least four or five times in my home-town *Commonwealth*. For non-Mississippians, it should be pointed out that the reason the newspaper story was reproduced in full in the advertisement was to call attention to the reference to the parents of the trainee as "Mr. and Mrs." As far as I know, no other Mississippi daily newspaper accords Negroes this courtesy title.

An advertisement widely reprinted as a circular consisted of an editorial from a magazine called *Mississippi Farmer*. This publication had offered us an editorial if we would buy an expensive page advertisement, but I couldn't afford it. Their editorial in favor of Whitten read in part:

Smith has the "honor" of being the only Mississippi congressman to consistently back the socialistic programs put forth by the New Frontier. This candidate is supposedly close to the men surrounding the President. If Kennedy had chosen upright men to help him this would be a real talking point—but look at the record.

Surrounding Kennedy are the lowest scum of this nation's socialists, fellow travelers, pinkos, and pro-communists that could possibly be found—men who have devoted their lives to fighting this country.

Two of my newspaper editorialist opponents started their attacks by describing me as a "fat slob," but most of them were content to skip the personalities and concentrate on painting me as an integrator and tool of the socialists and Communists. A lady editor at Ripley, where the Citizens Council was not too popular, and in a county which had voted Democratic in 1960, unloaded as follows:

> . . . Jamie Whitten has never left the ranks of the Democratic party, because he is what we know as a REAL Democrat, but he was USED as a tool of the very organization which was originated at Greenwood to help keep out intergration [sic], to give his own seat in the Congress to Frank Smith, a tool of the Kennedy administration, in order to help foster communism and socialism in the South. We happen to know that money is and has been moving South, but it will be used to help foster the belief in mankind, rather than to use the uneducated white person and the negro as a tool to secure votes, to turn America over to the Communists.

The Jackson *Clarion-Ledger* was a self-proclaimed neutral in the campaign, and columnist Tom Ethridge undertook to prove this neutralism by "surveying" the journalistic viewpoints of the contest. As Smith supporters he cited Hodding Carter and Hazel Brannon Smith, two of the reddest flags that could be waved at some 90 percent of the voters in the district.

Out in Texas, another campaign was going on. Will Wilson, the attorney general, was running a losing race for governor, and attempted to give it life by establishing a court of inquiry into the affairs of financier Billie Sol Estes. One of the witnesses was a Texas lawyer named Frank Cain, who represented one of the lending firms suing Estes after his indictment by a federal grand jury. Cain testified that Estes told him it would take between $100,000 and $200,000 a year in payoff to keep up his contacts for his agricultural program. To quote the Associated Press:

> Cain told the court of inquiry that Estes made the statement after receiving a telephone call from a man identified as Jamie Whitten.
>
> There was no further identification of Whitten although Cain quoted Estes as saying, "He really gets the job done on appropriations and agricultural programs."
>
> Cain further quoted Estes, "We've got this agricultural program wrapped up. It's a fortune. We've got such control that if they elected conservatives for every year it will take eight years to get us out."
>
> After Estes received the telephone call from the man identified as Whitten, Cain said he asked, "That was the pay-off, wasn't it?"
>
> He said that Estes agreed, and said, "I've got to retain my methods and ways if I am going to work things out."

Whitten at first denied any connection with Estes, but had to change his story after friends in Texas sent me a copy of a letter Estes had written him addressed "Dear Jamie" and a copy of a photograph printed in Estes's newspaper showing Whitten attending a dinner in Washington with Estes. The former clerk of Whitten's appropriation subcommittee was fired from the Department of Agriculture because of his connection with Estes, and Representative H. Carl Anderson, a veteran Minnesota Republican, was defeated in his primary largely because of his connections with Estes, but the issue was of very little benefit to me. Attorney General Wilson closed his court of inquiry after he lost out in the Texas primary, and nothing further than the Cain testimony developed. My only other source of information was a bitter local opponent of Estes, who couldn't break into locked records, even though there were authentic tips from people who had seen things now locked up. Whitten charged that I was using information fabricated by the Kennedys, but my Texas informant was actually a rabid Republican.

Anywhere else, with aggressive metropolitan newspapers to work on the story, Whitten's associations with Estes would have become a temporary sensation and a major factor in the congressional race. In Mississippi, Whitten convinced most of his supporters that Estes and I must have been fairly close ourselves, because we both supported Kennedy in 1960. I had never seen or heard of Estes before the Cain testimony was reported by the AP, but before the campaign ended Whitten was referring to me as the friend of Billie Sol Estes and Bobby Kennedy. At the subsequent congressional investigations and trials, Estes took the Fifth Amendment, so there never has been any exploration of whatever connections he had with the House Subcommittee on Agricultural Appropriations.

As my campaign developed in the eroded hill counties of the old Second District, my ideas of what could be accomplished if I won the election grew daily. Coordinated flood control and soil conservation programs, which we had started in the Watershed Development Subcommittee, would offer something for practically all of them. Recreational development on the Corps of Engineers reservoirs had only been touched. There was great need for industrial plants of the type which could be assisted by the ARA. Virtually every town and county could use community facilities under the pending Accelerated Public Works program. The new district was actually the poorest in the United States, with a mean income well below that of the worst regions of Appalachia. Several of the new counties had an average income per household more than a thousand dollars below average family income in the poorer counties of West Virginia. There would be a lot to keep me busy.

In the meantime, there were campaign speeches and daily headlines that had to be supplied from news releases. Some of our supporters cried out for harder-hitting attacks, and others decided that personal attacks did no good and shouldn't be used. The main effort each day was to get a good story in the *Commercial Appeal*. Outside the aegis of its Washington correspondent, I was getting reasonable coverage in the *Commercial*, which reached 90 percent of the voters, although it published only pro-Whitten letters to the editor. On the Saturday before the primary, the *Commercial Appeal* carried my statement that a victory for Whitten would "represent another triumph for the empty bombast of the Ross Barnett leadership in our state. Mississippi deserves a better face to the nation than this, and I believe the voters of the new district will demand it. . . . we have a district of patriotic and intelligent people who are not being fooled by the 'know-nothing, against everything' philosophy expressed by my opponent. The new second district is going to lead Mississippi ahead toward a new day of honest politics, striving to give our great state her rightful place on the national scene."

The Whitten speeches were all opened up with a choice little political ballad, written by his campaign manager, Sale Lilly, superintendent of schools at Charleston and a lay leader in the Methodist Church. The major rallies heard the song sung in person by the daughter of the Tallahatchie County state representative, and a sound-truck recording had to suffice for the whistle stops. The song went like this:

> Skunks in the stump holes,
> monkeys in the trees,
> Frank's crawled in bed with
> the Kennedys.

> Frank has Kennedys and their
>   money, too,
> But Jamie's good for me and
>   he's good for you.
> Jamie's got the ball, and he's
>   on the team,
> Let's run up the score on
>   the Kennedy machine!

The title of the epic was "How's Jamie Doin'." There were endless verses, but I was fortunate enough never to have to listen to any of them, exempted from at least some burdens of the campaign.

There are a few more excerpts from Whitten speeches worth reporting, for the benefit of both historians and future candidates for Congress:

> It was not merely the South which lost the Civil War, it was the Nation. It has taken a 100 years for us to fully see that might, when taken to be right, can destroy a Nation.

> Frank is desperately trying to keep the people from deciding on the basis of my 21 years' service compared to his 12; my key position on appropriations against his on authorizations, and our differences on the foreign aid giveaway and the United Nations. . . . The basic issue is Jamie Whitten's Southern conservatism, seniority and committee assignments versus Frank Smith's brand of one-world liberalism.

> Each day I become more and more proud to be a Mississippian with a true Mississippi viewpoint, believing in the right to work, in the right of management to run its own affairs so as to prosper and hire more and more Mississippi people.

> It is becoming more obvious every day that we are up against a big-money crowd in this election. In all the history of this state, there has never been a more concerted cam-

paign of political advertising than the one going on in Frank Smith's behalf right now.

Unfortunately, too many in Congress have reflected the views of the Hodding Carters, the Hazel Brannon Smiths and others among us right here in Mississippi who seem to feel that integration is inevitable and that our state must fall in line. It was Hazel Brannon Smith who wrote in an editorial that Frank "is closer to the Kennedy Administration because of his personal friendship with the president when the latter was a senator. . . . He is also an independent thinker who does not run with the mob—and in Mississippi that is an unpardonable sin."

I assume that "the mob" Mrs. Smith refers to is composed of Representatives Abernethy, Colmer, Williams, Winstead and myself, because it is against us, and the best interests in Mississippi, that Frank has voted so consistently. If this is the kind of "mob" Hazel Brannon Smith is talking about, then I'm proud to run with it, and Frank is welcome to her support.

Anyone who reads the Greenville newspaper knows where Hodding Carter stands. He has used his pen of vitriol to support the theory of integration and promote the policies of the enemies of the South. Frank is also welcome to backing such as this.

Despite the full onslaught of the attack, the outlook was surprisingly good up to two weeks before the balloting. The inroads into the hills were holding up, and a few of the fence-sitters were actually beginning to believe I could win. Unfortunately, the Whitten people began to get the same idea. A massive drive by Citizens Council telephone calls, mailing lists, and strategy meetings began to whip up new stories. An example—the sudden revelation that in return for the Kennedy millions I had promised to put a Negro in each post office in the district before the end of the year! The most effective weapon in this last-minute arsenal, however, was the ancient distrust of the Delta by the people of the red-clay hills. Although every element of the Delta that lay behind the traditional hostility of the hillmen was opposed to me, the fact remained that I was a Delta man. Walter Sillers and the group he headed—against me themselves in the Delta—were the people in state government who denied hill folks the programs they considered the answer to their needs as small farmers and poor men. The manager of the British-owned Delta Land and Pine Company, the 27,000-acre cotton plantation in Bolivar County, was active with Sillers in trying to defeat me in that county, but in the hills the word went out "we can't have a congressman who will only be interested in the Delta planters." The hill folk were told also that they had to get out the vote to overcome the thousands of Negroes in the Delta.

An added complication was the presence of a third candidate in the race, the Reverend Merrill Lindsey of Holly Springs. Lindsey was a Negro minister who was sponsored by the NAACP in an effort to persuade more Negroes to vote. Perhaps his presence on the ballot restrained some of the attacks on me as the "NAACP candidate," but it was small comfort to know that he might pull away votes that could be critically important if the outcome were close enough. The night before election, Lindsey took to television. I didn't get to hear it, but some of my friends said it was mighty good. "Mr. Smith and Mr. Whitten are knifing each other," Lindsey commented, "but they are using me for a whetstone."

The voting on June 5 gave Whitten 34,000 to my 21,000, and Lindsey received less than 2,000. I didn't make a respectable showing in any of the hill counties, and in half of them I received less than 10 percent of the vote. Whitten carried two of my old counties. I was proud of the fact that we had fought the Citizens Council crowd almost to a draw in their stronghold of Holmes, which I lost by only sixteen votes, but I was disturbed by the heavy loss of Quitman County, which contained a higher percentage of small white farmers than any other county in the Delta. I led narrowly in Bolivar and Coahoma Counties, where most of the local political pros had lined up with Sillers behind Whitten.

My best margin was in Washington County, which I led 5,197 to 976 for Whitten and 447 for Lindsey. There was no record of how many of the 1,762 Negroes registered in the county actually voted, but on the assumption that at least half did vote, I had outpolled Lindsey among them. My home county of Leflore gave me a margin of 3,322 to 1,109, a considerably smaller percentage than the better than 5 to 1 in Washington County. These were the only two counties which provided important margins, although my percentage was very good in Sharkey and Issaquena, two small counties at the south of the district. The estimates of my opponents before and after redistricting had proved true. Despite the opposition of another member of Congress, I had carried the old Delta district by a fair margin, making it clear that my vocal opposition through the years would not have been successful in opposing me. The architects of the 1962 redistricting had counted on the hill counties staying solidly with Whitten to my certain defeat, and they were right.

The redistricting and the vote which followed contain a lesson for future Delta politicians. They have nothing to gain in state and district politics by barring the Negro vote. In the purely political power struggles within the state, the Delta has no weapon commensurate with its population or its wealth. Before many years pass, this will be recognized as a burden too heavy to carry, and the local politicians will have to take the lead in advancing Negro voting if they are to increase the power of their communities in state affairs.

Any political defeat is bitter, and mine was no exception.

The hardest thing to take was the shattered hope of the friends who had shared my belief that a state political leadership built around hate, know-nothingism, and brazen power could be beaten.

Whitten said his victory marked the beginning of a conservative resurgence all over America. Ross Barnett announced, "Constitutional government still prevails. If Smith had won the newspapers would have come out with banner headlines 'Ross Barnett Repudiated.' I bet they don't say anything about me in connection with it now." *The New York Times* could understandably comment, "The outcome of the election indicated that the ultra-conservatives and the militant white-supremacists still hold considerable power." The London *Times* said the vote demonstrated that the electorate believed "the United Nations seems now to be nothing more than a tool of the Afro-Asian bloc, which is in turn seen as being manipulated by the Soviet Union."

The election didn't cause much of a flurry on the national scene, but I was very much pleased by a comment from Edward P. Morgan, "He was a breath of fresh air out of a political swamp." Tris Coffin said what I had been wanting to say and couldn't: "I don't suppose any Southern politician, even Leander Perez, really thinks that integration is going to be stopped or even slowed. There is a kind of desperation that sets in in many areas of the South, at the prospect of the enormous changes ahead. Mississippi . . . needs badly . . . statesmen who can make this change less painful, and win understanding in Washington. Frank Smith would have been worth his weight in gold. The old time Southern politicians—the kind who don't have too much trouble getting re-elected—are a dime a dozen in Washington, and are pointed out as curiosities by tourist guides. They are not taken very seriously. Frank Smith was."

Chapter XVII

NEVER!

The tragic horror of the night of September 30, 1962, on the University of Mississippi campus at Oxford was widely reported and is still being researched and written about. I hope that the future finds it the high water-mark of violent resistance to racial change in Mississippi. If this armed resistance to the military and legal forces of the federal government is exceeded in the future, the accompanying violence can serve no purpose but to compound the evidence against the state. Oxford saw the harvest of the seeds of hate and nihilism, carefully planted and tended for years by Mississippi's bankrupt leadership. The shout of "Never!" that the governor inspired on the Ole Miss campus was more than a shout; it was the official—and popular—death knell of the optimistic hope that Mississippi would gradually give effect to the laws of our society, even though the gradualism might be prolonged and agonizing.

For several years responsible members of the Board of Trustees of the Institutions of Higher Learning, who oversee the four-year colleges in Mississippi, were aware that all the legal delays to the entrance of a Negro student at the university were near exhaustion. After James Meredith's application was filed and began its movement through the courts, the question was not whether the order for admission would come but only when, at midyear in early 1962 or at the beginning of the fall semester. For a while the debate was whether Ole Miss would close rather than admit a Negro student, but that talk faded into the background when word leaked out that only Governor Barnett's appointees to the board of trustees, who were less than a majority, could be expected to vote for closure. Acting under orders from the trustees, working closely with state legal officials, and with volunteer legal advice thrown in from every direction, the university officials fought the order of admission down to the last step. They were obligated to carry out the orders of the board of trustees and state law until they received overruling federal court orders, but they were not obligated to swear to the court that the university had no policy barring students on account of race. At the same time this bare-faced declaration was being sworn to by officials of a school charged with training the future leadership of the state, Governor Barnett was renewing his pledge—"No school will be integrated in Mississippi while I am your governor!" No legalism or technicality can justify the immorality of this line of defense, completely contrary to obvious truth.

Governor Barnett flung down the gauntlet in a statewide radio and TV address on the night of September 13.

The Citizens Council reprinted the talk under the title "Mississippi Still Says 'Never!' " In addition to repeating his pledge that no school would be integrated while he was governor, Barnett pulled all the stops in asking Mississippians to follow the patriots who died at Valley Forge, Shiloh and Vicksburg, the Argonne, Guadalcanal, and Korea. The implication was clear: it was a call to physical battle. The people were told that Mississippians "will never submit to the moral degradation, to the shame and the ruin which have faced all others who lacked the courage to defend their beliefs. . . . We will not drink from the cup of genocide!" The college freshmen and the allied motley mob who charged across the Ole Miss campus with rocks, bricks, bottles, and Molotov cocktails against U.S. marshals and U.S. troops believed that they were Mississippi's version of the Hungarian freedom fighters, worthy heirs to the men of Valley Forge, or at least of Manassas.

One of Barnett's legislative leaders told the newspapers, "There are some people who don't mind dying for an honorable cause." A state senator proclaimed, "We must win this fight regardless of the cost in time, money, and human lives." A broadside was distributed to Ole Miss students advising them not to use force and violence until called for by the governor, and admonishing, "Do not permit yourself to be intimidated by any leftist school administrator." The Jackson *Clarion-Ledger* carried a headline predicting a possible gun battle at Ole Miss, and the Jackson *Daily News* printed the words of the "Never, No Never Song," with advice to clip them for further use:

> Never, Never, Never, Never, No-o-o Never
>   Never Never
> We will not yield an inch of any field
> Fix us another toddy, ain't yieldin' to no-body

Ross's standin' like Gibralter, he shall never
    falter
Ask us what we say, it's to hell with Bobby K
Never shall our emblem go from Colonel Reb
    to Old Black Jo!

In Washington, I was serving out the remainder of my last session, avoiding publicity, closing out my office, and packing up in my residence. But Barnett's incitement to madness was something I could not ignore despite every inclination to leave Mississippi's battles to those she was keeping in office. All the other members of the Mississippi delegation joined in praising the Barnett defiance. I replied that "Governor Barnett would lead our state down a blind alley. He would destroy our great university. The issue of state versus federal power was settled one hundred years ago."

With one important exception, my comment had the value of a straw tossed into a cyclone. I've found no evidence that it led anyone to stop and think. The exception was the blast of hot reaction I got for questioning Barnett. Telegrams came by the dozen, and the mildest of the epithets was "Judas."

As the President moved toward the inevitable moment of having to carry out the court order for Meredith's admission, Mississippi's offices in Washington reflected the growing tensions at home. In my office, we threw away most of the telegrams and letters, answering only when the girls were not busy with the closing chores. My colleagues in the House sent several telegrams to President Kennedy, denouncing him for his announced intention to enforce the court order and at the same time begging him not to do it. I was receiving four or five phone calls a day from Mississippi suggesting various ways of bringing Barnett into line without letting him make a martyr of himself or provoke violence. I talked to President

Kennedy. The idea of economic penalities against Mississippi, suggested by many, had been explored and rejected. The President thought that the best advice he had from Mississippi was to take the case directly to Barnett. As he well knew, I was not a Barnett expert, and I could offer no knowledgeable advice as what the governor would do. In essence, all I could say was that there were Mississippians who understood he had to enforce the law, and that they hoped he could do it with the least possible damage to the state.

The reaction of many otherwise intelligent Mississippians was hard to fathom. Hugh Clegg, a special assistant to the university chancellor and a former FBI official, called me to ask that I pass along to the President and the Attorney General the threat that Ole Miss would have the Southern Association of Colleges and Schools on them for citing the university officials in a motion for contempt. On the Saturday night before the fateful Sunday, he called me again, asking that the President agree to some mediation with friends of the governor. There seemed to be no realization that the admission of Meredith was beyond negotiation. At that time the governor, in his new capacity as school registrar, was already making agreements with the Attorney General, but he never bothered to pass this information to his school officials. My colleagues from Mississippi were giving advice to the President by way of the public press but were carefully avoiding seeking out the President in person. Fighting for Mississippi in Washington didn't require carrying things that far.

Oxford came, and before the tear-gas and cordite smells had left the campus a massive campaign was under way to convince Mississippians that they were the innocent victims of a subversive attack by brutal tyrants in Washington, intent upon destroying Mississippi because it was the last bulwark of constitutional government. The campaign was labeled a program to tell the Mississippi story to the world, but it was actually intended to save Mississippians from the doubts about their leadership that arose in the stunned aftermath at Oxford. There was loud talk about a congressional investigation, but none has ever been made. A few more Mississippians had spoken up in shock and dismay in the first reaction to Oxford, but most of those who did felt the lash of the Citizens Council's attack against anyone who dissented. My mail and telegrams of denunciation increased, but for a week the problem was how to get some relief from the telephone at home. A great many people seemed to take great satisfaction in spending money for long-distance calls to tell me how they were living in a police state under the dictatorial control of the Kennedys, with my assistance. I hung up when the calls became querulous or abusive, but most of the callers would brave the Washington Gestapo and replace the call immediately. I was never able to develop a rational conversation with any of these callers. I probably should have preserved the letters and telegrams for some future psychologist or historian studying mass hysteria, but the cleanest thing at the moment seemed to be to throw them away.

But there were a few heartening signs. A good dozen Mississippians I had never heard of before took the trouble to write expressing agreement. There were also a few dozen letters from former Mississippians in other states, approving my stand and telling of their sadness over our state. Perhaps the significant point of these letters was that people in the frame of mind to write them had left the state.

Oxford was a tragedy; the strength of the resistance that rallied thereafter is terror personified. It would perhaps be comforting to believe that the people who formed into that large body of resisters were only the pawns of the Citizens Councils and Governor Barnett, and the countless other hate peddlers who had crossed their formative years. But it is not so. For the traditional leaders of opinion in the state and for the majority of their followers, the response to the shout of "Never!" by the Ole Miss students was a resounding cheer of agreement and encouragement. A state of mind so conditioned will never voluntarily accept the end of discrimination against Negroes in Mississippi. Their demand is "Never!" and to them any means justifies their ends.

Under such conditions, it is no longer possible for a Mississippian to pay even lip service to the ideal of "liberty and justice for all," for the Mississippian will not accept the fact that liberty and justice are guaranteed and underwritten by the federal power. The state has resisted so completely even the first token steps toward elimination of basic discriminations that only a higher governmental power can ensure that elimination. I had hoped, through the years, that the gradual elimination of the more rank injustices against the Mississippi Negro would make possible the full acceptance of his rights as a citizen when Mississippi reached a level of education and economic progress comparable with the rest of the nation. The universal reaction in Mississippi—that the right of a state to discriminate is more important than the individual citizen's right to protection in the due process of the law— made it clear that the state would never comply with any voluntary plan for gradual establishment of civil rights. The problem with Mississippi is not whether the powers of the federal government should be used, but whether the enforcement of these powers will be resisted by force.

In the calmer days before anyone but the provocateurs foresaw the uproar of Oxford, I had prepared a final newsletter to my constituents, bidding them farewell as a representative and mildly offering the first really constructive advice on the race issue that I had ever felt free to give in all the years in Washington. I prepared the text of the letter in July, but the congressional session delayed on through August and September, past the fateful Sunday night at Oxford. The session was really ending now, and I reviewed the letter again and decided not to change it:

> In this last letter to my constituents after nearly twelve years in Congress, I want to take this opportunity to express my thanks for the opportunity that has been mine during this period. The honor and privilege has made the entire period of service very rewarding.
>
> I have been fortunate enough to be asked to enter a new field of public service, as a director of the Tennessee Valley Authority, and the challenge is a very inspiring one. I believe firmly in our country's future, and hope I can continue to make a contribution to its progress.
>
> I believe also in the future of our great state. We have a great heritage, and we also have a great potential. Mississippi's potential cannot be realized, however, if our state shuts its eyes to the reality of the world in which we live. We cannot isolate ourselves from the rest of the United States any more than the United States can isolate itself from the world. Only as a part of the mainstream of American life will our state and its people realize the heritage that is rightfully theirs as Americans.
>
> Our racial problems are going to remain for years to come, but the most certain thing about them all is that any solutions or remedies based on hate will merely aggravate the problems instead of simplifying them. Unless areas of mutual cooperation between the races can be worked out, Mississippi faces an era of continued bitterness that offers nothing good for the future.
>
> My parting message to you, as your representative in Washington, is to ask all Mississippians to look forward, not backward. We have nothing to fear for our country or from our country if we do our share to keep it free.

The same abusive responses came to this statement, a great many from people who economized by writing on the margins of the newsletter. One constituent economized completely by simply scrawling in huge letters across the entire page: "RED!" The abusive notes, however, were no greater in number than the letters of appreciation for what was said. There were more people willing to agree with my thesis. More Mississippians were speaking up. At Oxford, two young Episcopalian priests had been active in the effort to quell the riot, and in the aftermath they spoke out against the effort to absolve Mississippi of the blame. Few other churchmen in the state felt free to join them, and few did. When the leadership of the Methodist Church failed to speak up for that church on the issue, a group of 28 young pastors attempted to fill the void themselves by presenting a statement in the *Mississippi Methodist Advocate* expressing support for a section of the Methodist Discipline which says Jesus "teaches that all men are brothers. He permits no discrimination because of race, color or creed." The 28 were all young men and all native Mississippians. I wrote each a letter, expressing my appreciation for their stand as Mississippians and as fellow Methodists. Too many of their replies were tragically alike:

It now appears that I am faced with the alternatives of either leaving this church or be left to face empty pews. For over three years we labored productively together, but when the crisis came the only thing they have been able to remember is my stand on the race issue. During the past three years I have turned down over a dozen "calls" to other churches; now that I may need such a call none is pending. Such is life. . . .

We did not feel fit to make such a statement (or to suffer its consequences!). But we have not had the leadership on the state level, unfortunately, to give us a clear sense of direction and purpose for these times.

> You cannot realize the atmosphere of hate. . . . I am writing this from the hospital room of my wife who is here on account of her nerves because of the threats and vilification that have been heaped upon us. . . . Your letter is a welcome relief from the Citizens Council trash I have received. . . .

> No doubt you realize, as many of us do, that such a stand is not taken too early, as many claim—but, if anything, possibly too late. . . .

The record of the white Protestant church in Mississippi has not been a proud one. The ministers through the years have been conditioned to preach a gospel that does not disturb the conscience of their members, and I am sure that this has not been good for those men who sincerely believed in their mission and in the professions of their religion. In the years before the Civil War, pastors were dismissed from their churches for not defending slavery, and in the years since they have been removed for not defending segregation. For many the point of no return in harmonizing religious belief with the strictures of the community has been alarmingly close. Those who have found, or are finding, a way to teach a message of Christian brotherhood and retain their place in the local structures are entitled to a great measure of credit. They have kept a few candles burning through the years, but, in contrast with other parts of the country or even of the South, it is surprising how few of the voices for racial justice in Mississippi have been from the church.

The Christian churches of Mississippi have not been the only transgressors. For many years one of the cultural assets of the city of Clarksdale was Rabbi Alexander Kline, who not only led his temple but was one of the town's most articulate devotees of literature and the arts. I never had a chance to know this gentle man very well, but a few words with him after civic club speeches were always a pleasure. Rabbi Kline moved on in 1962, and the Clarksdale Jewry, evidently tired of the burden of a literate leader, turned to New York City for his successor. They brought in Benjamin Schultz, who through the years had gained some occasional national publicity as head of an organization called the Jewish Anti-Communist League. Rabbi Schultz, like many another new Mississippian, became one of the loudest converts to the Mississippi way of life. He proclaimed:

> If Mississippi had its way, Castro would not be in Cuba now. Washington would not have installed him there.
>
> If Mississippi had prevailed, the Berlin Wall would have been torn down as soon as it went up. But then, the Russians would not have been there in the first place.
>
> If Mississippi had prevailed, pro-Communists would be off American college faculties. Corruption of our youth would stop.
>
> If Mississippi with its States' Rights philosophy had its way, big government, provocative dictatorship and eventual national bankruptcy would be thrown out the window.
>
> If Mississippi had its way, "red-baiter" would not be a dirty word. Traditional patriotism would sweep the land to strengthen our people inwardly, and insure victory in the international crisis. As it is, America is losing, mostly because of decay among its own intellectuals.

With the added help of theologians like Rabbi Schultz, the Citizens Councils stepped up activity in the religious field. Bill Simmons's publication *The Citizen* provided religious doctrine as freely as political, and the council network to ferret out pastors who were weak on segregation was actively aided by a group of laymen's leagues established in the various denominations. One result was that six months after the declaration by the young Methodist pastors mentioned above, at least half had left the state or had been shifted into other churches.

In the state primaries of 1963 the few voices of moderation who had spoken up in the previous four years were eliminated, or prudently did not seek re-election. The entire tone of the campaign stepped up the intensity of hate against any position of moderation. The Republicans made a campaign for the governorship for the first time within the century. The Republican candidate ran as the chief supporter of Senator Goldwater within the state, and with a campaign motto of "K.O. the Kennedys!" yet most of the racial moderates voted for him in preference to the Democratic nominee as the lesser of the evils.

No matter what the real feelings, in all the years since World War II the official Southern syndrome in race matters has been, "Give us time to make progress in our own way." The congressmen who opposed "progress" for the Negro was as ruthlessly isolated by his fellow Southern members as one who spoke up for civil rights would have been suppressed by his constituents. Most Southern intellectuals who addressed the outside world used the same argument in varying degrees. Among those who saw beyond the shame of congressional resistance to civil rights, there were varying opinions as to the value of federal enforcement of civil rights laws and there were varying estimates of the time schedules, but none of us doubted that the South itself would eventually end segregation. What we did not see was the degree of inflamed opposition to any change that would develop behind the coldly efficient combination of state government and the far-flung apparatus of the Citizens Councils and its allies. The white people of Mississippi, speaking through both their officials and the mob at Oxford, not only opposed the admission of James Meredith as a student; they signaled their defiant opposition to segregation's ever being breached. "Never!" was the battle cry, and the conviction was firmly growing among the people who shouted the word that such tactics would make it possible for Mississippi to write her own ticket, no matter what the law or the practice was for all the other states of the Union. In different words, what were rights for American citizens in other states were not necessarily rights in Mississippi.

The Mississippi Advisory Committee to the United States Commission on Civil Rights has been composed of brave men and women. Only those willing to face physical threats and economic and social pressure could even contemplate serving on it. To add to the very real threats the group faced in Mississippi, the members had to endure in 1963 the ordeal of having one of its reports completely misunderstood and misinterpreted by the rest of the country. In despair over the bitter reaction to Oxford which was settling over the state, the committee turned to a recommendation for federal power as the last possible resort for justice within Mississippi. "When a State disregards a large segment of its population, the Federal government is compelled to intervene in behalf of the victims," their official report stated. The major new weapon which they proposed was the denial of federal funds for programs which involved continuing discrimination or otherwise abetted racial injustice. The recommendation was badly reported and widely misunderstood. The idea was spread that the committee had urged a flat embargo on all federal funds into Mississippi. This embargo idea had been proposed to me privately by a great many Mississippians as a way of dealing with the intransigence of Governor Barnett, but that was not what the Mississippi Civil Rights Advisory Committee had proposed. The committee asked for the denial of funds to programs operated on an entirely segregated basis.

Regardless of the actual request, the misinterpretation brought howls of protest from over the country, not simply from Mississippi politicians. It also resulted in very little serious study being given the real recommendation.

No state in the Union has a greater stake in federal expenditures than does Mississippi. No state's taxpayers furnish as small a share of the federal expenditures in the state as do those of Mississippi. In 1962, federal tax collections in Mississippi were $270,793,000 of which $219,380,000 was income tax. During the same period, federal expenditures in the state amounted to $644,617,217. In plain language, this means that for every $3 paid by Mississippians to the federal government in taxes, the government spent $6.50 in Mississippi, and this total of expenditures does not include many programs impossible to allocate precisely by state. Despite its role as chief support for the economy of Mississippi, no institution is abused as much by Mississippians and Mississippi officials. For years, the myth has been prevalent in the state that the federal government takes dollars from the taxpayers and returns pennies. All federal programs are wasteful to Mississippians. Each January, the newspapers print a release from a state business group giving Mississippi's share of the cost of the federal budget, but nothing is ever said about what Mississippi receives from that budget. I tried to make the explanation from time to time, but these explanations rarely got any attention. What attention there was came from people who imagined that I was attempting to justify my "big spending" proclivities.

When a state so dependent on federal funds uses a good part of them for programs denied to Negro citizens, or denied on an equal basis, the natural reaction for those interested in eliminating these injustices is to make use of those funds. It is not unreasonable for non-Mississippi taxpayers, or Negro taxpayers in Mississippi, to question the use of their money to perpetuate practices of discrimination officially proscribed by federal law or regulation. In the years ahead, there may not be specific embargoes of funds for Mississippi, but there are likely to be fewer and fewer programs in which Mississippi can participate without the elimination of segregation. The laws may not be spelled out in direct relation to a Mississippi situation, but in more and more cases the action taken will have the same effect. This may precipitate new showdowns on state policy, but financial considerations will continue to receive top attention in Mississippi. One of the underlying factors in Mississippi's defiance has been the reassuring belief that Mississippi could count on the largess of the federal government to sustain her economy, and thereby, her resistance.

The assassination of President Kennedy shocked Mississippi, but the reaction of many Mississippians was even more sickening to the rest of us. There were meetings where the announcement of the tragedy was greeted by applause. There were jokes in the streets, and cheers. In one town, two businessmen started to raise a fund of appreciation for Lee Oswald. The most revealing action was found among the school children. Eight-year-olds reported to their parents with obvious pleasure, "That bad man is dead, and I'm glad, too."

Some people remembered that the *Rebel Underground*, an anonymous sheet distributed on the campus at Ole Miss during the agitated demonstrations against Meredith, had once flatly appealed for the assassination of the President. On the day of the assassination, the official student newspaper had printed a letter from a student containing the admonition that it was the duty of all good Ole Miss students to hate the President.

Official Mississippi now shows a different face. When

Paul B. Johnson, Jr., was inaugurated as Governor of Mississippi on January 21, 1964, these lines were in his inaugural address:

> Hate or prejudice or ignorance will not lead Mississippi while I sit in the governor's chair. . . .
>
> You and I are part of this world whether we like it or not. What happens in it, through no fault of ours, affects us. We are Americans as well as Mississippians. As a practical matter we are at this moment in the mainstream of national life.

The words were there, but only the months ahead will demonstrate whether Mississippi's present leaders have the courage and the capability—and the intention—to return her into the mainstream of American life.

Chapter XVIII

LOOK AWAY FROM

DIXIE

Oxford ended any justification there might have been for denial or delay of the full rights of citizenship for all Negroes, including those in Mississippi. The confrontation between state and nation made it clear that the nation must and will prevail. The awareness of Oxford was part of the reason for the Birmingham demonstrations, and Birmingham made inevitable the full-scale Negro revolution of 1963. The success of the Negro revolution is just as inevitable—it must prevail if the visions of 1776 and the American system of government are to survive. Mississippi has one last opportunity to save itself from destructive turmoil by recognizing the revolution for what it is and devoting its political structure to the conquest of the moral and economic dimensions still to be mastered for the betterment of all its people.

In this concluding chapter of the story of a politician's failure to bridge the gap between Mississippi and reality, I want to discuss the need for Mississippi to act, the need for all the South to act. The chances that Mississippians will concern themselves with this counsel are remote, but I have based an entire public career on the remote, the optimistic, chance. This chapter, then, is directed to Mississippi and Mississippians, because it is Mississippi that I know best. Mississippi stands in greater need of the audacity to act than any other state, but there are other states and communities where the need, if unmet, will be no less corrosive. The Negro revolution is by no means confined to the South, but this whole book is a story of the South and of Southerners and of their relationship to the world, and of the difficulties which Mississippi and the South face in learning to use their infinite resources to achieve a society worthy of their potential.

The entire structure of political, economic, religious, and social life in Mississippi has for ten years been devoted to the creation of immutable resistance to integration. Symbolically and in fact, Mississippi's misguided crusade was lost at Oxford on the night of September 30, 1962, no matter how many the months that pass and are charged against us before resistance crumbles. No state's twentieth-century insurrection has been as militant as Mississippi's, but no other state has poured so much of its wealth and talent and energy into the effort. There is no way to measure the cost; the most expensive items are not susceptible to measurement—the money that could have become investment in new economic development, the opportunity for industrial expansion irretrievably lost because of business concern about the stability of the state, the enormous dissipation of talent perverted into fomenting hate and justifying injustice, and the millions upon millions of man-hours wasted in responding to the alarums and delusions by which segregation is sustained.

In return for this incalculable investment, what has Mississippi achieved? The state has assured itself of two, perhaps three, perhaps four years' delay in the coming of integration. In a generation, a man's lifetime, how much is this? In the long measure of a century, in the lives of the future generations who are so much orated about, will it be noted that Mississippi was a few years behind the pace? If the white political and economic structures do not move together to reform and rechannel the passions they have brought to fever pitch, Mississippi will only be handicapped the more by a cancerous burden of hate and distrust in dealing with a future in which the Negro citizen is going to possess far more in the way of ability, training, and political power, and in which his rights are going to be given far better protection by the federal government and by state and local governments. Like anyone on the lower end of the economic ladder, the Negro will be subject to exploitation, but it won't be as easy. The leaders of the coming Negro generation will carry the ancient scars of slavery, but they have made their bid—to carry them as we carry the more ancient scars of serfdom, proudly, for having wrested from such a foundation the highest form of society man has yet attained, a society of law, with an ethic which dictates that each man sacrifice absolute freedom that all men may be held safe in a common freedom. It is not to our advantage that they be made to carry as well the spurs of more real and more recent grievances. It would be worthwhile to work out a system of accommodation with these people rather than to continue a conflict that they will wage from an increasingly greater base of power to an inevitable victory. The potential areas of accommodation may seem distasteful now, but they will be made no less unpalatable by unceasing strife.

The people of Mississippi have conjured up fearful hallucinations of what equality for the Negro will mean to the social, political, and economic order they have known. There has never been an opportunity to explain or explore what these changes would actually mean to the state and its people. The whole subject has been so fraught with passionate ignorance that calm discussion or analysis has been impossible. The substitution of fact for fantasy would make the import of the coming changes far more easily understood, and we do not often fear what we understand.

To get the most explosive myth out of the way, it is not likely to lead to any significant increase in miscegenation. Despite scare stories to the contrary, miscegenation is very infrequent in every part of the country. Even in the areas where it occurs often enough for the discerning eye to notice, it is a result of urban cultural patterns far removed from Mississippi for the present or for the visible future. The attraction that it might hold is far more likely to develop in the stress of the struggle for Negro rights than in a society that routinely respects them. The South has a long history of extralegal miscegenation, a patronizing custom it will have to forego if it is effectively to achieve the individual and collective dignity for which we strive and to which we give voice in the creed we have worded justice for all.

The integration of schools in Mississippi will come very rapidly in the years immediately ahead; it will seem more rapid in Mississippi than elsewhere because in Mississippi not even a token start has been made. It will come, if it must, with court injunctions, police massed to avoid physical violence, and the loss of valuable school time to both white and Negro students. If we are to judge by the present climate in Mississippi and by experience in other states where conditions were similar, this is the way it will be. But far more orderly plans for integration on a peaceful basis, without a lifetime of scars for the children concerned, could be worked out. Mississippi allots large sums to the maintenance of two school systems. If those systems are combined with the same level of expenditure, better facilities, higher-quality teaching, and broader courses of instruction will be available for all. I am not an educator and I would not presume to lay down here the detailed procedures by which this should be achieved, but the possibilities are numerous. If, as the state says, the Negro teachers do not have the qualifications of their white colleagues, the state will have to underwrite the additional training that will give them those qualifications, and quickly. There is genuine disparity between the level of attainment in upper grades, but we could begin to overcome this now by some variation of the shared-time program, putting Negro students with potential aptitude into integrated classes on certain subjects while building up their fund of knowledge in other subjects, with a view to an ultimately normally integrated pattern. The means exist; they need only be selected and employed.

The Negro has been an underlying issue in Mississippi politics since 1845, and he has been the dominant issue throughout the lifetime of present-day Mississippians. In the past few years, he has become the only issue, with top prizes going to those who shout against him the loudest and demonstrate the most convincing hatred for his friends in national politics. If you set aside the racial characteristics, the quality of government in Mississippi is inferior to that in most of the states of the Union and in most of the states of the South. The level of public morality and ethics would win no prizes anywhere, and most Mississippians realize this in the moments when the red flag of racism is not obscuring their vision. If the race issue were eliminated, political candidates would have to stand on their own merit, and the electorate would have the opportunity to discriminate between qualified and inferior office seekers, to judge issues for what they are rather than for their relationship to race. As long as the Negro remains a major issue in state politics, there will be a natural and understandable policy on the part of those Negroes who do vote to cast their ballots for the candidate they consider at least the lesser of the evils. Only by removing race from politics will bloc voting be ended. The Negro is more interested in a sheriff who will give him the law's protection and a mayor who will pave his street than he is in anything else connected with his ballot, just as is the white man in a similar circumstance. It is the most responsible element in the Negro community who wants the vote the most, and the use of it will broaden the base of responsible Negro citizenship. The one way to be sure that responsible Negro citizens will vote with intelligent self-interest is to wipe out any suggestion that they have no community of interest with responsible white citizens.

American citizens in other parts of the country can comprehend, and sometimes sympathize with, every aspect of Southern discrimination against Negroes except the denial of the ballot. Future civil rights legislation will almost certainly be directed at elimination of the weak points in the present law which handicap the federal government in helping Negroes secure the right to vote. Since Mississippi has maintained the strongest bars to Negro voting, these future laws are likely to be designed specifically to meet the Mississippi challenge. In other words, federal power is more certain to break the barriers in Mississippi than anywhere else. Once again, why cannot this power be anticipated, and the Negro vote made a contribution to the community, so that the ballot will not be regarded by both races as a weapon of deprivation on the one hand and of retribution on the other?

The literacy test used by Mississippi to determine eligibility for voter registration will be outlawed, both because of the severity of the test and because of the way in which it is applied. Some registrars, seeking to prove the "equal severity" of the registration test, have gone so far as to disqualify registration applications submitted by white citizens who were graduates of the state's major colleges. Instead of proving equality of applications, this procedure has merely proved the unconstitutionality of the test itself. Despite the relatively high proportion of Negro population in Mississippi, there is nothing in the record of Negro voting practices to indicate that there would be a higher percentage of Negro voters than in other Negro population centers.

The elimination of economic discrimination should probably be the first step in a patterned process to end segregation and racial injustice, but the essence of the present situation is that all discrimination has been maintained too long, and the white people of Mississippi are not likely to be granted the luxury of gradual adjustment to the changing order. An end to economic discrimination against the Negro can only improve Mississippi's economic system. It will invoke incentives to efficiency that have been absent for so long that all our estimates are made without them. Too many people for too many generations have lived in relative comfort at the expense of exploited Negro labor, or at the expense of white labor competing only with exploited Negro labor. One of the ancient attractions of the plantation system for both planter and sharecropper was the undeniable fact that both could get by, after their fashion, with less than a full measure of either labor or skill. Improved efficiency of management has been the major gain in Mississippi farming in the post-World War II era, but there are still great improvements to be made. In the present economic order, the "have-nots," white and Negro alike, will benefit by an end to discrimination, and the only "haves" who will suffer are those who survive today in spite of their inefficiency and lack of skill. The soundly based economic operation of today, whether in agriculture, industry, or commercial trade, will simply gain a larger return in a more productive economy. New people and new classes may become wealthy, but one thing the history of the American economic system shows is that the only groups who lose ground in an expanding, more prosperous economy are those who stubbornly resist adaptation to new products and new methods. People who stick to building buggies, and by hand, invite the loss of their affluence.

The elimination of discrimination does not mean that every Negro worker will become a model of industry, decorum, and prudence, any more than every white worker now meets those standards. There will still be laziness, irresponsibility, and indifference to the future, because these long-fostered traits cannot be eliminated overnight. When the dead ends for the Negro are eliminated, however, the rewards attained by the skilled and the industrious are going to create the incentives for all workers that will rapidly break down the present pattern of limited effort and skill. As the Negro learns that he can improve his economic status and not have it suddenly jerked out from under him by either design or accident, he will inevitably respond to the opportunity. There is no way to separate the cumulative effect of discrimination on every aspect of life in Mississippi. For example, no equality of economic opportunity can be achieved under an unequal educational system. The present generation Negro cannot meet the challenge of new job opportunities in his present condition of rudimentary education and virtually no vocational skills. A crash program of training in both specific skills and simple reading and writing is essential if the Negroes coming into the work force are to use their opportunites. For most older Negroes, the chance is already gone. Every chance lost for every Negro is not a loss to him alone; it is as well a loss to the productive capacity of Mississippi and the United States.

Removal of race barriers will also help Mississippi rid herself of other facets of a static economy. The great wealth-producing soil of the Mississippi Delta was reclaimed from what had once been written off as useless swampland, and brought to a state of great productive value by a combination of private and governmental effort. From the productiveness of the land has grown every other segment of the area's economy. There is perhaps no better example of a dynamic, expanding economy kept moving with governmental assistance. In this case the assistance is flood control, drainage, and soil conservation programs—land reform, to use a shorter term. In such an economy is it worthwhile to continue to operate under a low-wage philosophy? The small-town business community in the South benefits more from federal minimum wage laws than any other business group in the country. The small-town merchant and tradesman gets the direct benefits from the payrolls which industrialization has brought to the South. For most of this industry in small towns, the going wage rate is the minimum prescribed by federal law. Collective bargaining rarely has anything to do with it. Every nickel added to the hourly rate means that much more into the local channels of trade, yet no group of people in the country fights an extension of coverage or increase in rate of the wage and hour law harder than do the small-town merchants and professional people. Mississippi is still trying to sell itself to industry on the basis of the nineteenth-century theory that low wages mean bigger profits and better business. Fewer and fewer industries are going to tie themselves to any such philosophy in the face of the realization that the nation as a whole will not for much longer tolerate this kind of exploitation of labor, whatever its color.

Negroes, of course, would be major beneficiaries of broadened minimum wage coverage, but the over-all Southern economy would be the biggest beneficiary. Mississippi would benefit most from an improved economic status for Negroes, because Mississippi has the largest proportion of Negro citizens, and Mississippi Negroes have the lowest incomes. These are more than sufficient reasons why Mississippi's white people should take the lead in eliminating economic discrimination.

Mississippi is fond of its paternalistic tradition that the responsible white people are the Negro's best friend. The tradition has been dishonored by both the unscrupulous and the innocently well-meaning who have used it to cover discrimination and injustice, but it is not all hollow falsehood. Mississippians also lay claim to being a people who profess Christianity and love of its doctrines. But some of those who make the strongest professions debase the Christian ideal by hypocritical defense of discrimination and injustice. Even most of those pastors who have condemned racial violence in principle have condoned it in fact by closing their eyes to its perpetration, literally within a stone's throw of their pulpits. If Mississippi honors religion, it must at least bring a halt to the system that so dishonors religion by making willing or unwilling hypocrites of those who lead in its profession. Today a pastor who attempted to prove a Christian justification for slavery would be laughed from his church, but there were Mississippi pastors doing it by the hundreds little more than a century ago. Does anyone believe that in the coming years any Christian religion will condone rejection of Christian brotherhood?

It has been the fashion for years to ignore the real bitterness that has been built between the races in the South, even while more was being engendered. Much of what has scarred so many minds and hearts can never be obliterated, but can we afford successive generations of strife and hatred, a bottomless cup of gall that every man must swallow? Mississippi has been losing a high percentage of her most talented young people who seek other homes as soon as they are old enough to do so. Some of them leave because of the lack of economic opportunity, and some of them leave because of the need for a more compatible intellectual climate. The two reasons are not unrelated. Every handicap from which Mississippi suffers has at least some of its roots in race.

In today's South, the most able and spirited Negro youth are entering wholeheartedly into leadership of the fight for Negro rights. That these young rights workers are endowed with a spirit of high adventure and bravery in the face of unknown physical threats is obvious. Their courage will become an American saga. Could not this energy, ability, and courage be far better utilized in schools and universities, churches, business, and politics? If the white posture within the state does not change, a great deal of the Negro leaders' effort will have to be spent in restraining recklessness within their own movement. Most of them have already demonstrated determined leadership in their exhibition of restraint. This brings us once more to the oft-repeated thesis of this chapter—the struggle is a great waste of human resource on both sides. Together, the qualities of the leaders can create a better society than could ever be hoped for under present circumstances.

Federal power is not going to transform either the South

as a whole or Mississippi in particular into a model of equal rights overnight, but anyone who imagines that the pressure to change will not be massive and constantly applied simply does not comprehend the strength of the national demand for lawful conduct. The bombers, the killers, the hate peddlers operate only in areas where they are tolerated by either official or community attitudes. National opinion will no longer countenance outbreaks like those of the past. Negro aggressiveness in both the North and the South may irritate and aggravate friends and the public in general, but the murderous violence which Southern white extremism has engendered spurs the national conscience. We in the South have made much of the race violence in Northern and Western cities, but we have used it as an excuse. We should be so conducting ourselves that violence anywhere would stand in sharp contrast to a South where race violence had been eliminated.

Many of us have said that true tolerance cannot be legislated, that moral issues will only be resolved by persuasion. This is true, if the quest is for the ideal. We in the South, however, have used state and local laws to impose discrimination and perpetuate injustice. Local law has enforced and reinforced custom, leaving the Southern Negro without power or privilege of protest, except to move North if he can afford the fare. The law, which stands between order and anarchy, has been used in the South to enforce discrimination; it can as easily be used to eliminate discrimination. If it is not, if perversion of the law is not reversed, the law will cease to serve and protect; it will, instead, enslave, until there will be liberty for no man. Already the white people of Mississippi are closing in upon themselves, eating away their own freedoms in their attempt to deny freedom to others. The national body cannot and will not tolerate so insidious a self-destruction. If the South will not save itself, the nation will have to redeem it.

If present federal power is not sufficient to end rapidly all forms of institutionalized segregation and discrimination, new power will be secured from the Congress. Any claim that additional power will not be made available is either wishful thinking or venal deceit. Southern leadership has too long been marked by a weakness which avoids speaking frankly about this outlook—to its own, if shortsighted, self-interest— and the Southern people have been afflicted with a willingness to be betrayed and yet betrayed again, victims of a cynical political system born of their own vanity. Most of the South's fight against civil rights has been made in the name of states' rights. If there are rights of the states in this field, they can exist only in tandem with the responsibilities. If the powers of the states merit protection from any new federal invasion, the states must exercise those powers to protect the rights of each individual citizen.

I have few illusions about the prospect of Mississippi's responsible white leaders turning their backs on segregation to take the lead in eliminating it. I make the appeal in hope, it is true, but I make it as much to bring the issue to discussion. Fair and frank discussion will ultimately make it clear to Mississippi that she has nothing to fear from the elimination of segregation. Any dialogue which could lead to full discussion is impossible, however, except when it is initiated from the outside, as I do this. Facing the fact that even the most responsible white leaders cannot bring themselves to voluntary elimination of segregation, even though they know it will be forced upon them by a combination of law and public opinion, what can be the minimum immediate request of them?

The barest minimum must be full political rights for every reasonably qualified Negro citizen, and the complete assurance of equal justice before the law. White leaders of Mississippi can join together in support of such a program and reclaim much of the ground lost to hate in the past ten years. It offers the opportunity to work with moderate Negro leadership toward building a better state and a generally better climate in which to live and work and raise children. For the responsible white citizen who has any awareness of his duties as an American citizen or as a child of God, it offers the one way to live at peace with his conscience. That peace is desperately needed by many Mississippians. The alternative is to live out the days and weeks and months in fear and trepidation, smothered by smoldering suspicion, beset by the danger that physical violence will erupt from any trivial incident. This is what has resulted already from the relatively minor demonstrations in Mississippi. It could accumulate to far greater grief as the final court orders for public school integration begin to come through, and as Negroes demonstrate for better job opportunities and for the right to register and vote. If the state does not act, these are the efforts that will be made in Mississippi. They are as inevitable as the tides, and their eventual success is just as certain. They could be averted by white and Negro leadership working together, aware of the human values on each side, and dedicated to the preservation of a common human dignity.

Among the white leaders of the state today are many who realize the necessity of taking this step, but who hold back from advocating it in fear of standing alone in the crowd or risking its vengeance. There are many more who would recognize the need and perhaps actively work to meet it, if it were explained to them. Most Mississippians have never heard any side of this issue except that of the professional bigots. These profiteers of hate have smothered all voices of dissent and barred outside viewpoints because they know their case will suffer most from open, fair, and dispassionate discussion. Thus, what is needed today are people willing to brave the calumny of the hate mongers and take the first bold steps toward racial understanding. They must move fore-armed with the knowledge that they can never satisfy the extremists, and that there must be no retreats.

Where can this leadership come from? Experience has fairly well demonstrated that it will not come from public officials, nor from the church, nor the bar. The group with the greatest stake in preserving the constitutional rights of citizens are the men of finance and the men of property. Among the ablest leaders of the propertied class in the Missis-sippi Delta, and in the state as a whole, are the planters. They are the least subject of all Mississippians to economic and social pressures. Whether they are first or fifth generation, most of them like to imagine themselves as part of a tradition of *noblesse oblige*. Their responsibility to actively live up to that tradition has never been greater.

The historian of a few years hence will refer to today as the South's heroic age, the age of the successful and dramatic struggle for the rights of the Negroes as American citizens and free men. Are the only heroes from Mississippi to be the martyred Medgar Evers, the host of obscure victims of strife, and the vigorous, if sometimes belligerent, young leaders of the demonstrations and protests? If the story of the future is to be this group's continuing fight and eventual triumph over a monolithic white power structure which falls without con-cession, it will be a tragedy, spared classic proportions only because Mississippi will still be part of the United States, and the suffering will be alleviated by the protection that all Mis-sissippians will share as Americans. The surest way to shorten the suffering and eliminate the chasm between black and white is for all citizens to join in the effort to assure all Mississippians their rights as Americans.

William Faulkner's words of nearly ten years ago put the challenge clearly:

> The question is no longer of white against black. It is no longer whether or not white blood shall remain pure, it is whether or not white people shall remain free.
>
> We accept insult and contumely and the risk of violence because we will not sit quietly by and see our native land, the South, not just Mississippi but all the South, wreck and ruin itself twice in less than a hundred years, over the Negro question.
>
> We speak now against the day when our Southern people who will resist to the last these inevitable changes in social relations, will, when they have been forced to accept what they at one time might have accepted with dignity and goodwill, will say, "Why didn't someone tell us this before? Tell us this in time?"

Now the challenge must be taken up. The time has come when Mississippi must look away from Dixie and look forward to America.

Index